FINALLY—AN EASY WA
POWERFUL YET COMP
ENOCHIAN MAGIC

MW01256454

Anyone can benefit from this beginner's guide to the complex magical system of Enochian Magic, originally formed by Dr. John Dee and Edward Kelly and used by the Golden Dawn and Aleister Crowley. The reader need have no background in magic at all.

One of the reasons why Enochian Magic is so hard to understand is that it has a special, complex vocabulary. To help beginning students, Enochian terms are explained in simple, everyday words, wherever possible.

✦ **Gain a solid background in Enochian Magic with the first book designed for the novice student**

✦ **Learn faster with the latest techniques in educational psychology**

✦ **Conduct selected rituals of Enochian Magic**

✦ **Learn two techniques for skrying**

✦ **Try your hand at Enochian Chess**

✦ **Use the Enochian Tarot as a focus for productive meditation**

✦ **Explore Enochian Physics—the laws and models behind how the magic works**

✦ **Examine the dangers associated with Enochian Magic**

The authors have employed the latest techniques in educational psychology to help students master the information in this book. *The Enochian Workbook* is comprised of 11 sections, containing a total of 43 lessons, with test questions following each section so students can gauge their progress. When you complete this book, you will be ready to tackle the more complex concepts contained in the other books in the series.

About the Authors

Gerald J. Schueler, born in Darby, Pennsylvania, and his wife, Betty Sherlin Schueler, born in Washington DC, currently reside in Maryland. Jerry is a systems analyst, freelance writer, and editor. He holds a BS degree in mechanical engineering and an MS in Administration. Betty is a computer consultant, freelance writer, editor, and artist. She holds a BS degree in psychology and sociology. The Schuelers have written many articles on anthropology, computers, children, dogs, philosophy, magic, theosophy, and other subjects.

To Write to the Authors

If you wish to contact the authors or would like more information about this book, please write to the authors in care of Llewellyn Worldwide and we will forward your request. Both the authors and the publisher appreciate hearing from you and learning of your enjoyment of this book and how it has helped you. Llewellyn Worldwide cannot guarantee that every letter written to the author can be answered, but all will be forwarded. Please write to:

Gerald and Betty Schueler
c/o Llewellyn Worldwide
P.O. Box 64383-719, St. Paul MN 55164-0383, U.S.A.

Please enclose a self-addressed, stamped envelope for reply, or $1.00 to cover costs.
If outside U.S.A., enclose international postal reply coupon.

Free Catalog from Llewellyn

For more than 90 years Llewellyn has brought its readers knowledge in the fields of metaphysics and human potential. Learn about the newest books in spiritual guidance, natural healing, astrology, occult philosophy and more. Enjoy book reviews, new age articles, a calendar of events, plus current advertised products and services. To get your free copy of the *New Worlds of Mind and Spirit*, send your name and address to:

New Worlds of Mind and Spirit
P.O. Box 64383-719, St. Paul, MN 55164-0383

Llewellyn's High Magick Series

The Enochian Workbook

An Introduction to the Enochian Magical System Presented in 43 Easy Lessons

Gerald and Betty Schueler

1993
Llewellyn Publications
St. Paul Minnesota 55164-0383, U.S.A.

FIRST EDITION

Cover painting by Lissanne Lake

Library of Congress Cataloging-in Publication Data

Schueler, Gerald J., 1942–
    The Enochian workbook : an introduction to the Enochian magickal
system presented in 43 easy lessons / Gerald & Betty Schueler.
        p. cm. -- (Llewellyn's high magick series)
    Includes bibliographical references and index.
    ISBN 0-87542-719-7
    1. Enochian magic. I. Schueler, Betty, 1944- . II. Title.
III. Series.
BF 1623.E55S36 1992
133.4'3--dc20   92-32369
                                                     CIP

Llewellyn Publications
A Division of Llewellyn Worldwide, Ltd.
PO Box 64383, St. Paul MN 55164-0383

About Llewellyn's High Magick Series

Practical Magick is performed with the aid of ordinary, everyday implements, is concerned with the things of the Earth and the harmony of Nature, and is considered to be the magick of the common people. *High Magick*, on the other hand, has long been considered the prerogative of the affluent and the learned. Some aspects of it certainly call for items expensive to procure and for knowledge of ancient languages and tongues, though that is not true of all High Magick. There was a time when, to practice High Magick, it was necessary to apprentice oneself to a Master Magician, or Mage, and to spend many years studying and practicing.

High Magick is the transformation of the Self to the Higher Self. Some aspects of it also consist of rites designed to conjure spirits, or entities, capable of doing one's bidding. Motive is the driving force of these magicks and is critical for success.

In recent years there has been a change from the traditional thoughts regarding High Magick. The average intelligence today is vastly superior to that of four or five centuries ago. Minds attuned to computers are finding a fascination with the mechanics of High Magical conjurations (this is especially true of the mechanics of Enochian Magick).

The Llewellyn High Magick Series has taken the place of the Mage, the Master Magician who would teach the apprentice. "Magick" is simply making happen what one desires to happen—as Aleister Crowley put it, magick "is the Science and Art of causing Change to occur in conformity with Will." The Llewellyn High Magick Series shows how to effect that change and details the steps necessary to cause it.

Magick is a tool. High Magick is a potent tool. Learn to use it. Learn to put it to work to improve your life. This series will help you do just that.

Other Llewellyn Books by the Authors

ENOCHIAN MAGIC: A Practical Manual
AN ADVANCED GUIDE TO ENOCHIAN MAGICK
ENOCHIAN PHYSICS: The Structure of the Magical Universe
ENOCHIAN TAROT (with card deck)
COMING INTO THE LIGHT: Rituals of Egyptian Magick
ENOCHIAN YOGA

Contents

FIGURES

TABLES

Introduction

The Enochian Workbook, our sixth book on Enochian Magic, is written for beginning and intermediate students of magic. It was written in answer to your many requests for an easy-to-understand workbook, with test questions to answer, so that you could gauge how well you were learning the material.

We realize that Enochian Magic is hard to understand. The early developers of Enochian Magic were very smart people. They wrote their books with the idea that they would only be read by people who were as well educated as they were. None of them foresaw that the day would come when books would be readily available to everyone—rich or poor, educated or uneducated.

One of the reasons why Enochian Magic is so hard to understand is that it has a special, complex vocabulary. Unfortunately, reading the various books on Enochian Magic, with a dictionary nearby, doesn't always help. Some words were coined by the early developers of Enochian Magic; other words were taken from the language of the day, but were given a slightly different meaning. To help beginning students, we have tried to explain Enochian terms in simple, everyday words, wherever possible. Later, as you progress in your studies, you can begin learning the traditional vocabulary of Enochian Magic.

Organization of the Book

This book covers the main teachings of Enochian Magic. The book is divided into 11 sections, which are in turn, each divided into lessons - making 43 lessons in all.

In Section 1, we look at the history of Enochian Magic and present the official sources for all Enochian information.

In Section 2, we present the Angelic Alphabet. This includes how the language is spoken and gematria methods.

Section 3 introduces the main terms and ideas of Enochian Magic.

Section 4 addresses magical weapons and tell how to make and use them.

Section 5 discusses talismans and magic squares, and shows you how to make them.

In Section 6, we present a few of the rituals of Enochian Magic, and show you how to conduct them.

Section 7 discusses the two magical techniques of skrying—skrying using a crystal, or other suitable medium, and skrying in the Spirit Vision. This will be one of the most exciting sections for novice users. The techniques are simple and most students will be successful. Many students will be amazed to find that skrying is as natural and easy as breathing.

In Section 8, we take a quick look at Enochian Chess; a brief history of the game, its purpose, and how to play. This section introduces Enochian material that we have not covered before.

In Section 9, we cover Enochian Tarot; a summary and description, several spreads for divination, and new meditations. Like skrying, most students will find they can easily use the Enochian Tarot cards as a focus for productive meditation.

Section 10 includes a brief look at Enochian Physics; the laws and models used to determine the laws behind how the magic works. Although physics is difficult for many, we present only the main concepts so that you can gain a deeper insight into how the magic works.

Section 11 discusses how to call on a deity. A step-by-step method is given along with an example. This final section represents a culmination of all of the lessons that you have learned up to this point.

We have included six special appendices at the end of this book. The first (Appendix A) contains color plates of the sixteen subquadrants of the Watchtowers. Although this material can be found in our previous books, and is included here in a new format, using color to denote the element (Fire is red, Air is yellow, Water is blue, Earth is black, and Spirit is white). The second appendix (B) contains the answers to the questions given at the end of each section. The third appendix (C) contains a collection of questions and answers which are especially suited for beginners. The fourth appendix (D) contains a short article that addresses dangers associated with the practice of Enochian Magic especially for beginners. The fifth appendix (E) contains a comprehensive listing of Enochian words listed by gematria value. Lastly, Appendix F includes a short section of references to our other Enochian books, to help beginners find information on key areas of interest.

Features

To help you learn about Enochian Magic, we have written this book using various educational features. Each section has an outline to acquaint you with the contents and organization of the material covered in the lessons. Each section begins with a statement of learning objectives. These are a list of things you should be able to do after finishing the reading.

Each section includes a summary, further suggested readings, a list of suggested things that you can do, and questions to answer. Important vocabulary words are printed in boldface type, the first time they are used, and a glossary of magical terms is included at the end of the book.

Some people find it hard to learn new information. If you are one of these people, there are a few tricks you can use to make the process a little easier. First, skim over the lesson outline, the learning objectives, and the summary. Second, read the headings and the first sentence of each paragraph in the lesson. Quickly look at each diagram, chart, or table. Third, read each paragraph of the lesson and then try to put the information into your own words. Pretend that you are teaching the information to someone else. Fourth, read the summary again.

When you think you know the information included in the section, try taking the test at the end of the section. Use a blank sheet of paper to write the answers. This allows you to go back and take the test again at a later date. Each time you successfully complete the test, give yourself a suitable reward. This helps make the process more fun. Learning new information can be easy, and fun, if you follow these simple steps.

If you find the information in a particular lesson too hard to understand, move on to another lesson. Never let learning about Enochian Magic become a chore. While Enochian Magic is a very serious subject, there is no reason why the process has to be tedious. For instance, the basis of deity names, and signposts from the Tablets, are especially tedious information for beginners to learn, but the central teachings are fairly easy and straightforward. Once these are understood, the details can be studied without confusion, at your own speed.

Acknowledgements

In our search for an overall practical system of Enochian Magic, we have borrowed heavily from the writings of three major sources: John Dee, the Golden Dawn, and Aleister Crowley (see Lesson 3 for a list of Enochian source material). We make no claims to present Enochian Magic, as taught by John Dee or the Golden Dawn or Crowley, per se; rather, we have blended together the best of these magical pioneers into an integral, workable system. We have also added new material, including our own interpretations and findings, to the available and often conflicting source material. Our system of Enochian Magic will agree in many areas with the source material but will disagree elsewhere.

Enochian Magic, like life, is a continually evolving system. We hope that others will continue to build on the system of magic we have presented here, just as we have built on the work of Dee, the Golden Dawn, and Crowley.

—Gerald & Betty Schueler

SECTION 1

History and Background

Section Outline

Learning Objectives

This section contains four lessons which address the general background material of Enochian Magic. In this section, you will learn what magic is, what Enochian Magic is, the basic source material used, and some of the basic teachings. Upon completing the reading you should be able to:

- Define magic and list three factors that separate magical acts from scientific acts.

- List the Three Primary Laws of Magic.

- Identify four major contributors to the development of Enochian Magic and two major magical groups who use Enochian Magic.

- List at least four primary, and two secondary source materials.

- List the eight Cosmic Planes of occultism, and the five Enochian regions and their corresponding Elements.

LESSON 1

Magic

Magic as Science and Art

Magic is both a science and an art. As a science, Magic is knowledge that must be learned. As an art, Magic has skills which add to the psychic abilities we are born with. Everyone has some hidden, mental ability but most people have to practice various magical skills to master their psychic talent.

What is Magic?

Magic is a means to control actions and situations with the Will. It allows you to control yourself and your surroundings (within limits, of course) with directed will power. This means that you can deliberately direct your life. You can rule your own destiny.

How Magic Becomes Science

Every deliberate, willful act is a magical act. Acts which are repeatable become ordinary and familiar—thus scientific. Acts are seen as either scientific or magical according to familiarity, availability, and viewpoint.

As we said before, all intentional acts are magical acts. It is only through familiarity, availability, and viewpoint that they lose their magical label and become scientific, but they are magical, nonetheless.

For example, if we want to talk with someone, we can call them on the phone. In the modern world, telephones are readily available, and thus, from our viewpoint, they are familiar. Therefore, the willed action of phoning a friend is by definition a magical act, but most modern people would consider it a scientific action. This is true of almost everything we do, we simply lose sight of the magical nature of the act due to our familiarity with the action. Our familiarity with the action is due to the widespread availability of telephones.

Now, let's take that same familiar act and see it from another viewpoint. Suppose you lived in the deepest, most inaccessible part of the Amazon, completely unaware of modern civilization. One day, a man dressed in funny clothes walks into your village. The man quickly signals with universal gestures that he is friendly. He wants to buy some of your village's carvings. Although you are scared of this funny looking man, he offers you a great deal on your carvings and you agree to trade with him. The man reaches into a bag he has brought along and brings out this small, rectangular box. He pulls up a shiny branch from the box, pushes something on the box and suddenly a voice is heard coming from within the box. You are terror struck. This is no ordinary man—he is a god or a great magician. He can shrink people and enclose them in a box.

Everyone in the village gathers around and watches in awe as the man talks to someone in the box. Some of the villagers start to panic. They think the man should be killed—before he shrinks anymore people. A smaller part of the tribe thinks the man is a god and wants to worship the god. Who is right and who is wrong? The modern man knows the phone is an example of scientific principle; the villagers think the phone is some sort of magical object. In reality, the use of the phone is both magical and scientific; it is all a matter of familiarity, availability, and viewpoint.

Scientific vs. Magical Actions

We need some way to distinguish scientific actions from magical actions. One way to do this is to consider all easily repeatable acts as scientific. Acts which are not always easily repeatable are magical acts. Let's use the phone example again, but with a new twist.

Use of the telephone is widely available and familiar and is considered a scientific action. On the other hand, only a very few people can easily communicate through the power of the mind—through telepathy. Because few people can communicate telepathically, it lacks availability and familiarity; therefore, it is considered a magical act. This does not mean that it isn't real, but from our current viewpoint, it falls into the realm of the magical rather than the scientific.

There are some who suggest that viewpoint is the only real difference between science and magic. If we took the same modern man, visiting an Amazon village of today, and time warped him into an Amazon village of the future, he would probably find telepathy the major means of communication. The principles of telepathy will probably become common knowledge in the future, making devices such as the telephone primitive in comparison. When that happens, telepathy will leave the classification of magic and become scientific.

The Amazon village scene illustrates the basic problem in separating science from magic—one person's magic is another person's science. Again, it is all a matter of viewpoint, familiarity, and availability.

Magic vs. Science vs. Miracles

Modern magic states that there is no such thing as a miracle. All events can be explained in terms of laws or principles. However, some laws are not known to modern science. This fact in no way prevents the law from working. In the same way, you need not understand how your telephone works to use it, nor do you need to know how your television set works in order to watch it. The principles of modern science work free of our ability to grasp them. Only one person has to understand the principle and be able to put it into use for the rest of us to benefit from that knowledge.

It is important, when trying to understand magic vs. science, to realize that most science was once considered magic. Imagine yourself saying the world was round back in the days of Copernicus. Such action would have led to a quick barbecue with you as the guest of honor on the spit. Even in the more modern days of John Dee, the founder of Enochian Magic, you could have been killed for using the plus or minus signs—both were thought to be signs straight from the devil. There have been times, in all of our lives, (usually around tax time) when we would like to go back in history and burn whomever came up with these devilish signs. So, while your friends might look at you funny for studying Enochian Magic, try to remember that today's magic is tomorrow's science. The terminology may be different, but the principles are the same.

The Three Primary Laws of Magic:

1. **The Law of Duality.** Good and evil, life and death, and day and night, are all examples of dualities. All forces and events in our universe are polar; each has an opposite and neither side can exist without the other.

2. **The Law of Periodicity.** This is sometimes called the Law of Cycles, the principle of cyclic change. All growth is cyclic. Growth and decline produce the Wheel of Life.

3. **The Law of Identity.** All things in our universe are basically identical. The core or essence of every person is spiritual, a spark of divinity. Differences are due to stages of development.

LESSON 2

The History of Enochian Magic

The Enochian language was first recorded by John Dee, the court astrologer to Queen Elizabeth I of England. Dee was born in England in 1527. He was educated at Cambridge University and became an authority on mathematics, navigation, astronomy, optics, astrology, and natural magic. He was friendly with Queen Elizabeth, and reportedly worked for her as a spy on several occasions.

In the course of his many studies, Dee became interested in crystal-gazing. He found that he could not do it successfully himself, so hired crystal-gazers to do the actual operations for him while he took notes. He used a variety of crystals and two of them can be seen today in the British Museum.

Working with Edward Kelly, his foremost psychic associate and partner, Dee recorded and translated the Enochian language. According to Dee's diary, the language was revealed to him by Angels. Kelly contacted the Angels in the subtle regions which he called the Watchtowers and Aethyrs.

While Kelly conducted the psychic operation known as skrying, Dee kept careful records of everything that occurred. Kelly would look deeply into a shewstone and describe aloud whatever he saw. Dee carefully wrote everything down. The shewstone is believed to have been a black crystal about the size of an egg. Although objects such as water and mirrors can often be used to skry successfully, the favored material is crystal. Dee is credited with being one of the first magicians to use a large polished crystal in the form of a sphere—a crystal ball.

One of the main results of Dee's research was a series of tablets sectioned into squares with letters on each square. These were the English-equivalent letters of the Enochian alphabet. They spelled out the names of those deities who rule over the regions symbolized by the squares. The tablets were maps of the invisible spheres that surround the physical world.

Little became of Dee's work until late in the nineteenth century when it was utilized by a mysterious and highly secret brotherhood of Adepts in England who called themselves the Hermetic Order of the Golden Dawn, or GD. This Order adopted the magical system created by Dee and Kelly. They invoked the Enochian deities whose names were written on the tablets. They also traveled in what they called their Body of Light, into these subtle regions, and recorded their psychic experiences in a scientific manner.

The Golden Dawn used the Angelic Language in its rituals, and elaborated on the definitions of the Tablets and the Squares of the Tablets. The advanced members of this Order skryed over the Tablets and visited the places in the invisible worlds represented by the Squares of the Tablets.

The Golden Dawn refined the Enochian Tablets of Dee and Kelly, probably under the direction of its leader, MacGregor Mathers. The Tablets used by the Golden Dawn are shown in Figures 1 through 5. Each Watchtower Tablet can be divided into subquadrants as shown in Figure 6, and each subquadrant can be divided further as shown in Figure 7. Perhaps their most important achievement was in founding an orderly approach for assigning characteristics to each of the Squares. They designed a system in which the Squares were assigned Elements (combinations of Earth, Water, Air, Fire, and Spirit), planetary, Tarot, and astrological correspondences as well as ruling deities. These are the signposts of the Watchtowers and they clearly show that order and logical structure prevail in the invisible planes beyond our physical world.

One member, Aleister Crowley, left the Order and was later the head of the Ordo Templi Orientis, or OTO. Crowley traveled through each of the 30 Aethyrs, and carefully recorded his experiences in a book called *The Vision and the Voice*.

Today, Enochian Magic is experiencing a rebirth of interest. While members of the OTO and the GD have studied it for years, many lone individuals have recently started to practice Enochian Magic because they are finding it is a useful tool in shaping the philosophy of their own lives.

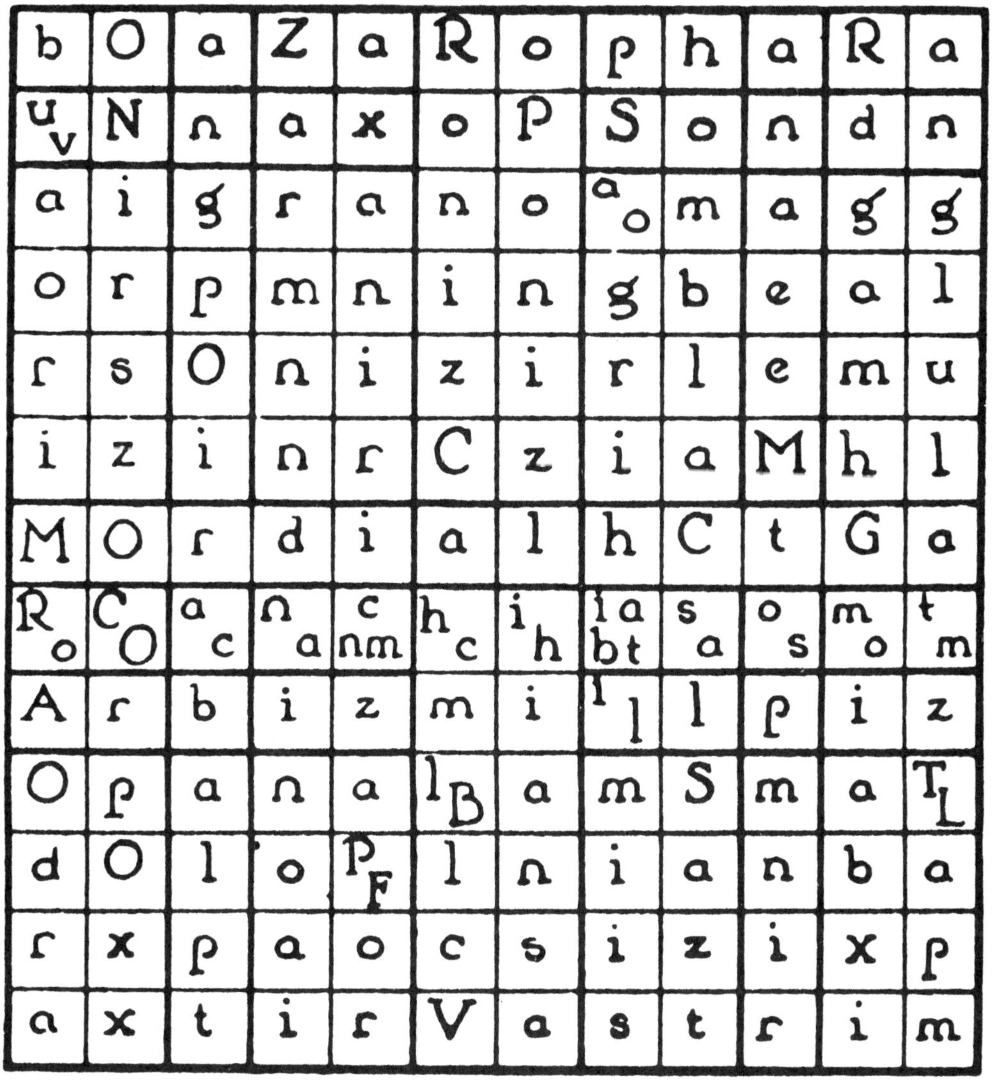

b	O	a	Z	a	R	o	p	h	a	R	a
u v	N	n	a	x	o	P	S	o	n	d	n
a	i	g	r	a	n	o	a o	m	a	g	g
o	r	p	m	n	i	n	g	b	e	a	l
r	s	O	n	i	z	i	r	l	e	m	u
i	z	i	n	r	C	z	i	a	M	h	l
M	O	r	d	i	a	l	h	C	t	G	a
R o	C O	a c	n anm	c h c	i h	ia bt	s a	o s	m o	t m	
A	r	b	i	z	m	i	l l	l	p	i	z
O	p	a	n	a	lB	a	m	S	m	a	T L
d	O	l	o	P F	l	n	i	a	n	b	a
r	x	p	a	o	c	s	i	z	i	x	p
a	x	t	i	r	V	a	s	t	r	i	m

Figure 1. The Great Watchtower of Earth in the North

T	a	O	A	d	u/v	p	t	D	n	i	m
a/o	a	b/l	c	o	o	r	o	m	e	b	b
T	o/a	g	c	o	n	x/z	m/i	n/a u	l	G	m
n	h	o	d	D	i	a	i	l/a	a	o	c
f/p	a	t/c	A	x	i	v/o	V	s	P	x/s	Y/l/N/b
S	a	a	i/z x	a	a	r	V	r	L/c	i	
m	p	h	a	r	s	l	g	a	i	o	l
M	a	m	g	l	o	i	n	L	i	r	x
o	l	a	a	D	n/a	g	a	T	a	p	a
p	a	L	c	o	i	d	x	P	a	c	n
n	d	a	z	N	z/x	i	V	a	a	s	a
r/i	i	d	P	o	n	s	d	A	s	p	i
x	r	i/t	n	h	t	a	r	n/a	d	i	L

Figure 2. The Great Watchtower of Water in the West

r	Z	i	l	a	f	A	$^{y}_{u}$	t	l_i	p	a
a	r	d	Z	a	i	d	p	a	L	a	m
C	z	o	n	s	a	r	o	$_v$Y	a	u	b
T	o	i	T	t	^z_x	o	P	a	c	o	C
S	i	g	a	s	o	^n_m	r	b	z	n	h
f	m	o	n	d	a	T	d	i	a	r	l_i
o	r	o	i	b	a	h	a	o	z	p	i
^t_c	N	a	b	^{r}a	V	i	x	g	a	^s_z	d
O	i	i	i	t	T	p	a	l	O	a	i
A	b	a	m	o	o	o	a	C	^u_v	c	a
N	a	o.	c	O	T	t	n	p	r	^u_a	T
o	c	a	n	m	a	g	o	t	r	o	i
S	h	i	a	l	r	a	p	m	z	o	x

Figure 3. The Great Watchtower of Air in the East

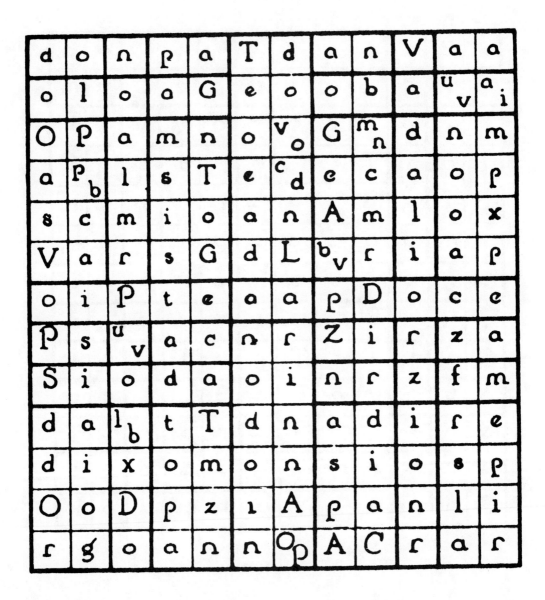

Figure 4. The Great Watchtower of Fire in the South

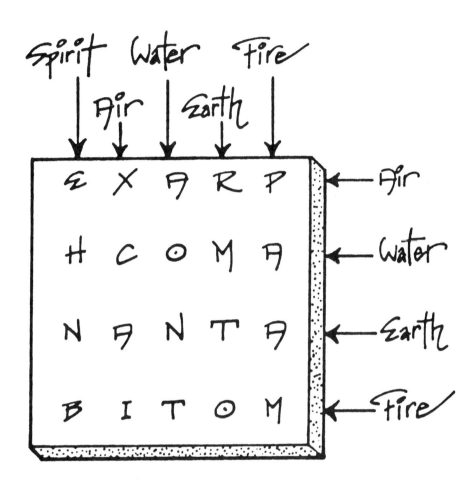

Figure 5. Tablet of Union or Squares of the Black Cross

Figure 6. The Subquadrants of the Watchtowers

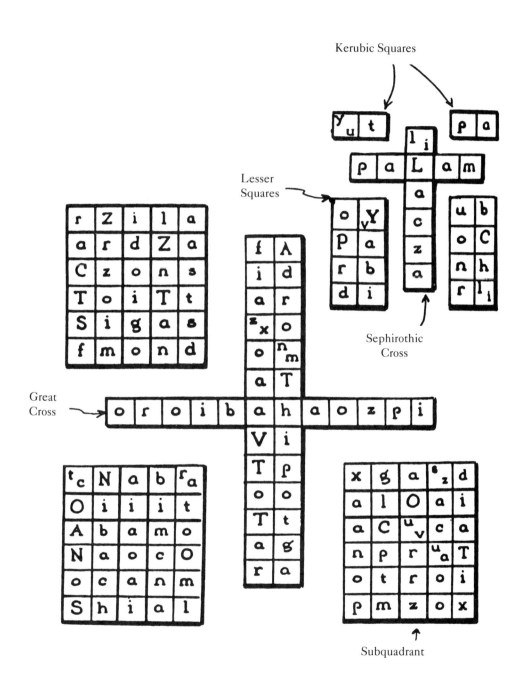

Figure 7. The Primary Divisions of the Great Watchtower of Air

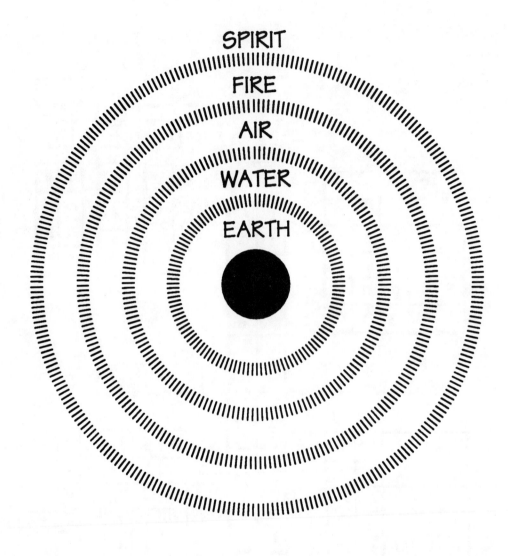

Figure 8. Diagram of the Cosmic Elements as Concentric Spheres

LESSON 3

The Source Teachings

The Primary Material

The primary source materials of Enochian Magic are as follows:

1. *Sigillum Dei Aemeth*. This is the Holy Pantacle or Great Seal. This Pantacle is used to derive the names of some Enochian deities. It is shown in Figure 2 of *Enochian Magic: A Practical Manual* (Llewellyn).

2. *Tabula Sancta*. This is called the Holy Table. It is shown in Figure 1 of *Enochian Magic: A Practical Manual* (Llewellyn).

3. *The Round Tablet of Nalvage*. This Tablet is shown in Figure 13 of *Enochian Yoga* (Llewellyn).

4. *Liber Enoch*. This contains the Enochian Tablets, the Tablets of the Four Watchtowers, and the Tablet of Union as shown in Figures 1 through 5.

5. *Liber Scientia Auxilii et Victoria Terrestris*. This contains the names of the Governors of the Aethyrs, and their planets and sigils. These are listed in Table 4.

6. *De Heptarchia Mystica*. This gives the names and sigils for Angels and Lesser Spirits of Enochian Magic. It provides additional Tablets of letters. It is not used by most magicians today.

7. *Liber Mysteriorum Sextus et Sanctus*. According to Israel Regardie, this is not used by most magicians today.

8. *Tabula Bonorum Angelorum Invocationes*. This contains various invocations for Angels of the Bonorum (see *Enochian Magic of the Golden Dawn*, Llewellyn).

9. *The Claves Angelicae*. This contains the Calls. A slightly modernized version of these Calls is given in Lesson 17.

10. The magical diaries of John Dee. These are stored in the British Museum.

Secondary Materials

1. *The Golden Dawn.* Vol 10, Israel Regardie, Llewellyn.
2. *The Vision and the Voice.* Aleister Crowley.
3. *Liber LXXXIX vel Chanokh.* Aleister Crowley.
4. *The Enochian Evocation of Dr. John Dee.* Ed. & Trans by Geoffrey James, Heptangle.
5. *Enochian* Magic: *A Practical Manual.* G. & B. Schueler, Llewellyn.
6. *An Advanced Guide to Enochian.* Magic G. Schueler, Llewellyn.
7. *Enochian Physics.* G. Schueler, Llewellyn.
8. *Enochian Yoga.* G. & B. Schueler, Llewellyn.
9. *Enochian Tarot.* G. & B. Schueler, Llewellyn.
10. *Golden Dawn Enochian Magic.* Pat Zalewski, Llewellyn.
11. *Mysteria Magica.* Denning & Phillips, Llewellyn.
12. The Enochian Tarot Card Deck. G. & B. Schueler & Sallie Ann Glassman, Llewellyn
13. *A True and Faithful Relation of What Passed For Many Years Between Dr. John Dee and Some Spirits.* Meric Casaubon, Askin.
14. *The Complete Enochian Dictionary.* Donald C. Laycock, Askin.
15. *Astral Projection, Magic, and Alchemy.* S. L. MacGregor Mathers and others, Ed. by Francis King, Destiny Books.

LESSON 4

The Cosmic Planes and Elements

Following are the primary teachings of Enochian Magic. The teachings are quite difficult but each one is followed by an easier-to-understand explanation. It is not really important that you consciously understand all of this information the first time you read it. Repeated readings will help you learn the important facts.

The fundamental teaching of Enochian Magic is that a spiritual intelligence exists beyond the ability of the human mind to conceive. That is, a god/goddess exists but we are unable to fully understand this being.

This being shows itself in a set of planes known as the Cosmic Planes of Manifestation. These planes are each more defined by time, space, and form from spiritual to the lowest and most gross, the physical plane which contains our planet, Earth. The various planes can roughly be compared to an onion. There is a core of the onion which is surrounded by layers of onion; on the outside of the onion is a brown, paper-thin skin. Each part of the onion looks different and has a different job but it is all still part of the onion. In this same way our planet is covered by layers of materiality and/or spirituality. The layers closest to the planet are the most material. The layers furthest away are the most spiritual. The layers between the material and spiritual are hard to tell apart, because they overlap each other, but they each have a different identity just like the layers of the onion.

The planes are each characterized by an element. The highest is Spirit—pure energy. The next element is Fire, followed in turn by Air, Water, and Earth. Figure 8 shows a diagram of these five planes and their respective elements.

The element Spirit is found in the highest plane—the spiritual plane which is said to contain the Tablet of Union. Below this plane is the element Fire which is found in the causal plane that contains a special region called the Watchtower of Fire. Causal is used in the sense of a form expressing cause. Below this plane is the element Air which is found in the mental plane that contains a special region called the Watchtower of Air. Mental is used in the sense of a form expressing reason. Below Air is the element Water which is found in the astral plane that contains a special region called the Watchtower of Water. Astral is used in the sense of a form expressing emotion. Below Water is the element Earth which is found in the etheric plane that contains a special

19

region called the Watchtower of Earth. Earth is used in the sense of a form expressing a life energy. Below all of these is our physical world of flesh and blood. The physical world is used in the sense of a form expressing solidity. Table 1 summarizes this flow of creative energy from Spirit to Matter.

Table 1
Cosmic Planes and Elements

Elements	Enochian Regions	Planes of Occultism
―――	―――	divine
Spirit	Tablet of Union spiritual	
Fire	Watchtower of Fire	higher mental/causal
Air	Watchtower of Air	lower mental
Water	Watchtower of Water	astral
Earth	Watchtower of Earth	etheric
―――	―――	physical

*The Holy Twelvefold Table containing seven
different talismans, as devised by Dee and Kelly*

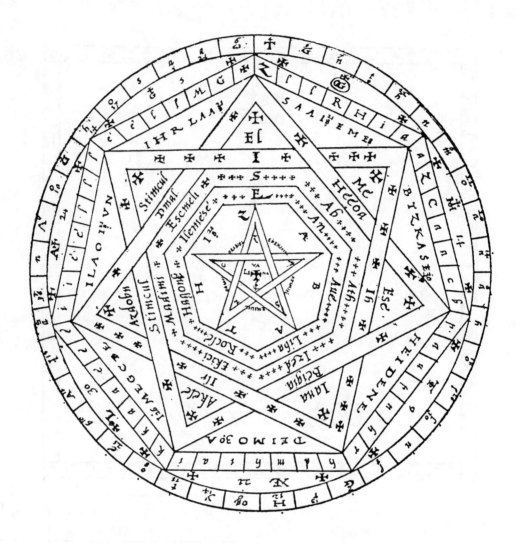

Figure 10. The Holy Pantacle, or Great Seal. This magical device was carved in wax and placed on top of the Holy Table during certain operations

Summary

Every deliberate, willful act is a magical act. Acts are seen as either scientific or magical according to familiarity, availability, and viewpoint. Easily repeatable acts are scientific; acts which are not easily repeatable are magical acts. All events can be explained in terms of laws or principles, but some laws are not known to modern science. The terminology is different, but the principles are the same.

There are three primary laws of Magic: the Law of Duality, the Law of Periodicity, and the Law of Identity. The Law of Duality states that all forces and events in our universe are polar. The Law of Periodicity states that growth is cyclic and it produces the Wheel of Life. The Law of Identity states that all things in our universe are basically identical and any differences are due to levels of growth.

The Enochian language was first recorded by John Dee working with Edward Kelly. The language was revealed to him by Angels in the subtle regions of the Watchtowers and Aethyrs.

One of the main results of Dee's research was a series of tablets sectioned into squares with letters on each square that spelled out the names of those deities who rule over the regions symbolized by the squares. The tablets were maps of the invisible spheres that surround the physical world.

Dee's work was later utilized by the Hermetic Order of the Golden Dawn which founded an orderly approach for assigning characteristics to each of the Squares. They designed a system in which the Squares were assigned Elements, planetary, Tarot, and astrological correspondences as well as ruling deities. These are the signposts of the Watchtowers.

One member, Aleister Crowley, left the Order and was later made head of the Ordo Templi Orientis. Crowley visited the thirty Aethyrs and recorded his experiences in *The Vision and the Voice*.

Primary source materials of Enochian Magic include: *Sigillum Dei Aemeth*, *Tabula Sancta*, the *Round Tablet of Nalvage*, *Liber Enoch*, *Liber Scientia Auxilii et Victoria Terrestris*, *De Heptarchia Mystica*, *Liber Mysteriorum Sextus et Sanctus*, *Tabula Bonorum Angelorum Invocationes*, the *Claves Angelicae*, and the diaries of John Dee.

A spiritual intelligence exists but we are unable to fully understand this being. This god/goddess shows itself in a set of planes known as the Cosmic Planes of Manifestation. These planes are defined by time, space, and form from spiritual to the physical. The layers closest to the planet are the most material. The layers furthest away are the most spiritual. The layers between the material and spiritual overlap each other but they each have a different identity. The planes are each characterized by an element: Spirit, Fire, Air, Water, or Earth.

Further Suggested Reading

In addition to the primary and secondary sources, the following are recommended reading for students:

The Shaman and the Magician. Nevill Drury, Arkana.

Magic White and Black. Franz Hartmann, M.D., Newcastle.

Ritual Magic. David Conway, E.P. Dutton.

Foundations of Practical Magic. Israel Regardie, Aquarian.

History and Practice of Magic. Paul Christian, Citadel.

The Magus. Francis Barrett, Citadel.

Man, Myth & Magic, Vol 18. Ed. by Richard Cavendish, Marshall Cavendish Corp.

John Dee. Peter J. French, Routledge & Kegan Paul.

Magick In Theory and Practice. Aleister Crowley, Castle.

The Alchemical Writings of Edward Kelly. Ed. by A.E. Waite, Weiser.

Things to Do for Section 1

1. Think about Magic as conscious action and see how you are already a magician. Do a consistently repeatable action, such as picking up a book and opening it. Now try to do an inconsistently repeatable action. Using the same book, close your eyes and see yourself opening the book to a desired page. With your eyes still closed, open the book to the same page. Record your efforts.

2. Answer the following questions as honestly as possible.

I want to be a magician because:

My goal is:

My reason for doing this is:

3. Consider the first Law of Magic. List some dualities, such as sweet/sour, below. Try to imagine what up would mean without down for comparison, or big without little.

4. Consider the second Law of Magic. List some of the things which cycle over time, such as sunrise/sunset. Do you believe in reincarnation? List the reasons for and against the concept of reincarnation.

For:

Against:

5. Consider the third Law of Magic. Do you believe that all people are born equal? Magic teaches that you have developed from the mineral, vegetable, and animal kingdoms into the human kingdom. Because of your past lives, you can share consciousness with all things. You are the smaller version of your larger world. Try to see how this ancient teaching is a direct result of the third law.

6. Study Table 1 carefully. Write down what you think may be the difference between each element and its corresponding Watchtower.

Questions for Section 1

1. How would you define magic?

2. True or False: Every planned act is a magical act.

3. List the primary difference between science and magic.

4. True or False: There is no such thing as a miracle.

5. List the three laws of magic.

6. True or False: John Dee was an authority on mathematics, navigation, astronomy, optics, astrology, and natural magic.

7. True or False: The Hermetic Order of the Golden Dawn adopted the magical system created by Dee and Kelly.

8. Who is the first person who claimed to have visited all 30 Aethyrs?

9. What are the Cosmic Planes of Manifestation?

10. Name the five most important Tablets of Enochian Magic.

11. Name the four cosmic elements according to Enochian Magic.

12. True or False: The Mental Plane is the Watchtower of Air.

13. True or False: The Watchtower of Earth is located on the etheric plane and is invisible to the physical senses.

SECTION 2

The Enochian Alphabet

Section Outline

LESSON 1: THE ANGELIC LANGUAGE

HISTORY

PRONUNCIATION

CORRESPONDENCES

THE ALPHABET

LESSON 2: GEMATRIA

HISTORY

THEORY

SUMMARY/FURTHER SUGGESTED READING/THINGS TO DO/QUESTIONS

Learning Objectives

This section contains only two lessons, but they are very important. The first will introduce you to the magical alphabet and language of Enochian Magic. The second lesson will introduce you to the technique called gematria, as it is used in Enochian Magic. Upon completing the reading you should be able to:

• Write a short paragraph on the history of the Enochian alphabet

• Pronounce Enochian words

• List letters of the Enochian alphabet and their various correspondences

• Write a short paragraph on the history of Enochian gematria

• Compute the numerical values of words and phrases using Enochian gematria

LESSON 5

The Angelic Language

History

In the late 1500s, the Enochian language was revealed by angelic beings to John Dee and his psychic partner, Edward Kelly. Using a magical technique known as skrying, Kelly would look into a shewstone and report what he saw and heard. Dee carefully recorded the results. Sometime Dee would have Kelly ask specific questions of the entities. The result of their several years of work was a series of tablets, criss-crossed by lines and notated by letters. These letters formed the Enochian alphabet.

No one knows for sure where the Enochian Language was originally developed. It may have been a language used hundreds of centuries ago on the lost continent of Atlantis. The Golden Dawn taught that traces of the Enochian alphabet could be found in the sacred mysteries of the world's oldest religions. Parts of it have been found on rock-cut pillars of ancient temples. Dee and Kelly called the language Enochian after the biblical patriarch, Enoch. Enoch was also the name of a group of Adepts who tended the flame of occultism during the Dark Ages. But, because the language was rediscovered with the help of Angels, it is also known as the Language of the Angels or the Angelic language.

Pronunciation

It is doubtful if Enochian was ever used as a spoken language; rather, it was probably used as a system of sigils and glyphs to record important ideas. It was the Golden Dawn that established a set of rules for pronunciation similar to the Hebrew language. The rules are:

Most consonants are followed by 'eh' (B is Beh, D is Deh). Most vowels are followed by 'h' (A is Ah, O is Oh). In general, each letter forms a syllable. The letters Y and I are interchangeable, as also are V and U, and S and Z. Z can be pronounced 'zod' (traditional) or 'zeh' (modern). S is pronounced either 'ess' or 'seh.' R can be either 'reh,' 'rah,' or 'ar.' I is pronounced 'ee' (TI is Teh-ee or simply Tee).

Pronunciation should be rich and full sounding, and flow easily—almost musically. The variations in the rules for pronunciation of letters allow for several possible ways to say most Enochian words and names. There is no right or wrong way, as long as the general rules are obeyed.

Correspondences

Each letter of the Enochian alphabet corresponds with a Tarot trump card and with a planetary, Zodiac, or elemental property. These correspondences are shown in Table 2.

Table 2
Enochian Alphabet Correspondences

Letter	Zodiac/Element	Tarot
A	Taurus	Hierophant
B	Aries	Star
C,K	Fire	Judgement
D	Spirit	Empress
E	Virgo	Hermit
F	Cauda	Draconis Juggler
G	Cancer	Chariot
H	Air	Fool
I,J,Y	Sagittarius	Temperance
L	Cancer	Chariot
M	Aquarius	Emperor
N	Scorpio	Death
O	Libra	Justice
P	Leo	Strength
Q	Water	Hanged Man
R	Pisces	Moon
S	Gemini	Lovers
T	Leo	Strength
	Caput Draconis	High Priestess
U,V,W	Capricorn	Devil
X	Earth	Universe
Z	Leo	Strength
	Caput Draconis	High Priestess

The Enochian Alphabet

The actual letters of the Enochian alphabet, together with their names, are shown in Table 3.

Table 3
Letters of the Enochian Alphabet

English	Name	Enochian
A	Un	⟩
B	Pe	Ꮩ
C, K	Veh	Ɓ
D	Gal	ꓛ
E	Graph	ꓶ
F	Orth	⨍
G	Ged	Ꮽ
H	Na-hath	ꓩ
I, J, Y	Gon	ꓶ
L	Ur	Ϲ
M	Tal	Ɛ
N	Drun	Ꝯ
O	Med	Ꮮ
P	Mals	ꓵ
Q	Ger	ꓸ
R	Don	Ɛ
S	Fam	ꓶ
T	Gisa	✓
U, V, W	Vau	ꓷ
X	Pal	Ꮁ
Z	Ceph	Ꮲ

LESSON 6

Gematria

History

Enochian Gematria was developed by one of the most famous (and some say infamous) modern day magicians, an Englishman named Aleister Crowley. Crowley was an experimenter. He tried many things just to see what their effects would be. His magical experiments included many investigations into Enochian Magic. Many of his works, such as *The Vision and the Voice*, form the cornerstone of modern Enochian Magic. The source for the gematria values shown in Table 4 can be found in his footnotes to *The Vision and the Voice*.

Theory

The theory of gematria states that each letter of an alphabet has a numerical value. By adding up the values of the letters that make up a word or phrase we can obtain the numerical value of that word or phrase. Words and phrases with equivalent numbers have direct relationships or correspondences. These correspondences are not obvious because they are hidden or occult. By computing the numeric value of words or phrases, all kinds of information can be learned that otherwise would remain unknown, making gematria a very powerful tool for the magician.

Table 4
Enochian Gematria

Letter	Gematria
A	6
B	5
C,K	300
D	4
E	10
F	3
G	8
H	1
I,J,Y	60
L	8
M	90
N	50

Letter	Gematria
O	30
P	9
Q	40
R	100
S	7
T	9, 3
U,V,W	70
X	400
Z	9, 3

Table 4 shows the gematric value of each Enochian letter. As you can see, letters T and Z both have two values, 9 and 3. The value of 9 is considered the primary value, while 3 is the secondary or alternate value. A comprehensive list of Enochian words is provided for your use in Appendix E. These words are listed by primary gematric value, and secondary values are included where appropriate (i.e., in all words with T or Z). Although not shown in Table 4, nor used in Appendix E, Crowley gave the letter D an alternate value of 31.

Let's look at an example of how gematria can be used. A key to the true nature of a deity can be obtained by knowing the deity's name. Let's look at the First Senior of Water whose name is LSRAHPM. Using the values in Table 4, we can compute that his name equals 221 (8+7+100+6+1+9+90 = 221). Appendix E of this workbook shows us that this is the value of the word MALPRG which means "fiery flames," thus, the Senior, LSRAHPM, has a fiery temper. The Enochian Tarot deck (card no. 60) shows this Senior. One of the meanings of this card is "a fire."

Enochian Gematria can also be used to compute the value of your name and the names of other people. By studying the correspondences between these names, you can learn information about the true nature of the individuals and their relationship to you.

Summary

In the late 1500s, the Enochian language was revealed by angelic beings to John Dee and his psychic partner, Edward Kelly. No one knows for sure, where the Enochian Language originated. It may have been a language used on the lost continent of Atlantis. Traces of the Enochian alphabet can be found in the sacred mysteries of the world's oldest religions.

It is doubtful if Enochian was ever used as a spoken language; rather, it was probably used as a system of sigils and glyphs to record important ideas. The Golden Dawn established a set of rules for pronunciation similar to the Hebrew language.

Pronunciation should be rich and full sounding, and flow easily—almost musically. Enochian words may be pronounced in several ways, as long as the general rules are obeyed.

Each letter of the Enochian alphabet corresponds with a Tarot trump card and with a planetary, Zodiac, or elemental property.

Enochian Gematria was developed by Aeister Crowley. The source for Enochian gematria values can be found in his footnotes to *The Vision and the Voice*.

Each letter of the Enochian alphabet has a numerical value. Some Enochian letters have a primary value and secondary value. By adding up the values of the letters in a word we can find out the hidden correspondences between words.

A key to the true nature of a deity can be obtained by knowing the name of a deity or person, and computing the numerical value of their name.

Further Suggested Reading

Man, Myth & Magic, Vol 5. Ed. by Richard Cavendish, Marshall Cavendish Corp.

Aleister Crowley: The Hidden God. Kenneth Grant, Weiser.

The Confessions of Aleister Crowley. Aleister Crowley, Various publishers.

The Eye of the Triangle. Israel Regardie, Llewellyn.

The Magician of the Golden Dawn. Susan Roberts, Contemporary Books, Inc.

777 and Other Qabalistic Writings of Aleister Crowley. Aleister Crowley, Weiser.

Things to Do for Section 2

1. Memorize each letter of the Enochian alphabet and practice writing them as shown in Table 3. To help memorize the letters, try and make a game of the process. First, think of the letter A and then think of some memory hook that will help you remember its title and glyph. You could think of A as *Un* flipped, slanted F wearing a hat (ﰧ). B is a *Pe* nosed V (ﰧ). C and K are a *Veh*-ry weird B with a nose (ﰧ). D is a *Gal* doing a split without any head (ﰧ). E is a *Graph*-ically flipped, upside-down L (ﰧ). F is an *Orth*-o-dontist's, forward-tipped F (ﰧ). G is *Geds*-ooks, a backwards J (ﰧ). H is a *Na-hath*-able, M with its legs scrunched together (ﰧ). I, Y, or J are *Gon*-zilla's L flying a flag behind (ﰧ). L is *Ur* C with an equal behind (ﰧ). M is a *Tal*-ky, backwards 3 (ﰧ). N is a *Drun*-ken lady getting ready to dive (ﰧ). O is a *Med*-ically approved Lady doing her sit-ups (ﰧ). P is the *Mals*-bent legs of a cowboy (ﰧ). Q is a *Ger*-iactric's legs upside-down (ﰧ). R is the *Don* of Es (ﰧ). S is the *Fam*-ily's backwards 7 (ﰧ). T is the *Gisa*-strip falling forward (ﰧ). U, V, or W are a *Vau*-lted H that is backwards and bent over (ﰧ). X is the L in *Pal* turned upside down, and backwards (ﰧ). Z is the fancy P in *Ceph* (ﰧ).

   Many of the memory hooks given here are weird, but they will work if you give them a chance. If you find them too bizarre to remember, make up your own. Not only will the memory process be more fun, but you will remember the letters better and with faster recall.

2. Practice speaking letters and words in Enochian until you can speak clearly and distinctly without making mistakes. Again, make up memory hooks to help you.

3. Table 5, in Lesson 10, page 61, contains a list of the names of the 30 Aethyrs and their Governors. Try to speak these names according to the rules of Enochian pronunciation.

4. Memorize the gematric values for each letter in the Enochian alphabet. (Use your memory hooks!)

5. Calculate the gematric values of the following Enochian words:

APILA _____	VOVIN _____	MOLAP _____
ABRAASSA _____	BABALOND _____	NANTA _____
EXARP _____	GRAA _____	BITOM _____
IADNAH _____	HKOMA _____	SOBOLN _____

6. Write the four Holy Names and the names of the four Kings in Enochian characters (these are given in English in Lesson 6).

Holy Names   **Kings**

_____   _____

_____   _____

_____   _____

_____   _____

Questions for Section 2

1. True or False. The Enochian Language is also called the Angelic Language.

2. How is the Enochian letter S pronounced?

3. Multiple Choice: Dee and Kelly conversed with Angels using a magical device called a

    a. magic circle.
    b. touchstone.
    c. shewstone.
    d. talisman.

4. True or False: John Dee was a gifted psychic.

5. True or False: John Dee acted as a scribe, carefully recording the results of every operation.

6. The Enochian language was created by

    a. the ancient Egyptians.
    b. the ancient Sumerians.
    c. no one knows for sure.

7. What letter corresponds to the Tarot card of the Fool? The Star?

8. What two Enochian letters did Crowley give two tarot and gematric correspondences?

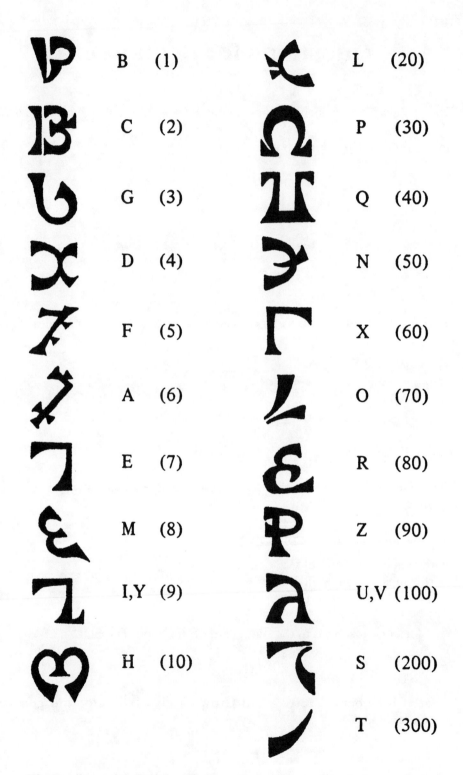

	B	(1)		L	(20)
	C	(2)		P	(30)
	G	(3)		Q	(40)
	D	(4)		N	(50)
	F	(5)		X	(60)
	A	(6)		O	(70)
	E	(7)		R	(80)
	M	(8)		Z	(90)
	I,Y	(9)		U,V	(100)
	H	(10)		S	(200)
				T	(300)

The Enochian alphabet, showing numerical values used in the Aurum Solis
(from *Mysteria Magica* by Denning & Phillips, Llewellyn)

9. True or False: Enochian should be pronounced sonorously and should flow smoothly like a musical chant.

10. What is the gematric value of the Enochian word ATH, meaning 'works?'

11. True or False: The gematric value of the name BABALON is 110.

12. True or False: The gematric value of the words ALAR, GRAA, and OM are all equal to 120, and thus have hidden correspondences.

13. The Enochian word TOANT means lust. What is the gematric value for this word? To what important goddess does this word correspond?

SECTION 3

Terms and Concepts

Section Outline

Learning Objectives

This section contains seven lessons that cover many of the basic concepts and techniques used in Enochian Magic. These include: the Watchtowers and Aethyrs, the aura or Body of Light, and Enochian god-forms. Upon completing the reading you should be able to:

- List the four Watchtowers and the main features of each Watchtower

- Divide each Watchtower into four subquadrants and label each subquadrant

- Define the Tablet of Union

- Make a Pyramid

- Name at least one Watchtower deity for each Watchtower and list their major characteristics and the regions they control

- Name four Egyptian Deities and their major characteristics

- Create a Sphinx for a Lesser Square

- Describe the signposts of one Square in each of the Watchtowers

- List the 30 Aethyrs by name, number, and meaning

- Travel in your Body of Light

LESSON 7

The Watchtowers

The Four Main Regions

The Watchtowers are the four main regions of unseen worlds that surround our physical world, Earth. Each Watchtower is divided into four parts or subquadrants. Each Watchtower can also be divided into a Great Cross of 36 Squares, and four subquadrants of 30 Squares each. Each subquadrant can be divided into a Calvary Cross of 10 Squares, 4 Kerubic Squares, and 16 Lesser Squares. This makes a total of 156 Squares per Watchtower. (See Figure 7)

The Great Cross contains the highest (most spiritual) of the Watchtower Squares. The Lesser Squares beneath the arms of the Sephirothic Crosses contain the lowest (most material) subplanes.

The four Watchtowers form a Magical Universe that is held together by a Black Cross of 51 Squares. Due to the repetition of letters on some of the Squares, the Black Cross is reduced to a Tablet of Union of 20 Squares (See Figure 5).

We cannot see the Watchtowers—they are invisible to our eyes. Our ears hear none of their sounds; our nose can not smell their scents. But the Body of Light can see their glory, and hear their music, and smell their fragrances.

The Watchtower of Earth

The Great Northern Quadrant of Earth is the first of the mighty Watchtowers that create and support our physical world (see Figure 1). It is a place of strong creative forces that give rise to all material things, but is not those things itself.

The Watchtower of Earth should not be confused with the planet, Earth, on which we live in the body of flesh. It is said that this Quadrant is located from the surface of our planet upward in all directions until the highest subplane touches the surface of the moon.

The Watchtower of Water

The Great Western Quadrant of Water is the Watchtower that reflects images upon our physical world (see Figure 2). The Water of this Watchtower should not be confused with the water that we drink. It is a region of strong life-creating forces that give rise to all living things but is not life itself. It is said that this Quadrant is located from the surface of the Earth upward in all directions until the highest subplane touches the surface of the planet Venus.

The Watchtower of Air

The Great Eastern Quadrant of Air is the Watchtower that pours thoughts and ideas upon our physical world (see Figure 3). It is a region of strong intelligent forces that give rise to the logic and reason of all living things.

The Watchtower of Air should not be confused with the air that we breathe. Each Square in the Watchtower of Air is a vast subtle region or subplane surrounding our physical world.

It is said that this Quadrant is located from the surface of the Earth upward in all directions until the highest subplane touches the surface of the planet Mercury.

The Watchtower of Fire

The Great Southern Quadrant of Fire is the Watchtower that causes constant change upon our physical world (see Figure 4). It is a region of strong creative and destructive forces that give rise to the ultimate growth of all living things.

The Watchtower of Fire should not be confused with the fire that we kindle. Each Square in the Watchtower of Fire is a vast subtle region or subplane surrounding our physical world. It is said that this Quadrant is located from the surface of the Earth upward in all directions until the highest subplane touches the surface of the Sun.

The Tablet of Union

The Tablet of Union is the Great Tablet that is the ultimate source of all things that exist upon our physical world. It is a region of strong causative forces that give rise to the entire universe of all living things (see Figure 5).

The Tablet of Union is composed entirely of Spirit that is not to be found in the physical world.

Each Square in the Tablet of Union is a vast subtle region or subplane surrounding our physical world. It is said that this Tablet is located from the surface of the Earth upward and outward in all directions until the highest subplane touches the farthermost fringes of the solar system.

Pyramids

In order to render a Watchtower Square closer to its real nature we make each Square a truncated pyramid. The top view of a typical truncated pyramid is shown in Figure 9. A template that can be used to make a typical pyramid is shown in Figure 10. The Square is used as its base. The top of the four-sided pyramid is then lopped off and the letter(s) of the Square is placed on the top surface. The corresponding elements are placed on the four sides to show the elemental makeup of the region (the rules to use in determining these elements are contained in *Enochian Magic: A Practical Manual*). All 16 subquadrants of the four Watchtowers as truncated pyramids are in the color plates.

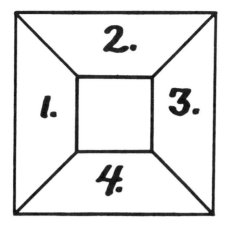

Figure 9. Top view of a typical tablet square made into a truncated pyramid

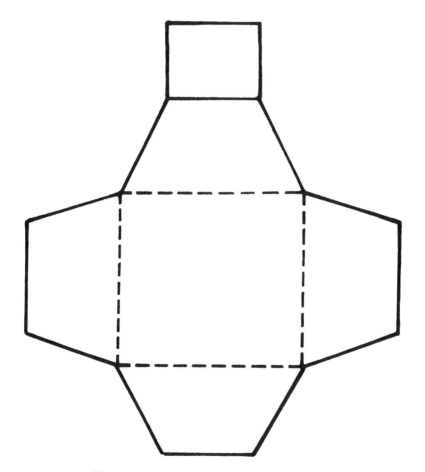

Figure 10. A truncated pyramid template

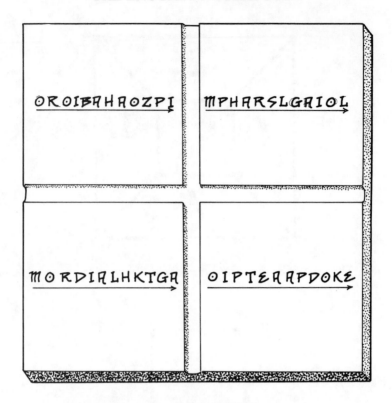

Figure 11. The Four Secret Holy Names of Divinity

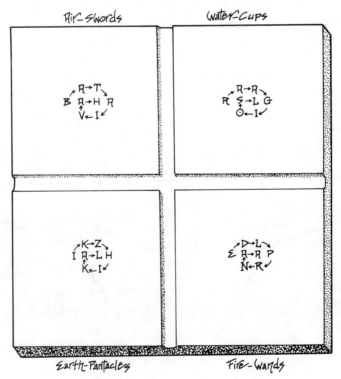

Figure 12. The Names of the Four Great Kings

LESSON 8

The Watchtower Deities

Enochian Deities

There are many Enochian deities in the four Watchtowers. In general, their names are all derived from the letters in the Squares. The highest names are the four Great Secret Holy Names and the four Kings as given below. Figure 11 shows how the four Holy Names are derived from the four Great Watchtowers. Figure 12 shows how the names of the Kings are derived from the four Great Watchtowers.

Element	Holy Name	King
Air	ORO-IBAH-AOZPI	BATAIVAH
Water	MPH-ARSL-GAIOL	RAAGIOSL
Earth	MOR-DIAL-HKTGA	IKZHIKAL
Fire	OIP-TEAA-PDOKE	EDLPRNAA

There are 24 Seniors, six governing each Watchtower as follows:

Air	Water	Earth	Fire
HABIORO	LSRAHPM	LAIDROM	AAETPIO
AAOZAIF	SAIINOV	AKZINOR	ADAEOET
HTNORDA	LAVAXRP	LZINOPO	ALNKVOD
AHAOZPI	SLGAIOL	ALHKTGA	AAPDOKE
AVTOTAR	SOAIZNT	AHMLLKV	ANODOIN
HIPOTGA	LIGDISA	LIIANSA	ARINNAP

Figure 13 shows how the names of the Seniors are derived from the four Great Watchtowers. Each Sephirothic Cross contains two names. Reading downward is a six-lettered name, and across is a five-lettered name. Figure 14 shows how these names are derived from the four Great Watchtowers. The Sephirothic Cross Angels are shown on page 54.

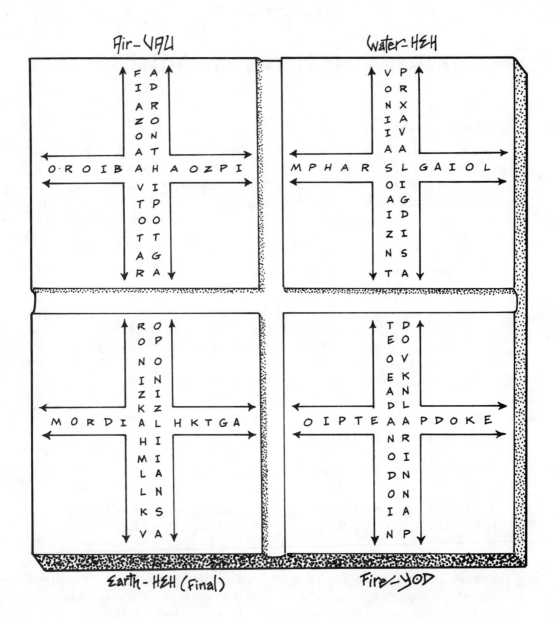

Figure 13. The Names of the 24 Seniors

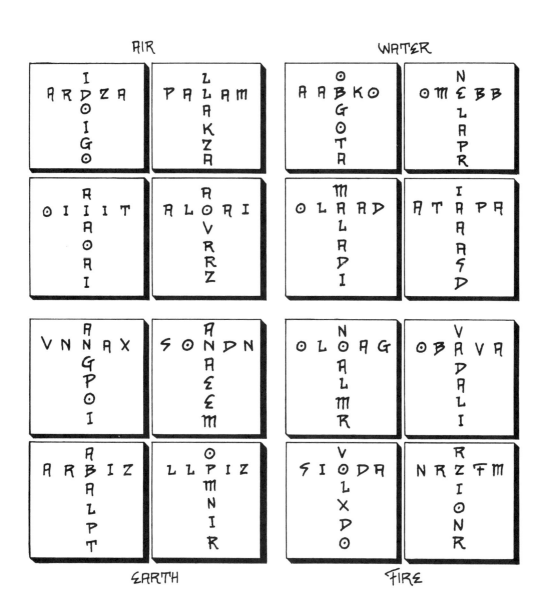

Figure 14. The Angels of the 16 Sephirotic Crosses

Watchtower of Air		Watchtower of Water	
Air:	IDOIGO, ARDZA	**Air:**	OBGOTA, AABKO
Water:	LLAKZA, PALAM	**Water:**	NELAPR, OMEBB
Earth:	AIAOAI, OIIIT	**Earth:**	MALADI, OLAAD
Fire:	AOVRRZ, ALOAI	**Fire:**	IAAASD, ATAPA

Watchtower of Earth		Watchtower of Fire	
Air:	ANGPOI, VNNAX	**Air:**	NOALMR, OLOAG
Water:	ANAEEM, SONDN	**Water:**	VADALI, OBAVA
Earth:	ABALPT, ARBIZ	**Earth:**	VOLXDO, SIODA
Fire:	OPMNIR, ILPIZ	**Fire:**	RZIONR, NRZFM

The letters above the horizontal bar of each Sephirothic Cross spell the name of a Kerubic Angel. These are anagramed by taking the first letter of each name to form the names of three more Kerubic Angels for a total of 64 Angels. There are also 64 Archangels. The names of the Archangels are formed by prefixing a letter (E, H, N or B depending on the Watchtower) from the Tablet of Union to the name of a Kerubic Angel. There are 64 Lesser Angels. Their names are formed from the letters in four rows beneath the horizontal bar of each Sephirothic Cross. There are 64 Ruling Lesser Angels. Their names are formed by prefixing a letter (X, A, R, or P to Air; K, O, M, or A to Water; A, N, T, or A to Earth; or I, T, O, or M to Fire) from the Tablet of Union to the name of a Lesser Angel. There are 128 demons. Their names are formed from the pairs of letters under the horizontal bar of each Sephirothic Cross to which is prefixed a letter from the Tablet of Union.

Egyptian Deities

In addition to Enochian deities there is also an Egyptian deity associated with each Lesser Square of each Watchtower. There are 16 Egyptian deities all together. Where they are located is determined by the elements that are on the sides of the truncated pyramid for that Lesser Square. Their names and when they are used are as follows:

The God Osiris. God of the Dead. Presides over all Squares where one pyramid side is of each element.

The Goddess Isis. Goddess of Nature and natural law. Presides over all Squares where at least three pyramid sides are of Water.

The God Horus. God of human evolution, government, and growth. Presides over all Squares where at least three pyramid sides are of Earth.

The Goddess Nephthys. Goddess of esoteric law. Presides over all Squares where at least three pyramid sides are of Fire.

The God Ur-Heru or the Elder Horus. Horus as humanity matured. Presides over all Squares where at least three pyramid sides are of Air.

The Goddess Hathor. Goddess of nourishment. Presides over all Squares that have two sides of Water and two sides of Earth.

The Goddess Sothis. Goddess of the Dog-Star (the star Sothis), goddess of initiation. Presides over all Squares that have two sides of Water and two sides of Fire.

The God Harpocrates or the Child Horus. God of silence and youth. Presides over all Squares that have two sides of Water and two sides of Air.

The Apis bull. God of lust and desire for life. Presides over all Squares that have two sides of Fire and two sides of Earth.

The God Anubis. God of the Tuat and guide through the Magical Universe. Presides over all Squares that have two sides of Air and two sides of Earth.

The Goddess Bast. Goddess of occultism and magic. Presides over all Squares that have two sides of Fire and two sides of Air.

The God Mestha. Protector. One of the four sons of Horus. Presides over all Squares with at least one side each of Fire, Water, and Earth.

The God Hapi. Protector. One of the four sons of Horus. Presides over all Squares with at least one side each of Fire, Water, and Air.

The God Tuamautef. Protector. One of the four sons of Horus. Presides over all Squares with at least one side each of Earth, Water, and Air.

The God Qebhsennuf. Protector. One of the four sons of Horus. Presides over all Squares with at least one side each of Earth, Fire, and Air.

The Sphinxes

Along with an Egyptian deity, each Lesser Square also contains a sphinx that is constructed in four parts according to the elements on the sides of the pyramid for the particular Square. The sphinxes are unnamed, and are considered to be living embodiments of the elements that comprise the Square.

The makeup of the sphinx is determined by the sides of the truncated pyramid. The four sides of a typical pyramid are shown in Figure 9.

1. Head. The element of Triangle 2 (see Figure 9) determines the head of the sphinx, and whether the sphinx has wings:

   Air—Human-headed with wings like an angel
   Water—Eagle- or hawk-headed with wings
   Earth—Bull-headed without wings
   Fire—Lion-headed without wings

2. Upper Body. The elements of Triangles 1 and 3 together (see Figure 9) determine the torso and arms or forelimbs:

   Air—Human torso/limbs with wings
   Water—Eagle or hawk torso with wings
   Earth—Bull-like torso/forelimbs without wings
   Fire—Lion-like torso/forelimbs without wings

3. Lower Body. The element of Triangle 4 (see Figure 9) determines the lower limbs (and tail for lion, bull, and eagle):

   Air—Human legs and feet
   Water—Eagle or hawk legs and tail
   Earth—Bull-like legs and tail
   Fire—Lion-like legs and tail

4. Sex. When Air and Fire are emphasized by the elements in the Triangles, the tendency of the sphinx is to be male. When Water and Earth are emphasized, the tendency of the sphinx is to be female. When these elements are equal, sex tends to be neutral and the sphinx is bisexual.

LESSON 9

The Signposts of Enochian Magic

Quite simply, signposts are those things in the Watchtowers and Aethyrs that are already known to exist. The Holy Tablets, made up of the four Watchtower Tablets and the Tablet of Union, for example, provide us with a crude map of these regions. When each Square is arranged as a truncated pyramid, we can determine a great deal about the tone or general atmosphere of each Square. For example, let's look at the Square A of AXIR, in Earth of Earth, in Appendix A. All four sides of the pyramid have the Earth element. This tells us that we would not expect to find great amounts of water in this Square. We would not expect to find fiery heat or blowing winds.

Now, let's look at some other signposts for this region. First of all, the astrological sign is Water and the Tarot card is The Hanged Man. Here 'water' is not meant in the sense of H_2O, because the element water is not found here. The astrological water is to be understood in the sense of nourishment. The Hanged Man usually implies a sacrifice of some kind. Together these signposts indicate that we would expect to see a region of fertility and growth where forms are sacrificed in order to produce new forms. We would expect to see seeds being sacrificed to produce plants, and plants being sacrificed to allow animals to live, and so on. The prototype of the entire food chain that we know on Earth is found in this Square. This conclusion is strengthened when we look at some other signposts.

For example, the ruling Egyptian deity is the god Horus who is associated with growth. The sphinx is a cow—a universal symbol of growth and nourishment. The sexual atmosphere of the Square is feminine which further clarifies the picture of this region. The Archangel, TAXIR, rules here and his chief administrator is the god, AXIR. (See the Ritual for Evoking the Watchtower Deities, Evocation Ritual: The Earth Angel, AXIR, beginning on page 345 of *An Advanced Guide to Enochian Magick* for details on AXIR.) The demon here is TAX who expresses motion. Motion is a good function in the Watchtower of Air or in the Air subquadrant of Earth. But in Earth of Earth it is bad and in this Square it is demonic. The entire Square reflects permanence and stability. But the seed of impermanence and transition is also found here, reflected in the demon TAX.

As you can see, we can gain a fairly good idea of the nature any Watchtower Square simply by looking at its known signposts. You will need to become familiar with the signposts of a region before trying to skry there. Otherwise you may go astray. The signposts should be used like you would use a map in a new city. They are necessary to guide you safely—to prevent you from becoming lost in the vast inner regions of the subconscious.

LESSON 10

The 30 Aethyrs

Along with the Watchtowers, a series of 30 subtle regions exists in the Magical Universe between our physical Earth and the highest spiritual regions of divinity. These are called the Aethyrs or Aires. The lowest is the 30th, called TEX. The highest is the first, called LIL. Table 5 contains the Enochian name, its English translation, and the ruling Governors for each of the 30 Aethyrs.

Table 5
The Aethyrs and Their Governors

Number	Name	Meaning	Governors
30	TEX	Aethyr in four parts	TAOAGLA GEMNIMB ADUORPT DOZIAAL
29	RII	Mercy of heaven	VASTRIM ODRAXTI GMOTZIAM
28	BAG	Aethyr of doubt	TABNIXP FOKLSNI OXLOPAR
27	ZAA	Aethyr of solitude	SAZIAMI MATHVLA KORPANIB
26	DES	Aethyr of acceptance	POPHAND NIGRANA BAZHIIM
25	VTI	Aethyr of change	MIRZIND OBVAORS RANGLAM
24	NIA	Aethyr of traveling	ORAKAMIR KHIASALPS SOAGEEL

Number	Name	Meaning	Governors
23	TOR	Aethyr of labor	RONOAMB ONIZIMP ZAXANIN
22	LIN	Aethyr of the void	OZIDAIA KALZIRG LAZDIXR PARAOAN
21	ASP	Aethyr of causation	KHLIRZPA TOANTOM VIXPALG
20	KHR	Aethyr of the wheel	ZILDRON PARZIBA TOTOKAN
19	POP	Aethyr of division	TORZOXI ABRAIOND OMAGRAP
18	ZEN	Aethyr of sacrifice	NABAOMI ZAFASAI VALPAMB
17	TAN	Aethyr of equilibrium	SIGMORF AYDROPT TOKARZI
16	LEA	Aethyr of the self	KUKUARPT LAUAKON SOKHIAL
15	OXO	Aethyr of dancing	TAHAMDO NOKIABI TASTOXO
14	VTA	Aethyr of semblances	TEDOAND VIVIPOS VOANAMB
13	ZIM	Aethyr of application	GEKAOND LAPARIN DOKEPAX
12	LOE	Aethyr of glory	TAPAMAL GEDOONS AMBRIOL
11	IKH	Aethyr of tension	MOLPAND VSNARDA PONODOL

Number	Name	Meaning	Governors
10	ZAX	Aethyr of the Abyss	LEXARPH KOMANAN TABITOM
9	ZIP	Aethyr of non-ego	ODDIORG KRALPIR DOANZIN
8	ZID	Aethyr of inner god	ZAMFRES TODNAON PRISTAK
7	DEO	Aethyr of love	OPMAKAS GENADOL ASPIAON
6	MAZ	Aethyr of appearances	SAXTOMP VAUAAMP ZIRZIRD
5	LIT	The godless Aethyr	LAXDIXI NOKAMAL TIARPAX
4	PAZ	Aethyr of manifestation	THOTANF AXZIARG POTHNIR
3	ZOM	Aethyr of self-knowledge	SAMAPHA VIRLOLI ANADISPI
2	ARN	Aethyr of fulfillment	DOAGNIS PAKASNA DIAIVOIA
1	LIL	The first Aethyr	OKKODON PASKOMB VALGARS

LESSON 11

The Body of Light

You have a body that is made of light, not flesh. You can move outside of the body of flesh and then return to it. As a magician or yogi, you must learn to do this at will. As the body of flesh lives in the physical world, so the Body of Light lives in the Magical Universe. As the body of flesh has senses to act and react in the physical world, so the Body of Light has senses to act and react in the Magical Universe. The Body of Light is invisible to physical eyes, but it can be seen with the inner vision. It is egg-shaped and permeates the body of flesh protruding from it in all directions.

The doctrine of the Body of Light is a very old one. It was well known, for example, in ancient Egypt. It is a general term for the subtle body that is actually composed of a divine body, a spiritual body, a causal body, a mental body, an astral body, and an etheric body. Table 6 shows the main parts of person's Body of Light used in Enochian Magic with Egyptian Magic and modern Theosophy for comparison.

Table 6
The Body of Light

Enochian	Egyptian	Theosophy
etheric	khaibit	linga-sarira
astral	ka	kama
mental	ba	lower manas
causal	sahu	upper manas
spiritual	khu	buddhi
divine	khabs	atma

LESSON 12

How to Assume
the God-Forms

Your Body of Light is plastic and can assume any form according to your will. This allows a magician or yogi to assume the form of any god or goddess while traveling in the Magical Universe.

You should select an appropriate Egyptian or Enochian deity and assume his/her form when entering your Body of Light. Then your Body of Light will naturally retain this shape throughout the operation.

In order to assist in constructing an appropriate god-form for the Greater and Lesser Angels of the Watchtowers, each letter in his/her name has the correspondences shown in Table 7.

Table 7
Enochian Letter
Telesmatic Correspondences

A	male	spiritual, wings
B	male	active
C, K	male	big, strong
D	female	beautiful, attractive
E	female	fierce, fiery
F	male	heavy, clumsy
G	female	beautiful, changing
H	female	undefined
I, J, Y	female	delicate
L	female	graceful
M	female	reflective, dreamlike
N	male	dark, determined
O	male	mechanical
P	female	fierce, resolute, strong
Q	female	thoughtful, intelligent
R	male	heavy
S	male	proud, dominant
T	male	fierce, active

U,V,W	male	dark
X	male	expressive, thin
Z	male	thin, intelligent

An Enochian god-form

Summary

Each Watchtower of the four main regions of unseen worlds that surround our physical world is divided into four subquadrants. Each Watchtower can also be divided into a Great Cross and four subquadrants. Each subquadrant can be divided into a Calvary Cross, Kerubic Squares, and Lesser Squares.

The Great Cross contains the most spiritual of the Watchtower Squares. The Lesser Squares beneath the arms of the Sephirothic Crosses contain the most material subplanes. The four Watchtowers form a Magical Universe that is held together by a Black Cross which contains a Tablet of Union.

The Great Northern Quadrant of Earth is a place of strong creative forces that give rise to all material things. This Quadrant is located from the surface of our planet upward in all directions until the highest subplane touches the surface of the moon.

The Great Western Quadrant of Water is the Watchtower is a region of strong life creating forces that give rise to all living things. This Quadrant is located from the surface of the Earth upward in all directions until the highest subplane touches the surface of the planet Venus.

The Great Eastern Quadrant of Air is the Watchtower is a region of strong intelligent forces that give rise to the logic and reason of all living things. This Quadrant is located from the surface of the Earth upward in all directions until the highest subplane touches the surface of the planet Mercury.

The Great Southern Quadrant of Fire is the Watchtower is a region of strong creative and destructive forces that give rise to the ultimate growth of all living things. This Quadrant is located from the surface of the Earth upward in all directions until the highest subplane touches the surface of the Sun.

The Tablet of Union is the Great Tablet that is the ultimate source of all things that exist upon our physical world. It is a region of strong causative forces that give rise to the entire universe of all living things. It is composed entirely of Spirit. This Tablet is located from the surface of the Earth upward and outward in all directions until the highest subplane touches the farthermost fringes of the solar system.

In order to render a Watchtower Square closer to its real nature, we make each Square a truncated pyramid.

There are many Enochian deities in the four Watchtowers. In general, their names are all derived from the letters in the Squares. In addition to Enochian deities there is also an Egyptian deity and a sphinx associated with each Lesser Square of each Watchtower. The sphinx is constructed in four parts according to the elements on the sides of the pyramid for the particular Square. They are unnamed, and are considered to be living embodiments of the elements that comprise the Square.

Signposts are those things in the Watchtowers and Aethyrs that are already known to exist. The Holy Tablets, made up of the four Watchtower Tablets and the Tablet of Union, provides us with a crude map of these regions. When each Square is arranged as a truncated pyramid, we can determine a great deal about the tone or general atmosphere of each Square. We can gain a fairly good idea of the nature of any Watchtower Square simply by looking at its known signposts.

Along with the Watchtowers, a series of 30 subtle regions exists in the Magical Universe between our physical Earth and the highest spiritual regions of divinity. These are called the Aethyrs or Aires.

As the body of flesh lives in the physical world, so the Body of Light lives in the Magical Universe. The Body of Light has senses to act and react in the Magical Universe. It is a general term for the subtle body that is composed of a divine body, a spiritual body, a causal body, a mental body, an astral body, and an etheric body. The Body of Light is plastic and can assume any form. A magician can assume the form of any god or goddess while traveling in the Magical Universe.

Further Suggested Reading

Magicians of the Golden Dawn. Ellic Howe, Weiser.

The Golden Dawn: The Inner Teachings. G.D. Torrens, Weiser.

The Golden Dawn. Ed. by Israel Regardie, Llewellyn.

Aspects of Occultism. Dion Fortune, Weiser.

Magick Without Tears. Aleister Crowley, Llewellyn.

Modern Magick. Donald Kraig, Llewellyn.

Mysteria Magica. Denning & Phillips, Llewellyn.

Transcendental Magic. Eliphas Levi (Trans. by A.E. Waite), Weiser.

The Gods of the Egyptians. E.A. Wallis Budge, Dover.

Tutankhamen. E.A. Wallis Budge, Bell.

Egyptian Mythology. Veronica Ions, Paul Hamlyn.

The Book of Celestial Images. A.C. Highfield, Aquarian Press.

Applied Magic. Dion Fortune, Weiser.

Coming into the Light. G. & B. Schueler, Llewellyn.

The Personal Aura. Dora van Gelder Kunz, Quest.

Man Visible and Invisible. C. W. Leadbeater, Quest.

Fountain-Source of Occultism. G. de Purucker, Theosophical University Press.

Things to Do for Section 3

1. The Enochian Tablets are "road maps" of the invisible worlds that surround our Earth. Make your own Tablets of the four Great Watchtowers and a Tablet of Union. At the end of this section we have included a master template you can use to make your Watchtowers and the Tablet of Union. Take these templates to your local copy center and have them reproduced. Make a number of copies of each template so that you can practice filling in the Squares with both letters and colors.

   Your ultimate goal is to be able to fill in all of the truncated Squares without having to reference this book. A set of the completed, truncated Watchtower Squares, with appropriate colors, is included in the color plates at the center of this book. Use these guides to complete your Squares.

2. Make your truncated pyramids as shown in Appendix A.

3. Using the template shown in Figure 10, make your own truncated pyramid out of cardboard. Typical examples are shown in Appendix A. Use colored construction paper to make replaceable sides that correspond to the elements. Use square pieces of paper with appropriate letters drawn on them to place on the truncated top. By changing the sides and the top, you can make a model of any of the Watchtower Squares.

4. Choose a Square in each Watchtower and list as many signposts for it as you can.

   Earth
   Square:

   Signposts:

Water
Square:

Signposts:

Air
Square:

Signposts:

Fire
Square:

Signposts:

5. List at least four signposts for the Lesser Squares of Earth of Earth.

6. Practice pronouncing each deity name presented in this section.

7. Calculate the gematria value of each Enochian King and Senior. Use Appendix D to find possible correspondences.

8. Calculate the gematria value of each Governor's name. Use Appendix D to find possible correspondences.

9. Using the gematria values given in an Appendix D. Try to establish some hidden correspondences with the deities that you calculated in 7 and 8 above.

10. Compare Tables 1 and 6. Notice that each of your four main subtle bodies and each of the four main cosmic planes corresponds to a Watchtower.

11. Practice making god-forms using the letter correspondences in Table 7. Make god-forms of the eight Sephirothic Cross Angels of Earth.

Questions for Section 3

1. True or False: The Watchtowers are invisible to our physical senses.

2. True or False: The Watchtower of Earth is a region of strong life creating forces.

3. Name the planet that is associated with each of the four Watchtowers.

    Watchtower of Earth _____

    Watchtower of Water _____

    Watchtower of Air   _____

    Watchtower of Fire   _____

4. What is the element of the Tablet of Union?

5. Name the four Kings of the Watchtowers.

    Watchtower of Earth _____

    Watchtower of Water _____

    Watchtower of Air   _____

    Watchtower of Fire   _____

6. True or False: Egyptian deities are only found in the Lesser Squares of the four Watchtowers.

7. True or False: Demons are only found in the Lesser Squares of the four Watchtowers.

8. Who is the Egyptian Goddess of the Dog-Star?

9. Who is the Egyptian God of the Dead?

10. Multiple choice: Each side of a truncated pyramid can contain
    a. up to four elements.
    b. two elements.
    c. only one element.
    d. all five elements.

11. Multiple choice: The top of a truncated pyramid should contain
    a. the name of the Egyptian deity.
    b. the Egyptian sphinx.
    c. the cosmic element.
    d. the Enochian letter of the Square.

12. What is the name of the 10th Aethyr and why is this Aethyr so important?

13. What is the difference between the Egyptian ka and the ba?

14. True or False: Your Body of Light is your own aura.

15. True or False: The Angel ATAPA has wings.

16. Name the Angel who designed the Enochian magical ring.

17. What Egyptian deity governs Square X of AXIR in the subquadrant Earth of Earth?

18. What Egyptian deity governs Square N of OPNA in the subquadrant Earth of Earth?

19. What are the names of the four main Kerubic Angels of the Watchtower of Earth?

Watchtower of Water?

Watchtower of Air?

Watchtower of Fire?

20. Describe the sphinx in the Squares A, X, I, and R of AXIR in the sub-quadrant Earth of Earth.

21. Who is the Egyptian ruler of Square P of OPNA in Earth of Earth? Describe the sphinx that is in this Square.

COLOR PLATE 1: Earth of Earth

COLOR PLATE 2: Water of Earth

COLOR PLATE 3: Air of Earth

COLOR PLATE 4: Fire of Earth

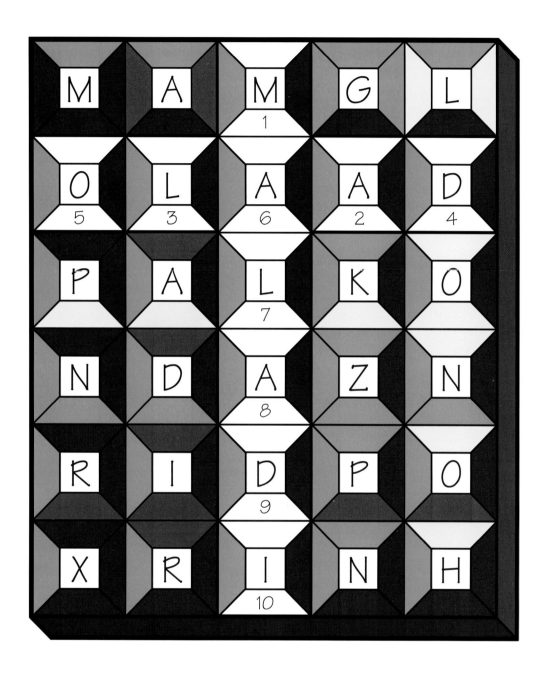

COLOR PLATE 5: Earth of Water

COLOR PLATE 6: Water of Water

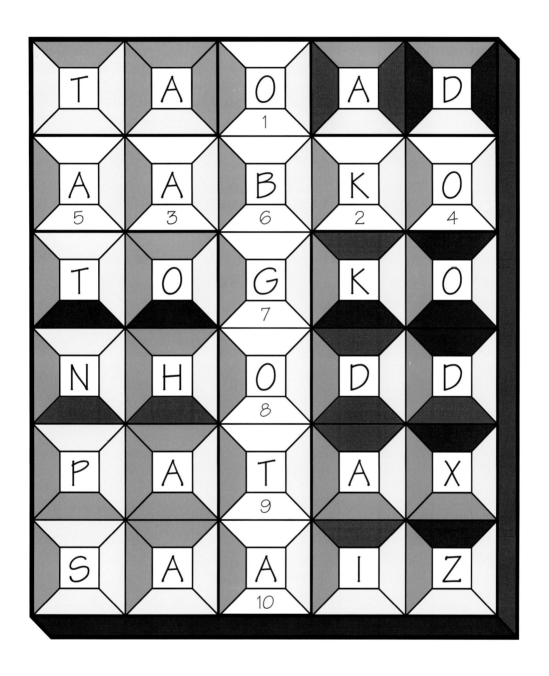

COLOR PLATE 7: Air of Water

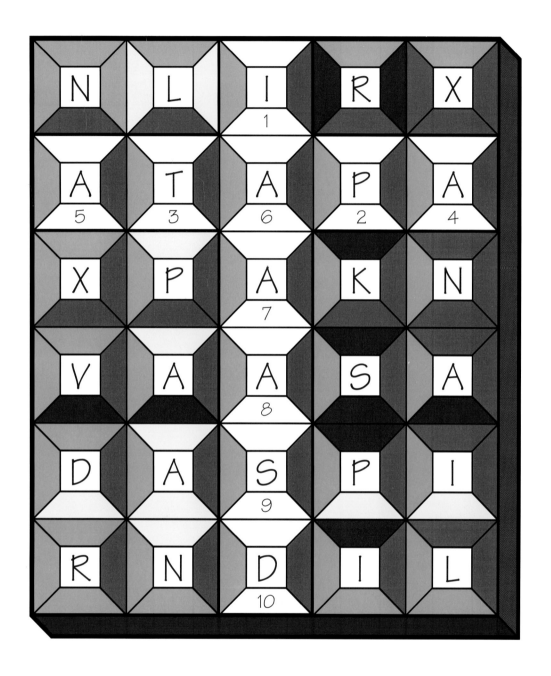

COLOR PLATE 8: Fire of Water

COLOR PLATE 9: Earth of Air

COLOR PLATE 10: Water of Air

COLOR PLATE 11: Air of Air

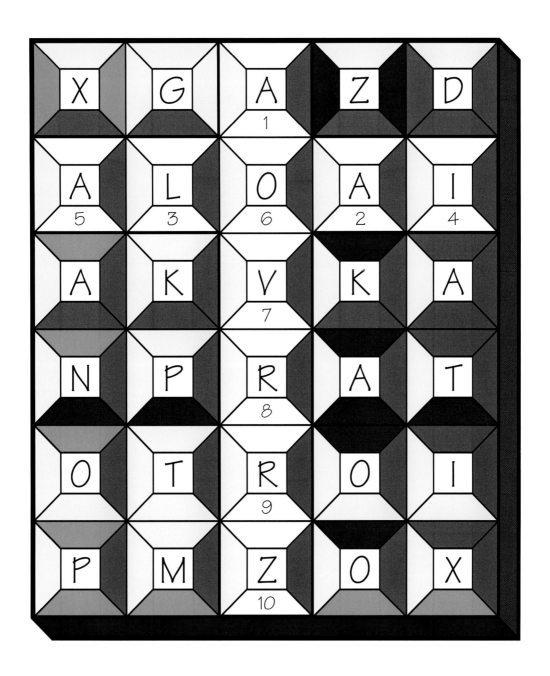

COLOR PLATE 12: Fire of Air

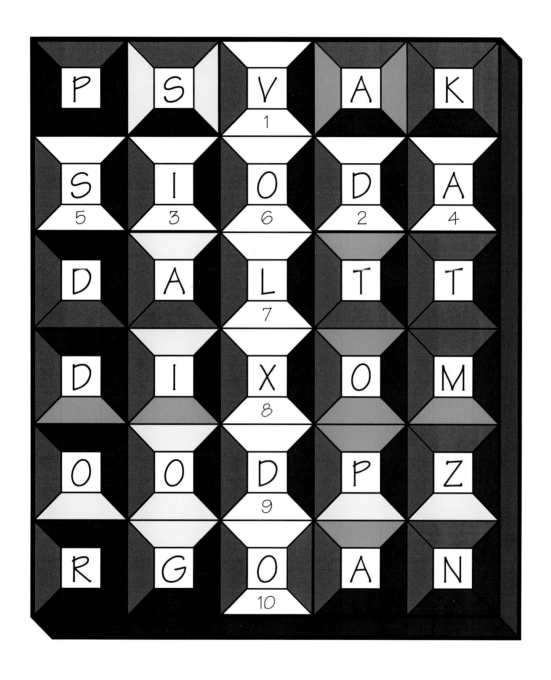

COLOR PLATE 13: Earth of Fire

COLOR PLATE 14: Water of Fire

COLOR PLATE 15: Air of Fire

COLOR PLATE 16: Fire of Fire

SECTION 4

Magical Weapons

Section Outline

LESSON 13: MAGICAL WEAPONS
THEORY

THE PANTACLE
HOW TO MAKE YOUR OWN

THE CUP
HOW TO MAKE YOUR OWN

THE SWORD & DAGGER
HOW TO MAKE YOUR OWN

THE WAND
HOW TO MAKE YOUR OWN

THE RING
HOW TO VISUALIZE THE MAGICAL RING

SUMMARY/FURTHER SUGGESTED READING/THINGS TO DO/QUESTIONS

Learning Objectives

This section has one lesson that deals with the magical weapons used in Enochian Magic. Upon completion of the lesson you should be able to:

- List the six magical weapons, their symbolism, and uses
- Construct your own magical weapons
- Visualize the use of the magical weapons and the ring

LESSON 13

Magical Weapons

Theory

Magical weapons are real or vividly imagined (visualized) props used as psychological devices to help focus the mind during magical operations. The Pantacle symbolizes food or nourishment; the Cup symbolizes understanding; the Sword symbolizes logic and reason; the Dagger symbolizes the penetrating power of thought; the Wand symbolizes the Will, and the Ring symbolizes protection.

The Pantacle

The Pantacle is your magical weapon for use in the Watchtower of Earth. It is a flat disk that, when fully charged, is a powerful source of energy and sustenance. The Pantacle symbolizes your body as a form of crystallized karma.

When properly constructed and consecrated, it will protect you from most of the evil forces that lurk in the Great Northern Quadrangle of Earth. A typical Pantacle is shown in Figure 15.

How to Make Your Own Pantacle

Use a round wooden disc that is four to five inches in diameter and about 1/4 inch in thickness. Sand until smooth. Paint the disc black. If you want, you can decorate the Pantacle by painting a white hexagram on each side. You can also write the Holy Name, MOR-DIAL-HKTGA, and the word for earth, NANTA, in Enochian letters somewhere on the Pantacle.

The Cup

The Cup is your magical weapon for use in the Watchtower of Water. The Cup is a passive weapon. It represents your understanding of Magic. It is feminine and can be used to counter attacks from the forces of masculine currents. It will protect you from most of the evil forces that lurk in the Great Western Quadrangle of Water. A typical Cup is shown in Figure 16.

How to Make Your Own Cup

Use any blue glass or blue crystal cup. Ideally, the cup should look like a flower with eight petals (i.e., it should have eight cuts or ridges). You should write the Holy Name, MPH-ARSL-GAIOL, and the word for water, HKOMA, in Enochian letters somewhere on the Cup in orange. Most office and art supply stores carry special pens that will write on glass.

Figure 15. A typical Pantacle

Figure 16. A typical Cup

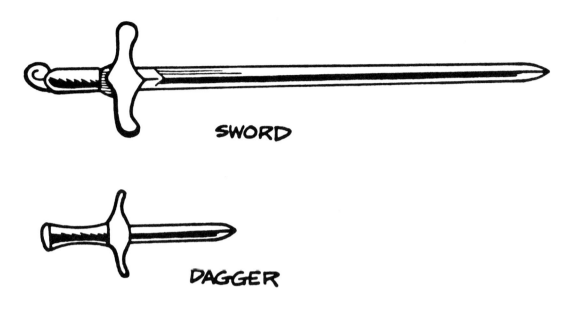

Figure 17. A typical Sword and Dagger

The Sword and Dagger

The Sword and Dagger are magical weapons to be used in the Watchtower of Air. The Sword cuts and dissects like the mind, when focused on a complex idea. Its nature is division and separation. The Dagger pierces like the penetrating power of thought against an illusion. Both weapons are used to counter illusion. The Dagger is often used by advanced magicians because, like a dagger's stab lets blood, so the Dagger's thrust can extinguish the emotions that often accompany a magician in the Watchtowers. The elimination of emotions is required in order to properly enter the Watchtower of Air. Either weapon will protect you from most of the evil forces that lurk in the Great Eastern Quadrangle of Air. A typical Sword and Dagger are shown in Figure 17.

How to Make Your Own Dagger

Use any knife or letter opener. Ideally, the Dagger should have a guard at the hilt. Paint the handle bright yellow. You should write the Holy Name, ORO-IBAH-AOZPI, and the word for air, EXARP, in Enochian letters somewhere on the Dagger in violet or in purple.

Figure 18. A typical Wand

The Wand

The Wand symbolizes the Magical Will. It is the principal weapon of the Magus and can be used for both invocations and evocations. It is the chief weapon used to combat all types of fiery energy and thus, is used for all operations associated with the Watchtower of Fire. The Wand will protect you from most of the evil forces that lurk in the Great Southern Quadrangle of Fire. A typical Wand is shown in Figure 18.

How to Make Your Own Wand

Use a wooden dowel about 10 to 12 inches in length, and 1/2 to 3/4 inches in diameter. Sand the dowel until smooth. Paint it bright red. Ideally, one end of the Wand should be cone-shaped and an iron or steel rod should be inserted along its central axis in order to obtain a magnetic effect. You should write the Holy Name, OIP-TEAA-PDOKE, and the word for fire, BITOM, in Enochian letters somewhere on the Wand in bright green.

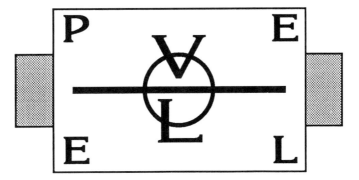

Figure 19. The magical Ring

The Ring

Figure 19 shows the design of the Enochian magical ring. This design was given to John Dee by the Angel Michael in a dream. It is made of gold and is magically designed to protect the wearer from all manner of evil influences. According to Dee's notes, Michael told Dee that this was the same ring "wherewith all miracles and divine works and wonders were wrought by Solomon."

How to Visualize the Magical Ring

Because the Enochian magical ring is made of gold, it cannot be easily reproduced. A picture of the ring is also shown on page 105 of *Enochian Yoga*, for those readers who want to have a copy of the ring made. Fortunately, it is not important to actually wear a physical ring. A properly visualized ring will work just as well and will not cost a cent. A yogic meditation of this ring's design can be found in *Enochian Yoga* (Llewellyn).

Summary

Magical weapons are real or visualized props used as psychological devices to help focus the mind during magical operations. The Pantacle symbolizes nourishment; the Cup symbolizes understanding; the Sword symbolizes logic; the Dagger symbolizes the power of thought; the Wand symbolizes the Will, and the Ring symbolizes protection.

The Pantacle is used in the Watchtower of Earth. It is a flat disk that is a powerful source of energy and sustenance. It symbolizes your body as a form of crystallized karma. It is used in the Watchtower of Water.

The cup is a passive weapon that represents your understanding of Magic. It is feminine and can be used to counter attacks from the forces of masculine currents.

The Sword and Dagger are used in the Watchtower of Air. The Sword cuts, when focused on a complex idea. Its nature is division and separation. The Dagger pierces illusion. It is often used because its thrust can extinguish emotions. The elimination of emotions is required in order to properly enter the Watchtower of Air.

The Wand symbolizes the Magical Will. It can be used for both invocations and evocations, and to combat all types of fiery energy. It is used in the Watchtower of Fire.

The Enochian magical ring design was given to John Dee by the angel, Michael, in a dream. The ring is made of gold and is magically designed to protect the wearer from all manner of evil influences.

Further Suggested Reading

The Golden Dawn: The Inner Teachings. G.D. Torrens, Weiser.

The Golden Dawn. Ed. by Israel Regardie, Llewellyn.

The Secret Temple. Robert Wang, Weiser.

Techniques of High Magic. F. King & S. Skinner, Destiny Books.

The Key of Solomon the King. S. Liddell MacGregor Mathers, Weiser.

Liber A. Aleister Crowley.

Book 4. Aleister Crowley.

Secrets of a Golden Dawn Temple. Chic Cicero and Sandra Tabatha Cicero, Llewellyn.

Things to Do for Section 4

1. Make your own Pantacle, Cup, Dagger, Wand, and if possible, Ring, using the guidance provided in Lesson 13.

2. Practice visualizing using your weapons and ring during a magical operations.

Questions for Section 4

1. True or False: The Enochian magician should construct and use magical weapons.

2. Match the magical weapons in the first column with the respective symbolism in the second column.

1. Pantacle	a. Power of thought
2. Wand	b. Protection
3. Cup	c. Will
4. Dagger	d. Food
5. Sword	e. Logic
6. Ring	f. Understanding

3. Match the magical weapons in the first column with the respective Watchtower in the second column. Items in the second column may be used more than once.

1. Pantacle	a. Watchtower of Air
2. Wand	b. Anywhere
3. Cup	c. Watchtower of Earth
4. Dagger	d. Watchtower of Water
5. Sword	e. Watchtower of Fire
6. Ring	

SECTION 5

Talismans
and Squares

Section Outline

Learning Objectives

This section contains three lessons. The first is on talismans, the second is on magic squares, and the third is about the magical dragon. In this section, you will learn how to make your own talismans, and how to use magical squares. You will learn the ultimate of practicing this magical system—to become a magical dragon. Upon completing the reading you should be able to:

- Differentiate between an amulet and a talisman
- Construct and charge a magic talisman
- Use a magic square

LESSON 14

Amulets and Talismans

Theory

Talismans and amulets are well-known devices that have been used by magicians for thousands of years. Amulets and talismans often have the same design; the primary difference between the two devices is how they are to be used.

Amulets are usually worn on the body as a form of magical protection—to ward away unwanted forces or hostile entities. They can be made and worn on the body without charging. The material they are made from influences you directly. An amulet should last for a long time.

Talismans are usually not worn on the body and are constructed and charged with magical force for a specific purpose. A talisman can be used once—then it is usually either carefully destroyed or recharged (much like a battery must be periodically recharged).

In Enochian Magic, amulets and talismans are used as a physical expression of your Magical Will. They are used to remind you of the power of your Magical Will. In addition, others who see it will also be moved consciously or unconsciously to carry out your Will.

Correspondences

The construction of an amulet or talisman depends on what it is to be used for. Its purpose usually determines the material from which it is made, the inscriptions that are placed on it, and the type of force or power that is invoked into it. Various metals, colors, gems, and the days of the week have magical correspondences with the subtle bodies and planets. These correspondences, shown in Table 8, must be considered when designing an amulet or talisman.

Table 8
Talisman Correspondences

Body	Planet	Metal	Color	Day	Gem
Physical	Sun	gold	orange	Sunday	carbuncle
Etheric	Mars	iron	red	Tuesday	diamond
Astral	Moon	silver	violet	Monday	crystal
Mental	Saturn	lead	green	Saturday	onyx
Causal	Venus	copper	indigo	Friday	emerald
Spiritual	Mercury		yellow	Wednesday	achate
Divine	Jupiter	tin	blue	Thursday	sapphire

Charging a Talisman

Talismans must be periodically recharged. The steps required to construct and charge an Enochian talisman are as follows:

1. On the day indicated in Table 8, make a pantacle-shaped talisman out of the metal shown in Table 8. If metals are not available, use a substitute such as wood or cardboard painted in the appropriate color as given in Table 8. This color serves as the background color of the talisman.

2. On the same day, inscribe the talisman with appropriate numbers and symbols. For example, if invoking a deity, use the gematria number of the god-name and sigil, if known.

3. On the appropriate day (see Table 8), conduct an invoking ritual to charge the talisman (a typical ritual for this purpose is given in Lesson 24).

4. After charging the talisman with the proper force, wrap it in white linen or silk and carefully store it in its own box to help keep the charge until it is used.

5. Use the talisman when and where necessary to effect the desired result. Usually this is during an appropriate ritual where the talisman is used to emphasize the desired purpose and assure a favorable result.

Examples

Let's look at two examples, but keep in mind there are no hard and fast rules. Use the symbols/signposts available from this and other books and place them together in a manner that is pleasing to you. A Golden Dawn rule was "In construction of a talisman, symbolism should be exact and in harmony with universal forces."

Figure 20. The talisman of ALHKTGA

Example 1. Figure 20 shows a talisman that can be used to obtain wealth, fertility, abundance, and general prosperity. It employs the magical power of ALHKTGA, the fourth Senior of Earth (see Enochian Tarot card 77 for a picture of this Senior). This talisman is designed with a seven-sided heptagon that has a letter of the Senior's name at each point. It should be made of copper and painted indigo (the metal and color of Venus because this Senior is associated with Venus as shown in his Tarot card as well as on page 43 of *Enochian Magic: A Practical Manual*).

The center of the talisman contains a green pentagram with the number 338 at its center. Emerald green is the special color of ALHKTGA, as given in *Enochian Tarot* (card 77). The pentagram symbolizes the number 5. (The gematria value of this Senior's name is 338 that reduces to 5 by theosophic addition. That is, you add the three numbers that make up the gematria value, 338, (3+3+8=14) and then add the numbers that make up the result, 14, (1+4=5), to get a value of 5.

The main symbols of this Senior are also included: a red rose and a red five-sided amulet. The rose and the Amulet of ALHKTGA are described on page 209 of *Enochian Tarot*. Red is used because it is the complement of green, the color of ALHKTGA. Beneath the star is the magical sign for the element Earth (this Senior's element); within it is the sign for Venus.

Figure 21. The talisman of LSRAHPM

Example 2.   Figure 21 shows a talisman that can be used to obtain magical power over others and for general personal gain. It employs the magical power of LSRAHPM, the first Senior of Water (see Enochian Tarot card 60 for a picture of this Senior). The talisman is designed with a seven-sided heptagon that has a letter of the Senior's name at each point.

This talisman should be made of iron and painted red (the metal and color of Mars because this Senior is associated with Mars as shown in his Tarot card as well as on page 42 of *Enochian Magic: A Practical Manual*). The center of the talisman contains an orange pentagram with the number 221 at its center. Orange is the special color of LSRAHPM as given in *Enochian Tarot* (card 60).

The pentagram symbolizes the number 5. The gematria value of this Senior's name is 221 that reduces to 5 by theosophic addition (2+2+1=5). The main symbols of this Senior are also included: a purple Rod of Power and a purple lightning bolt. The Rod of Power and the lightning bolt are described on page 175 of *Enochian Tarot*. Purple is used because it is the complement of orange, the color of LSRAHPM. Beneath the pentagram is the magical sign for the element Water (this Senior's element); within it is the sign for Mars.

LESSON 15

Magic Squares

Theory

An ancient Egyptian text says, "The life of a person is invested in his name." This ancient teaching expresses the idea that names have power in the sense that if you know the true name of something you have a degree of control over it. Names and words have always been regarded as important in magic.

Enochian Magic uses Enochian names and words. Some words can be put together in a special way to form a square. These are called Magic Squares. Figure 22 shows five typical Enochian Magic Squares. Descriptions of these squares can be found in *An Advanced Guide to Enochian Magick*. Additional Magic Squares can be found in *Enochian Yoga*.

Uses of Magic Squares

The use of such squares is variable. For example, many if not all Magic Squares can be made into talismans, suitably charged, and then used in magical rituals. According to Abramelin Magic, simply having such a square on your person and touching it, while making a corresponding wish, will help make that wish come true.

Many magicians, especially those who practice Enochian Magic, use them for meditation. Each letter stands for a special magical idea as shown in Table 2. Squares of letters can provide the basis for powerful meditations simply by concentrating on the letter- meanings and their arrangement within the squares. The following three examples are provided.

Examples

Example 1. The LAMA Square.

```
L   A   M   A
A   A   I   T
M   I   A   O
A   T   O   L
```

This square contains the Enochian words, LAMA-AAI-T-MI-AOA-TOL, that can be translated "the path that is within you leads to the power that is within everyone," or "the path in you is the power in all." This square contains the idea that we all have an inner source of power that we can use to overcome almost all problems that might arise if we but knew how. The gematria value of all 16 letters is 430 and that reduces to 7 (4+3+0=7), the number for wholeness and completeness. This square should be used whenever we feel unworthy or unsuccessful to increase our self-esteem and optimism.

Example 2. The PASHS Square.

```
P A S H S
A B R A M
S R O R N
H A R G A
S M N A D
```

This square contains the Enochian words, PASHS-ABRAM-S-ROR-N-HARG-A-SMNAD, that mean "Children are provided by the Sun. May I conceive such a one," or "Children are prepared by the sun. May I sow another." This square contains the idea that children are a gift of creative divinity because the Sun was taught by the ancients to be the highest creative deity in our solar system. The gematria value of all 25 letters is 802 that theosophic addition reduces to 1 (8+0+2=10, 1+0=1). The number 1 is the number for the monad, unity, and for male and female conjoined. Taken all together, this square should be used to assure fertility when trying to produce a child.

Example 3. The ZORGE square.

```
Z O R G E
O   I   L
R I T   Z
G       A
E L Z A P
```

This square represents a popular type of square, an incomplete square, in that not all of the positions contain letters. The square contains three Enochian words: ZORGE, meaning love; RIT, meaning mercy; and ELZAP, meaning the way. It suggests that the proper way to live is with mercy and love. The 19 Enochian letters have a total gematria value of 489 that reduces to 3 (4+8+9=21, and 2+1=3), the number of words used. The number 3 indicates intelligence and manifestation. It suggests that the intelligent way to live in this world is to express love and mercy. This square should be used by anyone who would like to see more love and mercy in their lives.

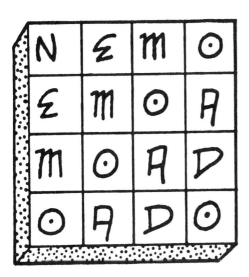

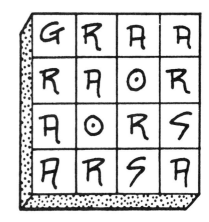

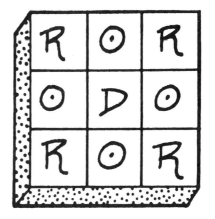

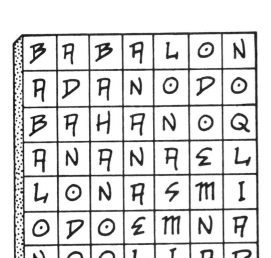

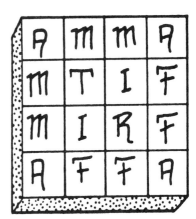

Figure 22. Examples of Enochian magic squares

LESSON 16

The Enochian Dragon

Who Qualifies as a "Dragon"

Enochian Magic is practiced by magicians of all levels of skill and expertise. Special levels or grades are called VOVIN (Voh-vee-neh), an Enochian word that means "dragon." The Magical Dragon is a title assumed by the advanced magician in Enochian Magic. The Dragon is aware of his/her True Will. S/he has had the Knowledge and Conversation with his/her Holy Guardian Angel— his/her inner divinity. S/he has successfully faced the Archdemon, KHORONZON, in the Great Outer Abyss, safely passed through to the spiritual realms beyond, and returned with full memory of his/her experiences. Such a one has successfully undergone at least five major ordeals. S/he has encountered both Angels and Demons. S/he has wandered the invisible pathways of the Watchtowers and Aethyrs. S/he is a qualified teacher and practitioner of his/her craft.

The history of humanity is steeped with the tales of mighty magicians. They are usually portrayed as solitary figures, full of years, with flowing beards and carrying a staff of some kind. Tolkien's Gandalf is a typical example of the magician or wizard found in folklore. Other magicians are said to carry bags containing all manner of spells and devices used in magical operations.

How does one become a magician? More to the point, how can you become a Magical Dragon? The path of the Dragon is long and hard. It begins with a serious study of the basics—the fundamental teachings and concepts. It winds through many regions of hard work and patient practice. The end is never really attained—only approached in degree.

Stages of Development

There are eight major stages of development as described in *Enochian Yoga*. The candidate begins at Grade I, the Novice. Here s/he learns the fundamental teachings of Enochian Magic and must successfully conduct several basic magical operations. If successful, the student reaches Grades II, III, and IV where s/he works to become a Dragon of Justice, Grade V. This is the first true level of the Magical Dragon. After passing the ordeals of this grade, s/he moves on to Grade VI. Now s/he must study to become the Dragon of Cycles. Success at this level will allow the magician to advance to Grade VII, the Dragon of Death.

Finally, after many years of hard work, the last level of Grade VIII is reached. Now the magician must earn the title of Dragon of Love, the last and highest rank. If s/he succeeds in all of this, s/he becomes a true Magical Dragon. S/he will be able to roam freely through all parts of the universe—both visible and invisible.

Summary

Talismans and amulets are magical devices that often have the same design but different uses. Amulets and talismans are physical expressions of the Magical Will.

Amulets are worn on the body for magical protection. They can be made and worn on the body without charging. The material they are made from directly influences the wearer.

Talismans are not worn on the body. They are constructed and charged with magical force for a specific purpose. A talisman is used once, then destroyed or recharged. Construction of an amulet or talisman depends on its use. Its purpose determines the material from which it is made, the inscriptions that are placed on it, and the type of force or power that is invoked into it.

Various metals, colors, gems, and the days of the week have magical correspondences with the subtle bodies and planets. These correspondences must be considered when designing an amulet or talisman.

Names have power. If you know the true name of something you have a degree of control over it. Enochian Magic uses Enochian names and words. Some words can be put together in a special way to form a square. These are called Magic Squares.

The use of squares is variable. Some are made into talismans and then used in magical rituals. Wearing a square on your person and touching it, while making a corresponding wish, may help make that wish come true. Some squares are used for meditation.

The Magical Dragon is a title assumed by the advanced magician in Enochian Magic. The Dragon is aware of his/her True Will and has had the Knowledge and Conversation with his/her inner divinity. S/he is a qualified teacher and practitioner of his/her craft.

Further Suggested Reading

The Golden Dawn. Ed by Israel Regardie, Llewellyn.

The Sacred Magic of Abramelin the Mage. Trans. by S.L. Macgregor Mathers, Dover.

The Magus. Francis Barrett, Citadel.

The Book of the Goetia of Solomon the King. Ed. by Aleister Crowley, Magical Childe.

Amulets and Superstitions. E.A. Wallis Budge, Dover.

Egyptian Magic, E.A. Wallis Budge, Citadel.

The Complete Book of Spells, Ceremonies & Magic. Migene González-Wippler, Llewellyn.

The Secret Lore of Magic. Idries Shah, Citadel.

The Book of Ceremonial Magic, a Complete Grimoire. A.E. Waite, Citadel.

The Legend of Aleister Crowley. P.R. Stephensen and Israel Regardie, Llewellyn.

The Eye in the Triangle. Israel Regardie, Llewellyn.

A Pictorial History of Magic and the Supernatural. Maurice Bessy, Spring Books.

The Complete Book of Amulets & Talismans. Migene González-Wippler, Llewellyn.

The Book of Ceremonial Magic: A Complete Grimoire. A. E. Waite. Citadel.

Things to Do for Section 5

1. Make your own Talisman of ALHKTGA and your own Talisman of LSRAHPM in accordance with the rules given in Lesson 15. Later in this workbook, you will learn how to charge them.

2. Make a talisman of the LAMA square. Later in this workbook, you will learn how to charge this talisman.

3. Carefully evaluate your motives. Why would you would like to work on the Path to the Magical Dragon? If not, why not? You can often tell a lot about your prospects for accomplishing magical goals if you first look at your purpose.

My purpose is:

4. If becoming a Dragon is one of your goals, establish a plan of action to achieve it. List all of the things that you would like to do.

Questions for Section 5

1. What is the difference between a talisman and an amulet?

2. True or False: Magic Squares can be used as magical talismans.

3. True or False: The construction of an amulet or talisman depends on what it is to be used for.

4. True or False: Magic Squares can be used for meditation.

5. What is a Magical Dragon?

SECTION 6

Rituals of
Enochian Magic

Section Outline

Learning Objectives

This section contains eight lessons which provide a background in rituals and how rituals are conducted in Enochian Magic. The section begins with the Calls, recorded by Dee and Kelly, and slightly modernized by the authors. The rules for when to use the Calls are also given. How to vibrate the Names of Power and how to make a magic circle are presented as introductory material for rituals. The section ends with several rituals for you to conduct in a step-by-step format for clarity and convenience. Upon completing the reading you should be able to:

- Make appropriate Calls for all Enochian deities.

- Make the four main magical Signs.

- Vibrate all Enochian names.

- Construct a Magic Circle.

- Consecrate your magical weapons.

- Conduct the pentagram and hexagram rituals for invoking and banishing Enochian deities.

- Magically charge your talismans.

LESSON 17

The Calls and
When to Use Them

The Calls

Following are 18 Enochian Calls to invoke or evoke the Watchtower deities. Before you begin a particular Call, you should first face the direction of the deity's Watchtower. Continue facing that direction while performing the Call. The 18 Calls are:

The First Call. "I rule over you," declares the God of Justice. His power is exalted above the torment of the world. In his hands, the Sun is like a sword and the Moon is like an all-consuming fire. He measures your clothing material among the available substances and draws you together like the palms of my hands. [Furthermore he says:] "I have decorated your seats with the Fire of Gathering, and have beautified your garments with admiration. I have made a law to govern the Holy Ones, and have delivered a Rod to you, with the Ark of Knowledge. Moreover, you have lifted up your voices and sworn obedience and faith to Him who lives and triumphs, whose beginning is not, and whose end cannot be, who shines like a flame in the center of your palaces, and who rules among you as the balance of righteousness and truth." [The magician addresses the appropriate angels and says:] Move therefore, and show yourselves! Unveil the mysteries of your creation! Be friendly to me, because I am a servant of this same God, a true worshipper of the Highest.

The Second Call. Can the winged wings understand your wondrous voices? You are the Second of the First. Burning flames outline you when I speak your names. I will treat you like cups for a wedding, or like beautiful flowers in the Chamber of Righteousness. Your feet are stronger than the barren stone, and your voices are mightier than many winds. You are becoming like a building which does not exist save in the Mind of the All-Powerful. [The magician addresses the appropriate angels and says:] The First commands you to arise and to move therefore toward his servant. Show yourselves, because I am of Him who lives forever.

The Third Call. "Behold," declares your God, "I am a circle on whose hands stand Twelve Kingdoms. Six of these are seats of life, the rest are like sharp Sickles, or like the Horns of Death. Because of this, the creatures of Earth live or die only in my own hands, which sleep and then rise again. In the beginning I made you stewards, and placed you in the twelve seats of government. I gave every one of you an appropriate level of power over the 456 true ages of time. My intent was that from the highest vessels, and the farthest corners of your governments, you might work my Power, and pour down the fires of life, and multiply upon the earth. Thus, you have become the skirts of justice and truth." [The magician addresses the appropriate angels and says:] In the name of this same God, lift yourselves up, I say. Behold, His mercies flourish, and His Name has become mighty among us. In Him we say, move, and descend. Apply yourselves to us as you would to partakers of His Secret Wisdom in your creation.

The Fourth Call. I place my feet in the South, and look about me and say, "Are not the thunders of increase numbered 33, and do these not rule in the Second Angle? I have placed 9639 servants under them. None have yet numbered them, but One. In them, the Second Beginnings of Things exists and grows strong. They are the successive Numbers of Time. Their powers are like those of the first 456. Arise, you Sons of Pleasure, and visit the Earth. I am the Lord your God, who is, and who lives forever." [The magician addresses the appropriate angels and says:] In the name of the Creator, move and show yourselves as pleasant deliverers, and praise Him among the sons of men.

The Fifth Call. Mighty sounds have entered into the Third Angle, and have become like olives on the Olive Mount. They look with gladness upon the Earth, and dwell in the brightness of the heavens like continual Comforters. On them I have fastened 19 Pillars of Gladness, and gave them vessels to water the Earth together with her creatures. They are the brothers of the First and Second. They have begun their own seats and have decorated them with 69,636 ever-burning lamps. The numbers are as the Beginnings, the Ends, and the Contents of Time. [The magician addresses the appropriate angels and says:] Therefore, come and obey the purpose of your creation. Visit us in peace and comfort. Perfect us as receivers of your mysteries. Why? Because our Lord and Master is the All-One.

The Sixth Call. The spirits of the Fourth Angle are nine who are mighty in the Firmament of Waters, who the First has planted as a torment to the wicked and a garland to the righteous. He gave them fiery darts to protect the earth, and 7699 continual workmen, whose courses visit the earth with comfort, and who are in government and continuance like the Second and the Third. [The magician addresses the appropriate angels and says:] Therefore listen to my voice. I have spoken of you, and I have advanced you in power and presence. Your works shall be a song of honor, and the praise of your God shall be in your creation.

The Seventh Call. The East is a House of Virgins who sing praises among the flames of the first glory. There, the Lord opened his mouth, and they became 28 living dwellings wherein the strength of man rejoices. They are clothed with ornaments of brightness, and they work wonders of all creatures. Their kingdoms and continuance are like the Third and Fourth; strong towers and places of comfort, the seats of mercy and continuance. [The magician addresses the appropriate angels and says:] O you Servants of Mercy, move and appear! Sing praises to the Creator, and be mighty among us, so that this remembrance will give power, and our strength will grow strong in our Comforter.

The Eighth Call. The Midday, where the First is like the Third Heaven, is made of 26 Hyacinthine Pillars. Here, the Elders become strong. "I have prepared them for my own righteousness," declared the Lord, whose long continuance is like a shield to the Stooping Dragon, and like the harvest of a widow. How many are there who remain in the Glory of the Earth, who live, and who shall not see Death until the House falls and the Dragon sinks? [The magician addresses the appropriate angels and says:] Come away! The Thunders have spoken. Come away! The Crowns of the Temple and the Robe of Him who is, was, and will be crowned, are divided. Come forth! Appear, to the terror of the Earth and our comfort, and to the comfort of such who are prepared.

The Ninth Call. A mighty guard of fire, with two-edged swords flaming, and with eight Vials of Wrath for two times and a half, and with wings of wormwood and with marrow of salt, have set their feet in the West. They are measured with their 9996 ministers. These gather up the moss of the Earth like the rich man gathers up his treasure. Cursed are they who have iniquities. In the eyes of those with iniquities are millstones greater than the Earth, and from their mouths run seas of blood. The heads of the Guard of Fire are covered with diamonds, and upon their hands are marble stones. Happy is he upon whom they frown not, because the Lord of Righteousness rejoices in them. [The magician addresses the appropriate angels and says:] Come away, but without your Vials, because the time is such that requires comfort.

The Tenth Call. The Thunders of Judgment and Wrath are numbered, and are contained in the North, in the likeness of an Oak whose branches are 22 nests of lamentation and weeping which are stored up for the Earth. These burn night and day, and vomit out the heads of scorpions and live sulphur mingled with poison. These are the Thunders that, 5678 times in the 24th part of a moment, roar with a hundred mighty earthquakes and a thousand times as many surges. They rest not, neither do they know any time here. One rock brings forth a thousand, just as the heart of man brings forth his thoughts. Woe! Woe! Woe! Woe! Woe! Woe! Yea, Woe to the Earth, because her iniquity is, was, and shall be great. [The magician addresses the appropriate angels and says:] Come away! But not your mighty sounds.

The Eleventh Call. The mighty Seat groaned, and there were five Thunders that flew into the East, and then an eagle spoke and cried aloud, "Come away!" And then they gathered themselves together and became the House of Death, which is measured, and they were like those whose number is 31. [The magician addresses the appropriate angels and says:] Come away! I have prepared a place for you. Therefore, move and show yourselves. Unveil the mysteries of your creation. Be friendly to me, because I am a servant of the same God, a true worshipper of the Highest.

The Twelfth Call. O you, who range in the South, and who are the 28 Lanterns of Sorrow, bind up your girdles, and visit us. Bring down your 3663 servants so that the Lord may be magnified. His name among us is Wrath. [The magician addresses the appropriate angels and says:] Move I say, and show yourselves! Unveil the mysteries of your creation. Be friendly to me, because I am a servant of this same God, a true worshipper of the Highest.

The Thirteenth Call. O Swords of the South, who have 42 eyes to stir up the Wrath of Sin, who make men drunken who are empty; Behold, the Promise of God, and his Power which is called among you a bitter sting. [The magician addresses the appropriate angels and says:] Move and appear! Unveil the mysteries of your creation, because I am a servant of this same God, a true worshipper of the Highest.

The Fourteenth Call. O Sons of Fury, O Children of the Just One, who sits upon 24 seats, who vex all creatures of the Earth with age, and who have 1636 servants under you; Behold, the Voice of God, the promise of Him who is called among you, Fury or Extreme Justice. [The magician addresses the appropriate angels and says:] Move and show yourselves! Unveil the mysteries of your creation. Be friendly to me, because I am a servant of this same God, a true worshipper of the Highest.

The Fifteenth Call. O Governor of the First Flame, under whose wings are 6739 servants, who weaves the Earth with dryness, and who knows the Great name of "Righteousness," and the Seal of Honor. [The magician addresses the appropriate angels and says:] Move and appear! Unveil the mysteries of your creation. Be friendly to me, because I am a servant of this same God, a true worshipper of the Highest.

The Sixteenth Call. O Second Flame, O House of Justice, who has His beginning in glory, and who comforts the Just, who walks upon the Earth with 8763 feet, and who understands and separates creatures. You are great, like the God of Conquest. [The magician addresses the appropriate angels and says:] Move and appear! Unveil the mysteries of your creation. Be friendly to me, because I am a servant of this same God, a true worshipper of the Highest.

The Seventeenth Call. O Third Flame, whose wings are thorns to stir up vexation, and who has 7336 living lamps going before you, and whose God is "Wrath in Anger." [The magician addresses the appropriate angels and says:] Gird up your loins and listen! Move and appear! Unveil the mysteries of your creation. Be friendly to me, because I am a servant of this same God, a true worshipper of the Highest.

The Eighteenth Call. O Mighty light and burning Flame of Comfort, who unveils the Glory of God to the center of the Earth, and in who the 6332 Secrets of Truth have their abode, and who is called in your kingdom, "Joy" and who is not to be measured. [The magician addresses the appropriate angels and says:] Be a window of comfort to me! Move and appear! Unveil the mysteries of your creation. Be friendly to me, because I am a servant of this same God, a true worshipper of the Highest.

The Call for the Aethyrs. There is only one Call to be used for the 30 Aethyrs. The name of the desired Aethyr is inserted into the blank space at the beginning of the Call as follows:

The Heavens that are in the (first, second, etc.) Aethyr, (LIL, ARN, etc.) are mighty in those regions of the universe, and they carry out the Judgement of the Highest. To them it is said: Behold, the Face of your God, the beginning of Comfort, whose eyes are the brightness of the Heavens. He enables you to govern the Earth, and her unspeakable variety, and furnishes you with the Power of Understanding so that you can carry out all things, according to the Provinces of Him who sits upon the Holy Throne, and who rose up in the Beginning, saying: The Earth, let her be governed by her parts, and let there be division in her, so that her glory may be both an eternal ecstasy and an inherent vexation.

Her course, let it run with the Heavens, and let her serve them like a handmaiden.

One season, let it mix with another, and let there be no creature upon her or within her that remains the same.

All of her members, let them have different qualities, and let no one creature be equal to another.

The creatures of reason who are on the Earth, such as man, let them disturb and eliminate one another; and their dwelling places, let their Names be forgotten.

The egotistical works of man, let them be destroyed.

His buildings, let them become caves for the beasts of the field.

Dim her understanding with darkness. Why? Because I am sorry that I made Man. The Earth is well known for awhile, and for another while, she is a stranger, because she is the bed of a harlot, and the dwelling place of him who is fallen.

O Heavens, arise! The Lower Heavens are beneath you. Let them serve you! Govern those who govern! Cast down those who are likely to fall. Bring forth with those who increase, and destroy those who are rotten.

Let no place remain in one number. Add and subtract until the stars are numbered.

Arise! Move! Appear before the Covenant of His Mouth which He has sworn to us in His Justice. Unveil the mysteries of your creation, and make us to be partakers of THE UNDEFILED KNOWLEDGE.

When to Use the Calls

Which Call(s) to use depends upon the name of the deity that you are addressing and the locality from which the name is derived. Depending on the deity or location, you may need to recite one, two, or three Calls.

The rules taught by the Golden Dawn for Watchtower Calls allow you to determine which Calls to recite for specific magical operations. Unfortunately these rules are hard to understand; therefore, we have simplified them for the novice magician. A complete list of the 18 original Golden Dawn rules are in Table VII of *Enochian Magic*.

1. For Archangels, use the First Call then the Second Call. The names of the Archangels are:

Archangels of the Watchtower of Air

ERZLM	EZLAR	ELARZ	EARZL	EYTPA	ETPAY
EPAYT	EAYPT	ETNBA	ENBAT	EBATN	EATNB
EXGZD	EGZDX	EZDXG	EDXGZ		

Archangels of the Watchtower of Water:

HTAAD	HAADT	HADTA	HPTAA	HTDIM	HDIMT
HIMTD	HMTDI	HMAGL	HAGLM	HGLMA	HLMAG
HNLRX	HLRXN	HRXNL	HXNLR		

Archangels of the Watchtower of Earth:

NBOZA	NOZAB	NZABO	NABOZ	NPHRA	NHRAP
NRAPH	NAPHR	NRONK	NONKR	NNKRO	NKRON
NIAOM	NAOMI	NOMIA	NMIAO		

Archangels of the Watchtower of Fire:

BDOPA	BOPAD	BPADO	BADOP	BANAA	BNAAA
BAAAN	BAANA	BPSAK	BSAKP	BAKPS	BKPSA
BZIZA	BIZAZ	BZAZI	BAZIZ		

2. Use the First, Second, and then Third Call for the Ruling Angels of (E)XARP (from the Watchtower of Air). They are:

XKZNS	XZNSK	XNSKZ	XSKZN	XTOTT	XOTTT
XTTTO	XTTOT	XSIAS	XIASS	XASSI	XSSIA
XFMND	XMNDF	XNDFM	XDFMN	AOYVB	AYVBO
AVBOY	ABOYV	APAOK	AAOKP	AOKPA	AKPAO
ARBNH	ABNHR	ANHRB	AHRBN	ADIRL	AIRLD
ARLDI	ALDIR	RABMO	RBMOA	RMOAB	ROABM
RNAKO	RAKON	RKONA	RONAK	ROKNM	RKNMO
RNMOK	RMOKN	RSHAL	RHALS	RALSH	RLSHA
PAKKA	PKKAA	PKAAK	PAAKK	PNPAT	PPATN
PATNP	PTNPA	POTOI	PTOIO	POIOT	PIOTO
PPMOX	PMOXP	POXPM	PXPMO		

Use the Third Call (only) for Angels from the subquadrant Air of Air as follows:

IDOIGO	ARDZA	RZLA	ZLAR	LARZ	ARZL	
KZNS	ZNSK	NSKZ	SKZN	TOTT	OTTT	TTTO
TTOT	SIAS	IASS	ASSI	SSIA	FMND	MNDF
NDFM	DFMN					

Use the Third Call then the Seventh Call for the following Angels of the subquadrant, Water of Air, from the Watchtower of Air. They are:

LLAKZA	PALAM	YTPA	TPAY	PAYT	AYTP	
OYVB	YVBO	VBOY	BOYV	PAOK	AOKP	OKPA
KPAO	RBNH	BNHR	NHRB	HRBN	DIRL	IRLD
RLDI	LDIR					

Use the Third Call then the Eighth Call for the following Angels of the subquadrant, Earth of Air, from the Watchtower of Air. They are:

AIAOAI	OIIIT	TNBA	NBAT	BATN	ATNB	
ABMO	BMOA	MOAB	OABM	NAKO	AKON	KONA
ONAK	OKNM	KNMO	NMOK	MOKN	SHAL	HALS
ALSH	LSHA					

Use the Third Call then the Ninth Call for the following Angels of the subquadrant, Fire of Air, from the Watchtower of Air. They are:

AOVRRZ	ALOAI	XGZD	GZDX	ZDXG	DXGZ	
AKKA	KKAA	KAAK	AAKK	NPAT	PATN	ATNP
TNPA	OTOI	TOIO	OIOT	IOTO	PMOX	MOXP
OXPM	XPMO					

3. Use the First, Second, and then Fourth Call for all Ruling Angels of (H)KOMA, (from the Watchtower of Water) as follows:

KTOKO	KOKOT	KKOTO	KOTOK	KNHDD	KHDDN
KDDNH	KDNHD	KPAAX	KAAXP	KAXPA	KXPAA
KSAIZ	KAIZS	KIZSA	KZSAI	OIAGM	OAGMI
OGMIA	OMIAG	OIAOK	OAOKI	OOKIA	OKIAO
OVSXN	OSXNV	OXNVS	ONVSX	ORVLI	OVLIR
OLIRV	OIRVL	MPAKO	MAKOP	MKOPA	MOPAK
MNDZN	MDZNN	MZNND	MNNDZ	MRIPO	MIPOR
MPORI	MORIP	MXRNH	MRNHX	MNHXR	MHXRN
AXPKN	APKNX	AKNXP	ANXPK	AVASA	AASAV
ASAVA	AAVAS	ADAPI	AAPID	APIDA	RIDAP
ARNIL	ANILR	AILRN	ALRNI		

Use the Fourth Call (only) for Angels from the subquadrant Water of Water as follows:

NELAPR	OMEBB	TDIM	DIMT	IMTD	MDTI	
IAGM	AGMI	GMIA	MIAG	IAOK	AOKI	OKIA
KIAO	VSXN	SXNV	XNVS	NVSX	RVLI	VLIR
LIRV	IRVL					

Use the Fourth Call then the Tenth Call for the following Angels of the subquadrant, Air of Water, from the Watchtower of Water. They are:

OBGOTA	AABKO	TAAD	AADT	ADTA	DTAA	
TOKO	OKOT	KOTO	OTOK	NHDD	HDDN	DDNH
DNHD	PAAX	AAXP	AXPA	XPAA	SAIZ	AIZS
IZSA	ZSAI					

Use the Fourth Call then the Eleventh Call for the following Angels of the subquadrant, Earth of Water, from the Watchtower of Water. They are:

MALADI	OLAAD	MAGL	AGLM	GLMA	LMAG	
PAKO	AKOP	KOPA	OPAK	NDZN	DZNN	ZNND
NNDZ	RIPO	IPOR	PORI	ORIP	XRNH	RNHX
NHXR	HXRN					

Use the Fourth Call then the Twelfth Call for the following Angels of the subquadrant, Fire of Water, from the Watchtower of Water. They are:

IAAASD	ATAPA	NLRX	LRXN	RXNL	XNLR	
XPKN	PKNX	KNXP	NXPK	VASA	ASAV	SAVA
AVAS	DAPI	APID	PIDA	IDAP	RNIL	NILR
ILRN	LRNI					

4. Use the First, Second, then Fifth Call for all Ruling Angels of (N)ANTA (from the Watchtower of Earth). They are:

AAIRA	AIRAA	ARAAI	AAAIR	AORMN	ARMNO
AMNOR	ANORM	ARSNI	ASNIR	ANIRS	AIRSN
AIZNR	AZNRI	ANRIZ	ARIZN	NOMGG	NMGGO
NGGOM	NGOMG	NGBAL	NBALG	NALGB	NLGBA
NRLMV	NLMVR	NMVRL	NVRLM	NIAHL	NAHLI
NHLIA	NLIAH	TOPNA	TPNAO	TNAOP	TROPN
TDOOP	TOOPD	TOPDO	TPDOO	TRXAO	TXAOR
TAORX	TORXA	TAXIR	TXIRA	TIRAX	TRAXI
AMSAL	ASALM	AALMS	ALMSA	AIABA	AABAI
ABAIA	AAIAB	AIZXP	AZXPI	AXPIZ	APIZX
ASTIM	ATIMS	AIMST	AMSTI		

Use the Fifth Call (only) for Angels from the subquadrant Earth of Earth as follows:

ABALPT	ARBIZ RONK		ONKR	NKRO	KRON	
OPNA	PNAO	NAOP	ROPN	DOOP	OOPD	OPDO
PDOO	RXAO	XAOR	AORX	ORXA	AXIR	XIRA
IRAX	RAXI					

Use the Fifth Call then the Thirteenth Call for the following Angels of the subquadrant, Air of Earth, from the Watchtower of Earth. They are:

ANGPOI	VNNAX	BOZA	OZAB	ZABO	ABOZ	
AIRA	IRAA	RAAI	AAIR	ORMN	RMNO	MNOR
NORM	RSNI	SNIR	NIRS	IRSN	IZNR	ZNRI
NRIZ	RIZN					

Use the Fifth Call then the Fourteenth Call for the following Angels of the subquadrant, Water of Earth, from the Watchtower of Earth. They are:

ANAEEM	SONDN	PHRA	HRAP	RAPH	APHR	
OMGG	MGGO	GGOM	GOMG	GBAL	BALG	ALGB
LGB	RLMV	LMVR	MVRL	VRLM	IAHL	AHLI
HLIA	LIAH					

Use the Fifth Call then the Fifteenth Call for the following Angels of the subquadrant, Fire of Earth, from the Watchtower of Earth. They are:

OPMNIR	LLPIZ IAOM		AOMI	OMIA	MIAO	
MSAL	SALM	ALMS	LMSA	IABA	ABAI	BAIA
AIAB	IZXP	ZXPI	XPIZ	PIZX	STIM	TIMS
IMST	MSTI					

5. Use the First, Second, then Sixth Call for all Ruling Angels of (B)ITOM (from the Watchtower of Fire). They are:

IOPMN	IPMNO	IMNOP	INOPM	IAPST	IPSTA
ISTAP	ITAPS	ISKIO	IKIOS	IIOSK	IOSKI
IVASG	IASGV	ISGVA	IGVAS	TGMNM	TMNMG
TNMGM	TMGMN	TEKOP	TKOPE	TOPEK	TPEKO
TAMOX	TMOXA	TOXAM	TXAMO	TBRAP	TRAPB
TAPBR	TRBRA	ODATT	OATTD	OTTDA	OTDAT
ODIOM	OIOMD	OOMDI	OMDIO	OOOPZ	OOPZO
OPZOO	OZOOP	ORGAN	OGANR	OANRG	OMRGA
MADRE	MDREA	MREAD	MEADR	MSISP	MISPS
MSPSI	MPSIS	MPALI	MALIP	MLIPA	MIPAL
MAKAR	MKARA	MARAK	MRAKA		

Use the Sixth Call (only) for Angels from the subquadrant Fire of Fire as follows:

RZIONR	NRZFM	ZIZA	IZAZ	ZAZI	AZIZ	
ADRE	DREA	READ	EADR	SISP	ISPS	SPSI
PSIS	PALI	ALIP	LIPA	IPAL	AKAR	KARA
ARAK	RAKA					

Use the Sixth Call then the Sixteenth Call for the following Angels of the subquadrant, Air of Fire, from the Watchtower of Fire. They are:

NOALMR	OLOAG	DOPA	OPAD	PADO	ADOP	
OPMN	PMNO	MNOP	NOPM	APST	PSTA	STAP
TAPS	SKIO	KIOS	IOSK	OSKI	VASG	ASGV
SGVA	GVAS					

Use the Sixth Call then the Seventeenth Call for the following Angels of the subquadrant, Water of Fire, from the Watchtower of Fire. They are:

VADALI	OBAVA	ANAA	NAAA	AAAN	AANA	
GMNM	MNMG	NMGM	MGMN	EKOP	KOPE	OPEK
PEKO	AMOX	MOXA	OXAM	XAMO	BRAP	RAPB
APBR	RBRA					

Use the Sixth Call then the Eighteenth Call for the following Angels of the subquadrant, Earth of Fire, from the Watchtower of Fire. They are:

VOLXDO	SIODA	PSAK	SAKP	AKPS	KPSA	
DATT	ATTD	TTDA	TDAT	DIOM	IOMD	OMDI
MDIO	OOPZ	OPZO	PZOO	ZOOP	RGAN	GANR
ANRG	MRGA					

Rule for Aethyr Calls

There is only one Call for the 30 Aethyrs. Substitute the correct Aethyr name in the blank at the beginning of the Call, and otherwise use the same Call for all 30 Aethyrs.

LESSON 18

How to Make
the Magical Signs

The following magical signs are used in rituals for special emphasis.

The Saluting Sign

Assume an appropriate god-form. Take one step forward while bringing your arms up over your head. As the step is completed, bring your arms over your head, forward, and thrust them together straight out before you at eye level. Your fingers should be straight, palms downward. Lower your head until your eyes look exactly between your thumbs.

The Sign of the Rending of the Veil

Stand facing forward with both arms outstretched in front of you. Turn your palms down—fingers together. Your hands should be a foot apart. Now take one slow step forward. This posture signifies forcing yourself through a barrier into the region beyond.

The Sign of the Closing of the Veil

Stand facing forward with feet together. Stretch both arms out in front of you with palms facing inward, fingers together. Bring your hands slowly together until the palms touch. This posture signifies forcing yourself out of an area and reclosing the barrier behind you.

The Sign of Silence

This is the sign of the Egyptian god, Harpocrates or Hor-Pa-Kraat, which means "Horus the Child." This is a sign of withdrawal, the complement of the Saluting Sign. Bring your left foot back against your right while tapping the heel firmly on the ground. Bring your left hand to your mouth and touch the center of your lower lip with your left forefinger. Close the other fingers and thumb. Drop your right hand to your side. Imagine that a watery cloud surrounds you.

LESSON 19

How to Vibrate
the Names of Power

The Enochian Names of Power should be spoken aloud using the proper pronunciation of each letter. The proper procedure is to vibrate the names as follows:

STEP 1. Give the sign of the Rending of the Veil that you learned in Lesson 18. Now visualize your body as being completely empty.

STEP 2. Breathe in deeply. Imagine the Name entering into your empty body with the breath.

STEP 3. Let the Name descend through your empty body until it settles at your feet.

STEP 4. Draw back your hands to the sides of your eyes and then lean forward. As you lean forward, shoot your arms outward in front of you and see the Name rushing upward while you exhale.

STEP 5. While speaking the Name aloud, see the Name leave your body and thunder outward into the far corners of the universe. Let it vibrate throughout the Magical Universe. Your mind should be one-pointed and fully focused on the Name.

STEP 6. Withdraw your left foot and stand up straight. Know that an occult link has been formed between yourself and the deity whose Name you have vibrated.

Figure 23. A magic circle for conducting Enochian magic

LESSON 20

How to Construct a Magic Circle

A typical magical circle is shown in Figure 23. The circle consists of two circles, roughly nine feet in diameter, and about 1 foot apart (i.e., the inner circle is nine feet and the outer circle is ten feet). The color of the circle can vary according to the operation, but green is typical. Written at the four corners, within the two circles, are the Enochian names of the elements that correspond with those corners. These are:

Fire is a red BITOM in the South
Earth is a black NANTA in the North
Water is a blue HKOMA in the West
Air is a yellow EXARP in the East

Optional embellishments include: placing a lamp at each of the four "corners"—just outside the circle; burning incense (see Section 10); writing appropriate deity names within the double circle; and writing an appropriate magical formula within the double circle.

If a circle such as the one shown in Figure 23 is not possible for you to draw, you can get the same magical effect by drawing a psychic circle. Draw a circle the size and description as given above by using your magical imagination. However, in order for this to work properly, your creative visualization ability must be highly developed. You must be able to actually "see" the circle clearly and without distortion in your "mind's eye." Successful creation of a psychic circle will allow you to conduct magical operations almost anywhere and at almost any time.

In general, beginners should actually draw their circle. After practicing creative visualization techniques (see *Enochian Yoga* for details), and after practice with a physical circle, you can feel more confident trying a psychic circle.

LESSON 21

Rituals to Consecrate Weapons

Ritual to Consecrate Your Pantacle

Use the ritual below to consecrate your Pantacle after you make it and before you use it in a ritual.

STEP 1. Consecrate a circle.

STEP 2. Hold the Pantacle in your right hand, face the Watchtower of Earth and say:

> IKZHIKAL, I invoke you from the Watchtower of Earth to come forward and instill the Power of Fruitfulness within my Pantacle. See the forces of fruitfulness entering into your Pantacle.

STEP 3. Address the Seniors and say:

> LAIDROM, I invoke you from the Watchtower of Earth to come forward and bestow the Desire of Mars upon my Pantacle.

See the forces of desire entering into your Pantacle.

> AKINZOR, I invoke you from the Watchtower of Earth to come forward and bestow the Generosity of Jupiter upon my Pantacle.

See the forces of generosity entering into your Pantacle.

> LZINOPO, I invoke you from the Watchtower of Earth to come forward and bestow the Memory of the Moon upon my Pantacle.

See the forces of memory entering into your Pantacle.

> ALHKTGA, I invoke you from the Watchtower of Earth to come forward and bestow the Fruitfulness of Venus upon my Pantacle.

See the forces of fruitfulness entering into your Pantacle.

AHMLLKV, I invoke you from the Watchtower of Earth to come forward and bestow the Reason of Mercury upon my Pantacle.

See the forces of reason entering into your Pantacle.

LIIANSA, I invoke you from the Watchtower of Earth to come forward and bestow the Concentration of Saturn upon my Pantacle.

See the forces of concentration entering into your Pantacle.

STEP 4. Know your Pantacle to be the physical embodiment of these Earthly qualities. Hold up your Pantacle before you and say:

KHR KAOSGN-KHIDAO
The Wheel is the Diamond of the Earth.

STEP 5. Know your Pantacle to be fully charged with the forces of the Seniors of Earth.

Ritual to Concecrate Your Cup

Use the ritual below to consecrate your Cup after you make it and before you use it in a ritual.

STEP 1. Consecrate a circle.

STEP 2. Hold your Cup in your right hand, face the Watchtower of Water and say:

RAAGIOSL, I invoke you from the Watchtower of Water to come forward and instill the Power of Reflection within my Cup.

See the power of passive reflectivity entering into your Cup.

STEP 3. Address the Seniors and say:

LSRAHPM, I invoke you from the Watchtower of Water to come forward and bestow the Passion of Mars upon my Cup.

See the forces of passion entering into your Cup.

SAIINOV, I invoke you from the Watchtower of Water to come forward and bestow the Benevolence of Jupiter upon my Cup.

See the power of benevolence entering into your Cup.

LAVAXRP, I invoke you from the Watchtower of Water to come forward and bestow the Receptivity of the Moon upon my Cup.

See the passive power of receptivity entering into your Cup.

SLGAIOL, I invoke you from the Watchtower of Water to come forward and bestow the Love of Venus upon my Cup.

See the power of love entering into your Cup.

SOAIZNT, I invoke you from the Watchtower of Water to come forward and bestow the Self-Expression of Mercury upon my Cup.

See the power of self-expression entering into your Cup.

LIGDISA, I invoke you from the Watchtower of Water to come forward and bestow the Stability of Saturn upon my Cup.

See the forces of stability entering into your Cup.

STEP 4. Know your Cup to be the physical embodiment of these Watery qualities. Hold up your Cup before you and say:

TALHO AFFA-ADPHANT
The Cup is an indescribable emptiness.

STEP 5. Know your Cup to be fully charged with the forces of the Seniors of Water.

Ritual to Consecrate Your Sword

Use the ritual below to consecrate your Sword after you make it and before you use it in a ritual.

STEP 1. Consecrate a circle.

STEP 2. Hold the Sword in your right hand, face the Watchtower of Air and say:

BATAIVAH, I invoke you from the Watchtower of Air to come forward and instill the Power of Discernment within my Sword.

See the power to discern and discriminate entering into your Sword.

STEP 3. Address the Seniors and say:

HABIORO, I invoke you from the Watchtower of Air to come forward and bestow the Courage of Mars upon my Sword.

See the power of courage entering into your Sword.

AAOZAIF, I invoke you from the Watchtower of Air to come forward and bestow the Wisdom of Jupiter upon my Sword.

See the discerning power of wisdom entering into your Sword.

HTNORDA, I invoke you from the Watchtower of Air to come forward and bestow the Instinct of the Moon upon my Sword.

See the discerning power of the instinct entering into your Sword.

AHAOZPI, I invoke you from the Watchtower of Air to come forward and bestow the Harmony of Venus upon my Sword.

See the forces of harmony entering into your Sword.

AVTOTAR, I invoke you from the Watchtower of Air to come forward and bestow the Intelligence of Mercury upon my Sword.

See the discriminative power of intelligence entering into your Sword.

HIPOTGA, I invoke you from the Watchtower of Air to come forward and bestow the Preservation of Saturn upon my Sword.

See the forces of preservation entering into your Sword.

STEP 4. Know your Sword to be the physical embodiment of these Airy qualities. Hold up your Sword before you and say:

NAZPZ TOL-TOH VAOAN
The Sword is all-victorious truth.

STEP 5. Know your Sword to be fully charged with the forces of the Seniors of Air.

Ritual to Consecrate Your Wand

Use the ritual below to consecrate your Wand after you make it and before you use it in a ritual.

STEP 1. Consecrate a circle.

STEP 2. Hold the Wand in your right hand, face the Watchtower of Fire and say:

> EDLPRNAA, I invoke you from the Watchtower of Fire to come forward and instill the Power of Change within my Wand. See the power to produce changes entering into your Wand.

STEP 3. Address the Seniors and say:

> AAETPIO, I invoke you from the Watchtower of Fire to come forward and bestow the Energy of Mars upon my Wand.

See the forces of creative energy entering into your Wand.

> ADAEOET, I invoke you from the Watchtower of Fire to come forward and bestow the Enthusiasm of Jupiter upon my Wand.

See the forces of energized enthusiasm entering into your Wand.

> ALNKVOD, I invoke you from the Watchtower of Fire to come forward and bestow the Imagination of the Moon upon my Wand.

See the power of imagination entering into your Wand.

> AAPDOKE, I invoke you from the Watchtower of Fire to come forward and bestow the Beauty of Venus upon my Wand.

See the forces of beauty entering into your Wand.

> ANODOIN, I invoke you from the Watchtower of Fire to come forward and bestow the Mobility of Mercury upon my Wand.

See the power of motion entering into your Wand.

> ARINNAP, I invoke you from the Watchtower of Fire to come forward and bestow the Ambition of Saturn upon my Wand.

See the forces of ambition entering into your Wand.

STEP 4. Know your Wand to be the physical embodiment of these Fiery qualities. Hold up your Wand before you and say:

KAB BITOM-ZIZOP
The Wand is a Container of Fire.

STEP 5. Know your Wand to be fully charged with the forces of the Seniors of Fire.

LESSON 22

Ritual of the
Pentagram

The following ritual is used to invoke the elemental forces of the Watch-tower deities. It is used at the end of a ritual to banish these forces, and to sever any psychomagnetic links that may have been established. The only difference between invoking and banishing is the direction used to trace the pentagram. Study Figure 24 carefully and memorize how to trace the pentagrams for each element before trying to conduct this ritual. While you trace each pentagram in the air before you, see it glow in the appropriate color using your magical imagination. The names of the four Kings at the end of this ritual should be vibrated as described in Lesson 19.

STEP 1. Stand. Touch your forehead and say ZAH.

STEP 2. Touch your left breast and say ONDOH.

STEP 3. Touch your right shoulder and say MIH.

STEP 4. Touch your left shoulder and say BUZD.

STEP 5. Touch both hands together on your right breast and say PAID.

STEP 6. Turn to the East, trace a yellow Pentagram of Air (see Figure 24) before you and say EXARP.

STEP 7. Turn to the South, trace a red Pentagram of Fire (see Figure 24) before you and say BITOM.

STEP 8. Turn to the West, trace a blue Pentagram of Water (see Figure 24) before you and say HKOMA.

STEP 9. Turn to the North, trace a black Pentagram of Earth (see Figure 24) before you and say NANTA.

STEP 10. Face the North, extend you arms outward to form a cross and say:

Before me IKZHIKAL
Behind me EDLPRNAA
On my right BATAIVAH
On my left RAAGIOSL
Behold, the four flaming pentagrams
And I alone in the midst.

Comments on the Pentagram Ritual The word ZAH can be pronounced either Zod-ah or Zah. It means "within is." The word ONDOH is pronounced Oh-en-doh and means "the kingdom." The word MIH is Mee-heh, "the power." The word BUZD can be either Boo-zod-deh or Booz-deh, "the glory." The word PAID is Pah-ee-deh, "forever." The message is that within you is the Kingdom of Power and Glory, forever.

An Enochian magician would use a consecrated magical weapon to trace the pentagrams. A yogi, a practitioner of yoga, would trace them with his mind. You should try several methods, such as tracing with a finger, a rod, and solely with your mind (i.e., a psychic tracing). Use whatever works best for you. However you do it, the result should be a shimmering pentagram clearly visible in your mind's eye.

Figure 24 shows how to draw the pentagrams. When invoking, the first line drawn is the line toward the point which corresponds to the operation. When banishing, the tracing begins at the corresponding point and the first line is drawn away from that point.

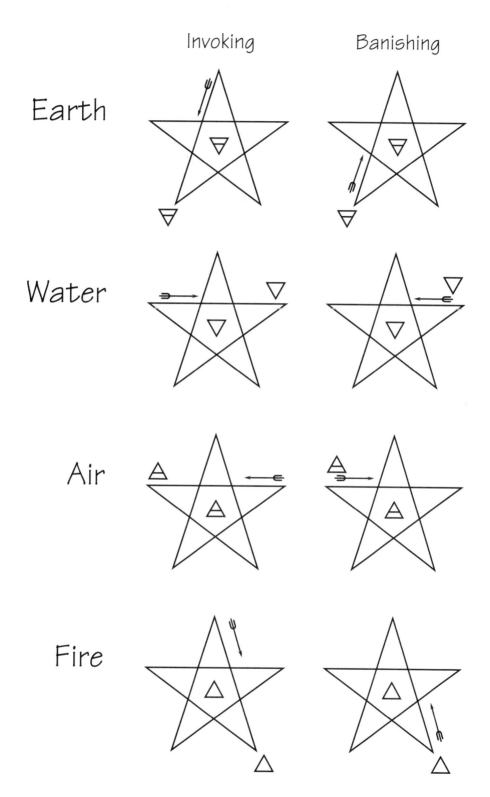

Figure 24. Invoking and banishing pentagrams

Air. Face the East and trace the hexagrams of Air as follows.

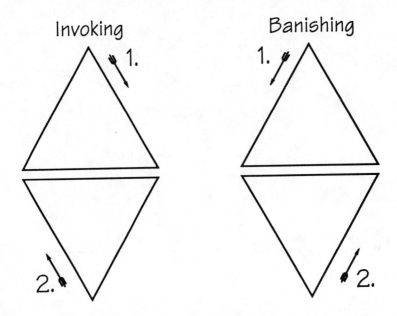

Figure 25. Hexagrams of Air

Fire. Face the South and trace the hexagrams of Fire as follows.

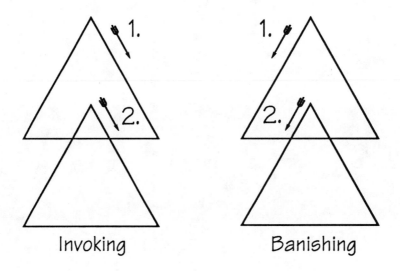

Figure 26. Hexagrams of Fire

LESSON 23

Ritual of the Hexagram

The following ritual is used in many Enochian Rituals. At the beginning of a ritual, it is used to invoke the planetary forces of the Watchtowers and is often used in conjunction with the pentagram ritual described in Lesson 21. At the end of a ritual, it is used to banish these forces, and to sever any psycho-magnetic links that may have been established. The only difference between invoking and banishing is the direction used to trace the hexagram. Study Figures 25 through 28 carefully and memorize how to trace the hexagrams for each element before trying to conduct this ritual. While you trace each hexagram in the air before you, see it glow in the appropriate color using your magical imagination. The four Holy Names at the end of this ritual should be vibrated as described in Lesson 19.

STEP 1. Stand with feet together, left arm down at your side, and right out arm before you.

STEP 2. Turn to the East and say IVITDT (Ee-vee-teh-deh-teh) while tracing the yellow Hexagram of Air before you as shown in Figure 25. Vibrate each letter of the formula while tracing a corresponding side of the hexagram and say:

> Behold, the Burning Flames of Truth
> that consume sorrow, sin, and death.

STEP 3. Turn to the South and say ZTZTZT (Zeh-teh-zeh-teh-zeh-teh) while tracing the red Hexagram of Fire before you as shown in Figure 26. Vibrate each letter of the formula while tracing a corresponding side of the hexagram and say:

> Behold, the Way of Love
> is to sacrifice All into the Cup.

STEP 4. Turn to the West and say IVITDT, in the same manner as in STEP 2, but trace the blue Hexagram of Water as shown in Figure 27.

STEP 5. Turn to the North and say ZTZTZT in the same manner as in

STEP 3, but trace the black Hexagram of Earth as shown in Figure 28.

STEP 6. Extend your arms outward in the form of a cross and say:

Before me MORDIALHKTGA
Behind me OIPTEAAPDOKE
On my right OROIBAHAOZPI
On my left MPHARSLGAIOL
Above me and below me,
My Magical Universe,
And behold, I alone
In the midst.

Note: In *An Advanced Guide to Enochian Magick* you will find that the formula IVITDT is from the Watchtower of Fire and ZTZTZT is from the Watchtower of Air. The pentagram ritual reverses the normal directional locations of these two formulas in order to achieve a union of polar opposites. The result is an overwhelming sense of oneness. The theory behind this ritual is the Monad Model described in *Enochian Physics*.

Water. Face the West and trace the hexagrams of Water as follows.

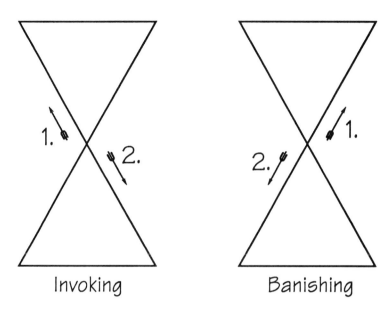

Figure 27. Hexagrams of Water

Earth. Face the North and trace the hexagrams of Earth as follows.

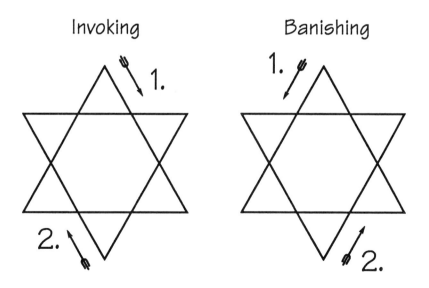

Figure 28. Hexagrams of Earth

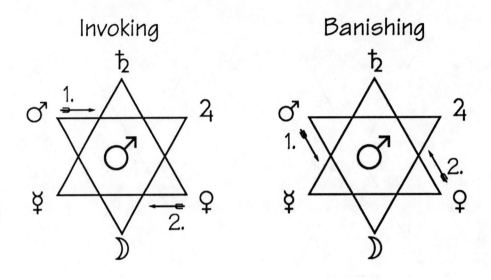

Figure 29. The hexagram of Mars

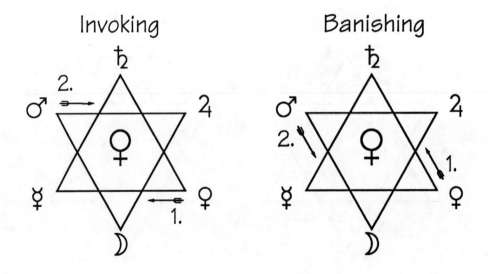

Figure 30. The hexagram of Venus

LESSON 24

Rituals to Charge Talismans

Ritual to Charge the Talisman of LSRAHPM

STEP 1. Make a Magic Circle. Put a table or altar at the center. Place the Talisman of LSRAHPM on the altar. Enter the circle.

STEP 2. Conduct the Invoking Pentagram Ritual from Lesson 22 and then the Invoking Hexagram Ritual from Lesson 23 to invoke the necessary Watchtower forces.

STEP 3. Face the Watchtower of Water in the West.

STEP 4. Enter your Body of Light.

STEP 5. Trace the Invoking Hexagram for Mars as shown in Figure 29.

STEP 6. Vibrate the names:

> MPHARSLGAIOL
> (Em-peh-heh Ar-ess-el Gah-ee-oh-leh)
> RAAGIOSL
> (Rah-ah-gee-oh-sel)
> LSRAHPM
> (Less-rah-pem)

STEP 7. Assume the character and god-form of LSRAHPM. Let your Body of Light take on the appearance of this Senior, who is shown on card number 60 of the Enochian Tarot deck as well as in *Enochian Tarot*. Although all Seniors are male, LSRAHPM is rather feminine. His body is well proportioned and graceful but the lower half shimmers as though indistinct. His god-form has a small pair of wings. He wears an orange robe. In his right hand he carries an oak spear and in his left hand is a lighting bolt. His overall impression is one of fierce determination.

STEP 8. Recite an invocation:

> O LSRAHPM, Senior of Water,
> Come to me and assist me.
> Help me to slay
> All that opposes my progress.
> Grant me your great boon

Of Occult Powers.
Assist me in my Magical Will
And tear asunder my enemies.

STEP 9. Assume the character of LSRAHPM (see yourself as if you were LSRAHPM). This Senior bestows occult powers. He has the energy of Mars and his spear and lighting bolt can destroy the enemies of truth. His presence stirs the desire to control one's life and to attain all manner of magical powers (Siddhas).

STEP 10. Acting as LSRAHPM, stretch out your right hand over the Talisman and see a blue mist, flecked with orange. Leave your hand and enter the Talisman charging it with your powers and abilities.

STEP 11. Return to your own form. Return to your physical body.

STEP 12. Trace the Banishing Hexagram of Mars as shown in Figure 29.

STEP 13. Conduct the Banishing Pentagram Ritual from Lesson 22 and then the Banishing Hexagram Ritual from Lesson 23 to banish the Watchtower forces.

Ritual to Charge the Talisman of ALHKTGA

STEP 1. Make a Magic Circle. Put a table or altar in the center of the circle . Place the Talisman of ALHKTGA upon the altar. Enter the circle.

STEP 2. Conduct the Invoking Pentagram Ritual and then the Invoking Hexagram Ritual to invoke the necessary Watchtower forces.

STEP 3. Face the Watchtower of Earth in the North.

STEP 4. Enter your Body of Light.

STEP 5. Trace the Invoking Hexagram for Venus as shown in Figure 30.

STEP 6. Vibrate the names:

MORDIALHKTGA
(Moh-ar-Dee-ah-leh-Heh-keh-teh-gah)
IKZHIKAL
(EE-keh-zeh-hee-kal)
ALHKTGA
(Ah-leh-hek-teh-gah)

STEP 7. Assume the god-form of ALHKTGA. Let your Body of Light take on the appearance of this Senior who is shown in card 77 of the Enochian Tarot deck as well as in *Enochian Tarot*. He is very strong and sexually attractive. His body is well proportioned and muscular. His god-form does not have wings. He wears an emerald green robe. In his right hand he carries a rose and in his left hand is an aphrodisiac in the form of an amulet. His overall impression is one of strong sexual attraction and physical fitness.

STEP 8. Recite an invocation:

O ALHKTGA, Senior of Earth,
Come to me and assist me.
Help me to find healing
And general prosperity.
Grant me your two boons
Of wealth and fertility.
Assist me in my Magical Will
And grant me all of my desires.

STEP 9. Assume the character of ALHKTGA (see yourself as if you were ALHKTGA). This Senior bestows wealth and fertility. He has the energy of Venus and his Rose of Riches can make anyone wealthy beyond measure. His Amulet will bestow fertility on anyone it touches. His presence stirs the desire for wealth, health, and fertility.

STEP 10. As ALHKTGA, stretch out your right hand over the Talisman. See a black mist, flecked with emerald green, leave your hand and enter the Talisman charging it with all of your powers and abilities.

STEP 11. Return to your own form. Return to your physical body.

STEP 12. Trace the Banishing Hexagram of Venus as shown in Figure 30.

STEP 13. Conduct the Banishing Pentagram Ritual from Lesson 22 and then the Banishing Hexagram Ritual from Lesson 23 to banish the Watchtower forces.

Ritual to Charge the Talisman of LAMA

STEP 1. Make a Magic Circle. Put a table or altar in the center. Place the Talisman of LAMA on the altar. Enter the circle.

STEP 2. Conduct the Invoking Pentagram Ritual from Lesson 22 and then the Invoking Hexagram Ritual from lesson 23 to invoke the necessary Watchtower forces.

STEP 3. Recite the Call for the second Aethyr, ARN.

STEP 4. Invoke the goddess BABALON, who dwells in ARN, by reciting the following verses from THE BOOK OF BABALON (this book is given in *Enochian Yoga*):

I am the One Goddess. I am Space at midday. I am the stars that shine at night. I am called the Womb of the Babe. The Pathway of the Stars is my name. I am the Womb and I am the Tomb.

My three names are Beauty and Desire and Magic. Fear me in my name of She-who-is-the-beauty-of-the-night. Come to me in my name of She-who-is-most-desired. Know me in my name of She-who-wields-the-universe. Behold, I am the Maiden in the morning, the Temptress and Mother at noon, and the Crone in the evening.

I am the Lust of Kosmos for Kaos, the fourfold seduction that lies within light; that which charms the moth, draws him in, promises him life everlasting, and then devours him heartily.

Come to me through joyous dance and music.

I am the most beautiful goddess in the universe.

STEP 5. Imagine BABALON hovering above you. See a red mist descend from her right hand and enter your Talisman.

STEP 6. Know that your Talisman of LAMA is fully charged with the feminine power of BABALON.

STEP 7. Return to your own form. Return to your physical body.

STEP 8. Conduct the Banishing Pentagram Ritual from Lesson 22 and then the Banishing Hexagram Ritual from Lesson 23 to banish the Watchtower forces.

Summary

Which Call(s) to use depends upon the name of the deity that you are addressing and the locality from which the name is derived. Depending on the deity or location, you may need to recite one, two, or three Calls.

The rules taught by the Golden Dawn for Watchtower Calls allow you to determine which Calls to recite for specific magical operations.

A typical magical circle consists of two circles, roughly nine feet in diameter, and about one foot apart. The color of the circle can vary according to the operation, but green is typical. Written at the four corners, within the two circles, are the Enochian names of the elements that correspond with those corners.

The Pentagram ritual is used at the beginning of a ritual to invoke the elemental forces of the Watchtower deities. It is used at the end of a ritual to banish these forces and to sever any psycho-magnetic links that may have been established.

The Hexagram ritual is used at the beginning of a ritual to invoke the planetary forces of the Watchtowers and is often used in conjunction with the pentagram ritual. It is used at the end of a ritual to banish these forces and to sever any psycho-magnetic links that may have been established.

The only difference between invoking and banishing is the direction used to trace the pentagram.

Further Suggested Reading

Techniques of High Magic; A Manual of Self-Initiation. Francis King and Stephen Skinner, Doubleday.

Applied Magic. Dion Fortune, Weiser.

The Sword and the Serpent. Denning & Phillips, Llewellyn.

The New Magus. Donald Tyson, Llewellyn.

The Golden Dawn. Ed. by Israel Regardie, Llewellyn.

The Key of Solomon the King. S. Liddell MacGregor Mathers, Weiser.

The Secret Rituals of the O.T.O. Ed. by Francis King, Weiser.

The Book of the Goetia of Solmon the King. Trans. by Aleister Crowley, Magickal Childe.

Buckland's Complete Book of Witchcraft. Raymond Buckland, Llewellyn.

A Witches Bible Compleat. Janet and Stewart Farrar, Magical Childe.

Planetary Magick. Denning and Phillips, Llewellyn.

Things to Do for Section 6

1. Practice making the four signs or positions as given in this lesson.

2. Vibrate the name of the Angel AXIR, from the subquadrant Earth of Earth, according to the step-by-step procedure given in Lesson 19. Note the results, if any.

3. Consecrate the weapons that you made in Lesson 13 using the rituals given in Lesson 21.

4. Conduct the Ritual of the Pentagram. Try it with a drawn circle, and with a psychic circle. Determine which you like best.

5. Conduct the Ritual of the Hexagram. Try it with a drawn circle, and with a psychic circle. Determine which you like best.

6. Charge the three talismans that you made in Lessons 14 and 15 using the rituals provided in Lesson 24.

Questions for Section 6

1. What Call(s) should be made to address the Angel AXIR in the subquadrant Earth of Earth?

2. What Call(s) should be made to address the Angel PALAM in the subquadrant Water of Air?

3. What is the Call for the 29th Aethyr, RII?

4. What does the Sign of Rending the Veil signify?

5. What does the Sign of Closing the Veil signify?

6. What magical sign should you use when vibrating a name?

7. True or False: A psychic circle can be just as effective as one painted on the floor.

8. Multiple choice: To consecrate a Cup, you would invoke the forces of the Watchtower of:
    a. Earth.
    b. Water.
    c. Air.
    d. Fire.

9. Multiple choice: To consecrate a Dagger, you would invoke the forces of the Watchtower of:
    a. Earth.
    b. Water.
    c. Air.
    d. Fire.

10. Multiple choice: To consecrate a Wand, you would invoke the forces of the Watchtower of:
    a. Earth.
    b. Water.
    c. Air.
    d. Fire.

11. Multiple choice: The Enochian word for Air is:
    a. EXARP.
    b. BITOM.
    c. HKOMA.
    d. NANTA.

12. Multiple choice: The King of the Watchtower of Earth is:
    a. RAAGIOSL.
    b. BATAIVAH.
    c. EDLPRNAA.
    d. IKZHIKAL.

13. True or False: Every Enochian ritual should end with a banishing ritual.

SECTION 7

Skrying

Section Outline

Learning Objectives

This section contains four lessons on how to experience the Watchtowers and Aethyrs. Two magical techniques are presented. The first is crystal gazing; the second is traveling in the Spirit Vision or astral traveling. You should begin with crystal gazing, which is easy and without danger. Detailed instructions are given so that you can enter the Watchtowers and Aethyrs, described by Enochian Magic, and see these subtle regions and their inhabitants for yourself. Upon completing the reading you should be able to:

- Crystal gaze

- Travel in the Spirit Vision

- Skry into or visit the Watchtowers

- Skry into or visit the Aethyrs

LESSON 25

Crystal Gazing

The word skrying means "seeing." When you skry into a crystal ball or shew-stone you are trying to see something. Traditionally skrying has been used for divination—to see into the future. The crystal ball has become stereotyped as a tool of the gypsy or fortune teller. However, Dee and Kelly used the technique to look into the Watchtowers and Aethyrs of Enochian Magic with great success.

There are many forms of skrying. For example, hydromancy is skrying into water; leconomancy is skrying into oil which is poured onto water; catoptromancy is skrying into a mirror, and so on.

Dee's shewstone, which he called his "angelical stone," was about the size of an egg. According to tradition, it was solid black.

Before you begin skrying, you should purchase your own quartz crystal. A clear or rose quartz crystal can also work well. Ideally, you should experiment with several kinds until you find one that works best for you.

There are no hard rules for crystal gazing. It can be held in your hands, or set on a stand in front of you, or simply placed on a table so long as it doesn't roll.

Adding frills to the skrying process should be done with care. For instance, William Lilly was reported to have a crystal on a silver stand with the names of Angels engraved on it. However, you don't want to add so many frills that they become a distraction. For example, you can burn candles, or use a round table with an appropriate covering, or burn incense (see Section 10). You might want to conduct an appropriate purification ritual beforehand to help you focus your mind on the desired goal. All of these frills can be helpful, but don't let them distract you.

Whatever your preparation and equipment, the actual operation is simplicity itself—just gaze into the crystal and note what, if anything, you see there. This sounds easy enough, but you may see nothing at all, or you may see the wrong things. Illusion and deception abound on the astral and mental planes and this is why signposts are so necessary. While gazing into the crystal, concentrate on the known signposts of where you want to see. These will help direct your mind to the right place.

Most successful crystal gazers report that their crystals first appear cloudy or misty. Then they detect movement—like clouds being blown by the wind. As the mist recedes, a vision appears. These visions can range from an abstract feeling to a clear picture.

A Sample Worksheet for Crystal-Gazing

Date:

Time:

Place:

Crystal used:

Intended Watchtower Square:

Known Signposts:

Results:

Comments:

LESSON 26

Spirit Vision

The magical technique known as "skrying in the spirit vision" is more advanced than simple clairvoyance or psychic vision. Once you have mastered crystal gazing, you should be ready to advance to skrying in the spirit vision. Basically the difference is this: when crystal gazing, your Body of Light remains within your physical body. When skrying in the spirit vision, your consciousness leaves the physical body and enters your Body of Light which then goes to the location desired. Skrying in the Spirit Vision is identical to astral traveling. The process is like falling asleep, except that you remain conscious and return to your physical body with full memory of your experiences.

As we have seen, Enochian Magic teaches that an invisible world surrounds us. We cannot see this world with our physical eyes but we can see it more or less clearly with our astral sight or inner vision.

We are more than just a physical body. We each have seven bodies or "sheaths." The seventh, the most gross, is our physical body. Within the physical body is an ethereal body which contains the prana of Yoga and the chi of acupuncture. This is called the etheric body. Within the etheric body, is another which is less dense. This is the astral body, the body of our feelings and emotions. Within the astral body is another which is less dense. This is the mental body, the body of our thoughts. Within the mental body is the causal body which is within the spiritual body which, in turn, is within our divine body.

Table 9 shows all seven bodies. Each body is comprised of elements from a different plane, and each body functions with a full set of senses on that plane. Thus, the astral body has astral senses that function on the astral plane. The mental body has psychic senses that function on the mental plane, and so on. Notice that the body and the standard occult plane names are identical.

Notice that only five Enochian planes are given. The physical plane has no special Enochian equivalent simply because it is our normal physical world. The highest plane, corresponding to the Divine, is also not mentioned in Enochian Magic. This plane was regarded as too lofty to speak about in words and was usually kept secret.

Table 9
The Bodies and Planes

Cosmic Plane

Body	Occultism	Enochian
Physical	Physical	——
Etheric	Etheric	Watchtower of Earth
Astral	Astral	Watchtower of Water
Mental	Mental	Watchtower of Air
Causal	Causal	Watchtower of Fire
Spiritual	Spiritual	Tablet of Union
Divine	Divine	——

Table 9 provides us with the theoretical basis for skrying in Enochian Magic. The goal is to experience, in some degree, the worlds of the Watchtowers. Enochian Magic also teaches that there are 30 special states, in these inner planes, called Aethyrs or Aires. As shown in Table 5, these range from the lowest and most dense, called TEX, to the highest and most spiritual, called LIL. The Enochian magician learns to skry in the Watchtowers Squares and the Aethyrs. The primary reason for doing this is to learn firsthand the truth about yourself and your universe.

LESSON 27

Skrying/Visiting the Watchtowers

The four Watchtowers and 30 Aethyrs of Enochian Magic are planes and subplanes within the Magical Universe. They are regions of inner space. They can be visited by you in your Body of Light. To enter the Watchtowers, you can skry using a crystal or visit in your Body of Light. In general, skrying is easier and safer and is therefore the recommended procedure for beginners.

The following is an outline for how an Enochian magician would enter the Watchtowers:

STEP 1. Recite the appropriate Call or Calls.

STEP 2. Vibrate the appropriate Names of Power.

STEP 3. Gaze into a crystal shewstone or enter your Body of Light as follows:

  a. Etheric body for Watchtower of Earth

  b. Astral body for Watchtower of Water

  c. Mental body for Watchtower of Air

  d. Causal body for Watchtower of Fire

  e. Spiritual body for Tablet of Union

STEP 4. Make the Sign of the Rending of the Veil to enter a Square.

Comments. Enter the Watchtowers in serial order. Always enter Earth first, then Water, then Air, then Fire, and only then the Tablet of Union. The correct Call to use for the Watchtowers depends on the Square being visited. Use the Calls for the deity of the Square to be visited. After success has been obtained, and you have gained sufficient practice in the Watchtowers, you will find that merely thinking about the Call will have the same effect as reciting it.

Ritual for Skrying the Square "O" of "OPNA" in Earth of Earth

Now let's put together all of the different magical techniques that we have learned, and conduct a ritual that will let us skry (visit in the mind's eye) the subquadrant Earth of Earth in the Watchtower of Earth. We will visit the Lesser Square O of OPNA. You can find this Square in Figure 1. Begin at the lower left-hand corner of the Watchtower, as shown in Figure 1, and count four rows upward, counting the bottom row as the first. The same Square, drawn as a truncated pyramid, can be found in the subquadrant, Earth of Earth, in Appendix A. As shown, the truncated pyramid has four sides, three of Earth and one of Fire.

STEP 1. Begin by drawing a magic circle in which to work. You learned how to do this in Lesson 20. Place an altar (a table with an appropriate covering will do) in the center. Place a quartz crystal on a black cloth on the altar. You will also need your Pantacle. In addition, place two black candles on the altar behind the crystal. Make up the truncated pyramid that you constructed in Things to Do for Section 3, for Square O, and place it behind the crystal and between the two candles.

STEP 2. Consecrate the circle by conducting the Pentagram Invoking Ritual that you learned in Lesson 22. When you conduct the invoking ritual, use your Pantacle to trace the pentagrams.

STEP 3. Recite the appropriate Call. You are going to skry in the sub-quadrant Earth of Earth. According to the rules given in Lesson 17, you need only recite the Fifth Call (the words to this Call are given in Lesson 17).

STEP 4. Vibrate the appropriate Names of Power, as learned in Lesson 19. Vibrate each of the following names in the order shown:

IKZHIKAL (Ee-keh-zeh-hee-kal)
LAIDROM (El-ahee-dar-oh-em)
AKZINOR (Ah-keh-zee-noh-rah)
LZINOPO (El-zee-noh-poh)
ALHKTGA (Ah-leh-hek-teh-gah)
AHMLLKV (Ah-mel-el-keh-veh)
LIIANSA (Elee-ee-ah-ness-ah)
ABALPT (Ah-bah-el-peh-teh)
ARBIZ (Ah-rah-bee-zeh)
NRONK (En-roh-en-keh)
RONK (Roh-en-keh)

STEP 5. Make the Sign of the Rending of the Veil that you learned in Lesson 18. Gaze into your crystal and record what you see or hear.

STEP 6. If you have success at this point, you should see something like a volcano or fiery flames coming from the ground. Now let's look at some of the signposts for this region. The Egyptian deity is Horus, the hawk-headed god of growth and physical manifestation. The sphinx will be a cow with a lion's legs and tail. The Archangel is TOPNA (Toh-peh-nah) who is very similar to Horus. TOPNA wears an orange robe. He is very strong and terrible to look at. He carries an arrow and uses it to point to the flames of his alchemical processes. The Angel here is OPNA (Oh-peh-nah). He also wears an orange robe. Both

TOPNA and OPNA are fast moving, having small wings on their feet. The Demon in this Square is TOP (Toh-peh). The primary forces working through this region are creative, having to do with the physical manifestation of life. But, while a volcano is ultimately creative by making more land, in the short term it is highly destructive and dangerous. The astrological forces of Cancer operate in this Square, but they are opposed or complimented by the forces of death, which are also here (suggested by the element Fire, but also by the letter N (see Table 2) in the names of the Angels.

STEP 7. Close by conducting the Banishing Ritual of the Pentagram. Check your results against the known signposts.

A Sample Worksheet for
Skrying/Visiting the Watchtowers

Date:

Time:

Place:

Watchtower Visited:

Intended Watchtower Square:

Known Signposts:

Method (Check One):

    Skrying via crystal ____
    Visiting via Body of Light ____

Results:

Comments:

LESSON 28

Skrying/Visiting the Aethyrs

The following is an outline for how an Enochian magician would enter the Aethyrs:

STEP 1. Recite the proper Call.

STEP 2. Invoke the appropriate Governors.

STEP 3. Enter your Body of Light for a visit or gaze into a crystal shewstone for skrying.

STEP 4. Concentrate on the known signposts.

STEP 5. Make the Sign of the Rending of the Veil to enter the Aethyr.

Comment. Enter the Aethyrs in serial order. Always enter TEX first, then RII, and so on.

Entering TEX

1. Stand facing West—the Watchtower of Water contains the four governors of TEX.

2. Recite the Call for TEX: "The Heavens that are in the Thirtieth Aethyr, TEX, are mighty in those regions of the universe..." (see Lesson 17 for the complete Call).

3. Vibrate the following two names:

MPH-ARSL-GAIOL (Em-peh-heh-ar-ess-el-gah-ee-oh-leh)
RAAGIOSL (Rah-ah-gee-oh-sel)

4. Vibrate the name TAOAGLA (Tah-oh-ah-geh-lah) and trace his sigil in the air before you (see figure 31). The sigil should be blue, the color of the Watchtower of Water. This Governor is kindly and righteous.

5. Vibrate the name GEMNIMB (Gem-nee-em-bah) and trace his sigil in the air before you (see Figure 31). The sigil should be blue, the color of the Watchtower of Water. This Governor is very judgmental, but his judgements are often temporary and can be changed.

6. Vibrate the name ADUORPT (Ah-du-oh-rah-peh-teh) and trace his sigil in the air before you (see figure 31). The sigil should be blue, the color of the Watchtower of Water. This Governor has a feminine nature and passive like the moon.

169

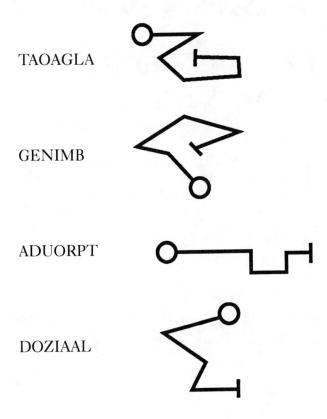

TAOAGLA

GENIMB

ADUORPT

DOZIAAL

Figure 31. The sigils of the four Governors of TEX

7. Vibrate the name DOZIAAL (Doh-zee-ah-ah-leh) and trace his sigil in the air before you (see Figure 31). The sigil should be blue, the color of the Watchtower of Water. This Governor is very emotional and he can bestow either pleasure or pain, joy or sorrow.

8. Concentrate on TEX, a region that is divided into four parts:

TAOAGLA governs the West.
ADUORPT governs the South.
DOZIAAL governs the East.
GEMNIMB governs the North.

9. Gaze into your crystal or enter your Body of Light. Try to see yourself in the Aethyr. If necessary, you can use card number 30 from the Enochian Tarot deck to focus upon. If you still have trouble, make the Sign of Rending the Veil as given in Lesson 18.

A SAMPLE WORKSHEET FOR VISITING THE AETHYRS

Date:

Time:

Aethyr:

Governors:

Known Signposts:

Method (Check One):

    Skrying via crystal   ____
    Visiting via Body of Light ____

Results:

Comments:

Summary

The word skrying means "seeing." When you skry into a crystal ball or shew-stone you are trying to see something. Traditionally skrying has been used for divination.

There are many forms of skrying. Hydromancy is skrying into water; leconomancy is skrying into oil which is poured onto water; catoptromancy is skrying into a mirror, and so on.

There are no hard rules for crystal gazing. It can be held in your hands, or set on a stand in front of you, or simply placed on a table so long as it doesn't roll.

Adding frills to the skrying process can be helpful in focusing but should be added with care.

Illusion and deception abound on the astral and mental planes and this is why signposts are so necessary.

The magical technique known as "skrying in the spirit vision" is more advanced than simple clairvoyance or psychic vision. When crystal gazing, your Body of Light remains within your physical body. When skrying in the spirit vision, your consciousness leaves the physical body and enters your Body of Light which then goes to the location desired.

Skrying in the Spirit Vision is identical to astral traveling. The process is like falling asleep, except that you remain conscious and return to your physical body with full memory of your experiences.

An invisible world surrounds us which we can only see with our astral sight or inner vision.

We each have seven bodies or "sheaths": the physical body, the etheric body, the astral body, the mental body, the causal body, the spiritual body, and the divine body. Each body is comprised of elements from a different plane, and each body functions with a full set of senses on that plane. The astral body has astral senses that function on the astral plane. The mental body has psychic senses that function on the mental plane, and so on.

While traditional occult schools list seven planes and bodies, Enochian magic only lists five. The physical plane has no special Enochian equivalent simply because it is our normal physical world. The highest plane, corresponding to the Divine, is also not mentioned because it was considered too lofty to speak about in words and was usually kept secret.

The goal of skrying is to experience the worlds of the Watchtowers Aethyrs. The primary reason for doing this is to learn firsthand the truth about yourself and your universe.

The four Watchtowers and 30 Aethyrs of Enochian Magic are planes and subplanes within the Magical Universe. They are regions of inner space. They can be visited in the Body of Light. To enter the Watchtowers, you can skry using a crystal or visit in your Body of Light. In general, skrying is easier and safer and is therefore the recommended procedure for beginners.

Further Suggested Reading

Cunningham's Encyclopedia of Crystal, Gem & Metal Magic. Scott Cunningham, Llewellyn.

Secrets of Gypsy Fortunetelling. Raymond Buckland, Llewellyn.

Crystal Enlightenment. Katrina Raphaell, Aurora.

Crystal Awareness. Catherine Bowman, Llewellyn.

Crystal Power, Michael G. Smith, Llewellyn.

Astral Projection, Magic and Alchemy. Ed by Francis King, Weiser.

Of Skrying and Traveling in the Spirit-Vision. Golden Dawn Paper found in Regardie's *Golden Dawn*, Vol 4, Llewellyn.

The Confessions of Aleister Crowley. Eds. John Symonds and Kenneth Grant, Bantam.

The Llewellyn Practical Guide to: Astral Projection. Denning & Phillips, Llewellyn.

Psychic Self-Defense & Well-Being. Denning & Phillips, Llewellyn.

The Llewellyn Inner Guide to Magical States of Consciousness. Denning & Phillips, Llewellyn.

The Llewellyn Practical Guide To: The Development of Psychic Powers. Denning & Phillips, Llewellyn.

Things to Do for Section 7

1. Try to skry into one of the Lesser Squares of Earth of Earth using a quartz crystal. Use the worksheet provided in Lesson 27 to record your results.

2. Try to travel in the spirit vision to one of the Lesser Squares of Earth of Earth. Use the worksheet provided in Lesson 27 to record your results. Compare the results of spirit vision with crystal gazing.

3. Using one of the two magical techniques, that you have learned in this section (i.e., crystal skrying or entering your Body of Light), visit the first Aethyr TEX and record your results.

Questions for Section 7

1. Multiple choice: The word "skrying" means
   - a. knowing.
   - b. seeing.
   - c. calculating.
   - d. flying.

2. True or False: Hydromancy is the technique of skrying into water.

3. True or False: The shewstone used by John Dee was the size of an egg.

4. Why are signposts necessary when skrying the Watchtowers and Aethyrs?

5. What is the difference between crystal gazing and traveling in the Spirit Vision?

6. Which subtle body corresponds to the Watchtower of Air? The Watchtower of Fire?

7. True or False: You can skry into the Watchtowers and Aethyrs by staring at a bowl of water.

8. True of False: Entering your Body of Light and traveling in your Spirit Vision is as easy as gazing into a crystal.

9. True of False: When entering an Aethyr, you do not have to recite a Call.

10. True or False: When entering an Aethyr, you do not have to address the Governors.

11. How many Governors are in TEX? What are their names?

12. What is the first Aethyr that every student should enter first?

13. What is the first Watchtower that every student should try to enter first?

SECTION 8

Enochian Chess

Section Outline

179

Learning Objectives

Enochian Chess was developed and practiced by the early leaders of the Golden Dawn. In this section we present a simplified version of the game. The lessons contain all that you should need to make your own game board and pieces, and play the game. At the completion of the reading you should be able to:

- Write a brief paragraph on the history of Enochian Chess

- Make your own game pieces

- Play a game of Enochian Chess

LESSON 29

Enochian Chess

Purpose

Enochian Chess is an extremely complicated board game based loosely on the classic game of chess. It can be used for entertainment as well as for meditation and divination. The Golden Dawn carefully worked out a complex system for using Enochian Chess for divination which will not be addressed in this introductory workbook.

History

Israel Regardie, once a member of the Golden Dawn, was of the opinion that only a few of the highest Adepts of the Golden Dawn fully understood the game of Enochian Chess. The game was created by the original leaders of the Golden Dawn, but exactly who created which aspects, are unknown. The origin of the game of chess is obscure, but the Golden Dawn taught that it began in Egypt and Persia with the oldest recorded chess game in the Sanskrit literature of India. All known forms of chess use an eight by eight checkerboard pattern of 64 squares. Enochian Chess uses four 64-square boards, one for the 64 Lesser Squares of each Watchtower. Thus, each board corresponds to the lower portions of a Watchtower. The game pieces correspond to Egyptian god-forms and the play itself simulates various forces and powers moving through the Lesser Squares of the Watchtowers. While you play, if correspondences between the Watchtowers and their forces come intuitively to you, so much the better.

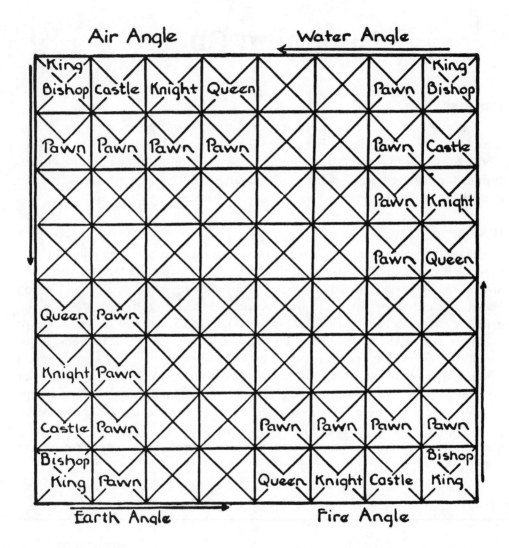

Figure 32. A subboard of the Enochian chessboard.
(The arrows indicate the direction of play.)

LESSON 30

How to Make
Your Own Game Pieces

The Board

Enochian Chess uses four boards, one for each element or Watchtower, without the connecting Black Cross. Each board contains 64 squares (8x8, the same number as a normal chess board) and is itself divided into four 4x4 sections. Each board represents one of the Watchtowers without its Central Cross or Sephirothic Crosses or Kerubic Squares. In other words, each board contains the 64 Lesser Squares.

The entire game board represents the lower four cosmic elements and avoids Spirit completely. Spirit, is taken into account by the game pieces and their movements. Each Square of each subboard is made into a pyramid by drawing a cross on it as shown in Figure 32.

The Game Pieces

There are five sets of nine game pieces—one set for each cosmic element and Watchtower. The nine pieces are shown in Figures 33 through 38. Their correspondences are given in Table 10.

Table 10
Correspondences of the Chess Pieces

Chess	Tarot	Element	Suggested Deity	G.D Deity
King	Ace	Spirit	Osiris	Osiris
Queen	Queen	Wate	Isis	Isis
Knight	King	Fire	Nephthys	Horus
Bishop	Knight	Air	Shu	Ur-Heru
Rook/Castle	Knave	Earth	Horus	Nephthys
Knight's Pawn	—	Fire	Qebhsennuf	Qebhsennuf
Bishop's Pawn	—	Air	Hapi	Hapi
Queen's Pawn	—	Water	Tuamautef	Tuamautef
Castle's Pawn	—	Earth	Mestha	Mestha

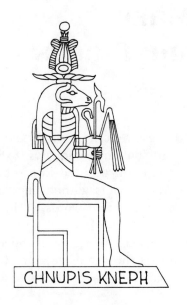

CHNUPIS KNEPH

Figure 33. The King

SATI ASHTORETH

Figure 34. The Queen

RA

Figure 35. The Knight

TOUM

Figure 35. The Bishop

ANOUKE

Figure 37.The Rook/Castle

Drawings by Richard Dudschus for Enochian Chess of the Golden Dawn *by Chris Zalewski*

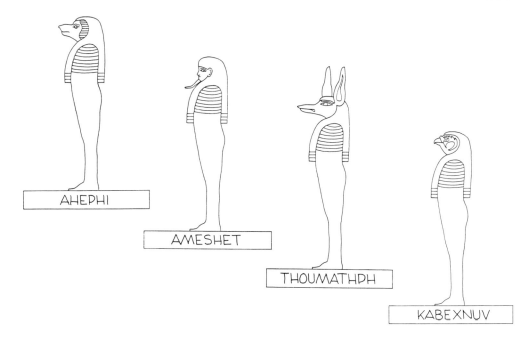

Figure 38. The Four Pawns

Drawings by Richard Dudschus for Enochian Chess of the Golden Dawn *by Chris Zalewski*

The Suggested Deities are in keeping with known correspondences (Horus and Nephthys are reversed and Ur-Heru, the Elder Horus, is replaced with the more familiar god of air, Shu). You may use the traditional Golden Dawn version, as shown, if you prefer. The four pawns are represented by the four sons of Horus. The deities are:

Osiris. God of the Dead. He has a mummy-like form, carries a crook and scourge, and a Phoenix wand (or winged miter). He sits on a throne to befit his kingly position. His color is pure white (see Figure 33).

Isis. Goddess of Nature. She sits on a throne and wears a throne and vulture headdress. Her color is watery blue (see Figure 34).

Horus. God of Growth and Victory. He has a hawk's head, stands upright, and carries a double miter. His color is earthy black (see Figure 35).

Shu/Ur-Heru. God of the Air. Like Horus, he stands erect and carries a double miter. However, this deity has a human head. His color is airy yellow (see Figure 36).

Nephthys. Goddess of Sacrifice. She wears an altar-shaped headdress. Like her sister, Isis, she sits upon a throne. However, this figure is surrounded by a rectangular frame to represent her throne-room. Her color is fiery red (see Figure 37).

Mestha. A god of protection. He has a human head.

Hapi. A god of protection. He has the head of an ape.

Tuamautef. A god of protection. He has the head of a dog or jackal.

Qebhsennuf. A god of protection. He has the head of a hawk.

Note. The four pawns should be standing, in mummy-like form (without arms) as shown in Figure 38. Each game piece should be painted appropriately, using white for spirit, red for fire, and so on.

The figures can be made from almost any material, but the easiest is probably cardboard. They should be mounted on square wooden or cardboard bases so that they each stand upright. Color the base of each figure the appropriate element color depending on where that set of figures is placed on the board. There are four sets of figures, one for each element. Thus, one set of figures will be mounted on a red base and will be initially placed in the Fiery subsection of whichever subboard play begins on. For example, the King of Air will be a white Osiris on a yellow base, while the Queen of Earth will be a blue Isis on a black base.

LESSON 31

How to Play

Placement of Pieces

The game pieces can be placed on the game board in any of 16 possible ways. One player, acting as the main player, chooses the section of the subboard that he/she wants to use and the other players place their pieces accordingly. For example, if the main player chooses Air of Fire, the players would arrange their pieces as shown in Figure 32. This arrangement is not haphazard. It is exactly the same as the YHVH arrangement used to make pyramids from the Lesser Squares (see *Enochian Magic: A Practical Manual*, Figure 25 on page 111).

The main player can begin on any of the four subboards that he/she wishes, and the other three players must follow that arrangement on the same subboard. The Air pieces face downward to the Earth pieces, who face across to the Fire pieces, who face upward to the Water pieces, who face across to the Air pieces. The vertical lines of Squares are called columns, while the horizontal lines of Squares are called ranks. Air and Fire are active vertical forces, while Water and Earth are passive horizontal forces.

How the Pieces Move

King. The King can move one square in any direction. This represents the motion of spiritual force which is purposeful, unhurried, and balanced.

Queen. The Queen moves three squares in any direction (horizontal, vertical or diagonal) counting the square where she is located as the first. This represents the undulating motion of the sea.

Knight. The Knight moves three squares diagonally counting the square where he is located as the first. This represents the jumping or leaping motion of fire. The Knight moves the same as the Knight in traditional chess.

Bishop. The Bishop moves, like the Bishop in regular chess, along any diagonal for as many open squares as desired. This represents the speedy motion of the wind.

Castle/Rook. The Castle or Rook moves, like the Castle/Rook in regular chess, along any rank or column (horizontal or vertical) for as many open squares as desired. This represents the strong ponderous motion of the earth.

Pawns. The pawns move forward one square at a time. They capture diagonally, like pawns in regular chess except in regular chess pawns may open movement with two squares forward while Enochian Chess only allows one square. The pawns represent the four occult connections that exist between

Spirit and the four cosmic elements. If a player manages to move a pawn all the way to the eighth square of its column, it may be exchanged for its corresponding major piece. For example, the Knight's pawn may be exchanged for a new Knight (a second Knight, if the first is still on the board, otherwise a reincarnation of the first Knight).

Note: If an opponent's piece is on the square where your piece moves, it is captured and removed from the board just like in regular chess. There is no castling allowed in Enochian Chess.

The Play

The main player moves first. The others follow in turn, clockwise around the board. Although the King begins play with another piece in his square, once he moves he can never again share a square with another piece. A stalemate occurs when a player cannot move a piece without moving into check. In such a case, that player loses a turn until the stale-mate is over. A checkmate occurs when a player captures an opponent's King, just like in regular chess.

There are at least four main ways to play:

1. Four players each taking a set.
2. Four players with partners; Fire and Air vs Water and Earth.
3. Two players where one takes Fire and Air, and the other player takes Water and Earth.
4. One player who moves all four sets. This can be an excellent mediational exercise if you concentrate on the Watchtower forces and signposts while you move the pieces over the board.

Summary

Enochian Chess is a board game based loosely on the classic game of chess. It can be used for entertainment as well as for meditation and divination. The game was created by the original leaders of the Golden Dawn.

Enochian Chess uses four 64-square boards. Each board corresponds to the lower portions of a Watchtower. The game pieces correspond to Egyptian god-forms and the play itself simulates various forces and powers moving through the Lesser Squares of the Watchtowers. The entire game board represents the lower four cosmic elements and avoids Spirit completely. Spirit, is taken into account by the game pieces and their movements.

There are four sets of nine game pieces—one set for each cosmic element and Watchtower. The game pieces can be made from almost any material. The game pieces can be placed on the game board in any of sixteen possible ways. One player, acting as the main player, chooses the section of the subboard that he/she wants to use and the other players place their pieces accordingly. The main player can begin on any of the four subboards that he/she wishes, and the other three players must follow that arrangement on the same subboard.

The main player moves first. The others follow in turn, clockwise around the board. A stale-mate occurs when a player cannot move a piece without moving into check. In such a case, that player loses a turn until the stalemate is over. A checkmate occurs when a player captures an opponent's King, just like in regular chess.

There are at least four main ways to play: (1) Four players each taking a set. (2) Four players with partners; Fire and Air vs Water and Earth. (3) Two players where one takes Fire and Air, and the other player takes Water and Earth. (4) One player who moves all four sets.

Further Suggested Reading

Instructions on Chessman, a Golden Dawn Lecture by G.H. Fraters D.D.C.F. and N.O.M.

Upon the Rosicrucian Ritual of the Relation Between Chess and Tarot, a Golden Dawn Lecture by G.H. Frater S.R.M.D.

Part Four of the Concourse of the Forces, Enochian or Rosicrucian Chess, a Golden Dawn Lecture.

Things to Do for Section 8

1. Make your own chessboard and four sets of chessmen as shown in Lesson 30.

2. Learn the rules of play and try to play a few games. As you play, think of the pieces as powerful god-forms moving through the Watchtowers.

3. Teach Enochian Chess to at least one other person.

Questions for Section 8

1. True or False: The main board used in Enochian Chess is divided into four subboards having 64 squares each, for a total of 256 squares.

2. How many game pieces are used in Enochian Chess?

3. The King corresponds to what element? To what Egyptian god?

     Element: _____

     God: _____

4. Which Egyptian goddess wears a throne on her head?

5. What is the color attributed to Horus?

6. What are the names of the four pawns (the four sons of Horus)?

7. True or False: Enochian Chess can be played on any of 16 possible locations of the board.

8. How does the King move? The Queen?

    The King:

    The Queen:

9. True or False: The Castle in Enochian Chess moves exactly like the Castle moves in regular chess, except for castling.

10. True or False: The Pawns in Enochian Chess move exactly like the Pawns move in regular chess.

11. Multiple choice: Which of the following is not an accepted way to play Enochian Chess?
    a. One player
    b. Two players
    c. Three players
    d. Four players

12. True or False: When four players play, the second player is the player seated to the right of the first player.

13. Why is Shu suggested as an alternative to the Golden Dawn use of Ur-Heru?

14. Who created Enochian Chess?

SECTION 9

Enochian Tarot

Section Outline

Learning Objectives

This section is included to give interested readers a brief look at Enochian Tarot. While we encourage serious users of Enochian Magic to be aware of the basics of Enochian Tarot, it is not a required subject. Although it can be used for divination, the chief strength of Enochian Tarot is that it can help the student become familiar with the Enochian deities.

This section contains five lessons in Enochian Tarot. The Enochian Tarot deck was developed by the authors as a valid tarot using Enochian regions and deities. This section briefly discusses how the deck is constructed and how it may be used. We will look primarily at divination (foretelling the future). However, the card deck is also a powerful device for meditation. With this in mind, we have provided two new meditational exercises that you can use with the card deck.

The card deck is an excellent way for the beginning student to become more familiar with the 30 Aethyrs and the Kings and Seniors of the Watchtowers. Upon completing the reading you should be able to:

- Predict future events

- Use the Enochian Tarot Deck for meditation

- Improve your health

- Increase your magical power

LESSON 32

A Look at
Enochian Tarot

The tarot is an ancient magical tool for divination and meditation. It is a powerful magical tool which is capable of harm, if used in too light a manner, so learn to use the tarot cards with care and respect. This is especially true for those who seem to have little natural psychic ability or who have had limited exposure to the psychic sciences. Regular use of the tarot can help you develop your latent psychic abilities.

There are three steps in learning to use the tarot. First, you must learn the card meanings; then how to lay out the cards in a simple spread; and last, how to decode (interpret) a spread of cards.

You do not have to be a master of Enochian Magic to use the Enochian Tarot deck. Enochian Magic need only be understood on a very broad, non-verbal level. Trying to describe Enochian Magic is much like trying to explain the nature of a sunbeam. It is not necessary to understand the details of the sunbeam to value its wonderful power. The same is true of Enochian Magic and Enochian Tarot.

Visualization and imagination are important parts of Enochian Tarot. They can help you grasp the cosmic meaning and significance of each of the cards in the Enochian Tarot deck. With their help, you can become a part of each card you study.

If you have a good imagination, you will find it easy to learn the meanings of each card in the tarot deck. First, you have to find yourself a quiet, comfortable place to study the cards. Next, select an interesting card to study. Look at the card and see yourself gently drifting out of your body and into the card.

You want to become a part of the action of the card. If the person in the card is floating above a peaceful lake, imagine yourself floating along with that character. See what the character sees. Talk freely with the character in the card. Come to know and value the character's individual nature—be it evil or good. Remember that the universe is a balance of good and evil and that both are necessary for our level of being.

As you progress, you will find that it is important that you learn to listen to the "still small voice" within. You must learn to "silence the steady chatter of your conscious mind" so that the knowledge of your unconscious mind can shine forth and teach you.

In order to understand the full meaning and symbology of the tarot cards, it is important to understand the history of the tarot deck. There are many theories about the development of the tarot, but for our purposes, we will discuss only esoteric tradition.

The tarot is held to be the oldest book in human history. It was written in ancient Egypt, at the end of the Egyptian empire, in an attempt to save the sacred teachings. The sacred teachings were reduced to symbols and drawn on papyrus leaves. The author of the book was thought to be Hermes Trismegistus (the ibis-headed god, Thoth), and its original title was The Book of Thoth. Whatever the actual origin, the tarot cards are ancient human wisdom carefully saved in symbolism and glyph.

The Enochian Tarot has a much shorter history. It was not part of John Dee's original discovery and it was not used by Aleister Crowley, or by the Golden Dawn. It was designed by the authors in 1988. However, the design combines the ancient tarot tradition with the powerful magical system of Dee—it is the ancient Book of Thoth blended with the more modern system of Enochian Magic.

Today, the tarot is used for self-understanding. We use the tarot as a map into the realms of psychic and spiritual reality, and as a record of our relationship with the universe. For instance, the major arcana is a symbolic map of inner space, describing the highways of consciousness, from the lofty spiritual heights of divinity, down to the material world of human beings and matter. In this respect, the traditional tarot and Enochian Tarot are identical. Although the "pathways" are slightly different, they take consciousness over the same terrain and allow the user to reach similar states and stages of consciousness.

LESSON 33

The Enochian Tarot Deck

The Enochian Tarot deck has 86 cards: 30 cards for the major arcana and 56 cards for the minor arcana as shown in Table 11.

Table 11
The Cards of the Enochian Tarot Deck

Arcana	Cards	Basis
Major	30	Aethyrs
Minor		Watchtowers
Court	28	King and Seniors
Suit	28	Deities

The major arcana has 30 cards; one for each of the 30 Aethyrs. The 30 Aethyrs and the Qabalistic Tree of Life are both maps of the same subtle regions. Although they vary in details, they show the makeup of the subtle planes and subplanes that exist between spirit and matter.

The 30 Aethyrs and the Tree of Life are very much alike, therefore, it is not surprising to find that the Aethyrs can help us foretell the future. By knowing where we currently are, we are able to see where we are going. The 30 Aethyrs, like the 22 paths of the Tree of Life, provide a source of inspiration that can be used for either divination or meditation.

The minor arcana of the Enochian Tarot deck has 56 cards; 28 court cards and 28 suit cards. It contains the hierarchy (chain of command) for each Watchtower, as shown in Table 12. The minor arcana has seven court cards and seven suit or deity cards for each of the four Watchtowers.

There are many deities in the Watchtowers and Aethyrs ranging from Kings down to Demons. The deities form a hierarchy, from the spiritual to the material, as shown in Table 13.

Each card of the Enochian Tarot deck has a sexual current or tone associated with it (see *Enochian Physics*, pages 314-316, for an explanation of sexual currents). Each card in the Enochian Tarot deck has an Enochian name, an English title, a card number, a gematria number, and a sexual current.

Table 12
Minor Arcana Hierarchy

Court
   King
   Six Seniors
Suit
   Higher Sephirothic Cross Angels
   Lower Sephirothic Cross Angels
   Kerubic Angels
   Archangels
   Ruling Angels
   Lesser Angels
   Demons

Table 13
Enochian Hierarchy

Kings
Seniors
Sephirothic Cross Angels
   Higher
   Lower
Kerubic Angels
Archangels
Ruling Angels
Lesser Angels
Demons

LESSON 34

The Main Layouts
for Divination

The tarot is popularly used for divination. Each card has an individual set of possible meanings—depending on whether it is shown in its normal position or reversed (i.e., upside down) during the layout (laying the cards out on the table). These meanings can be found in *Enochian Tarot* as well as in the instruction booklet that comes with the card deck.

The normal method of divination is to let the questioner (the person wanting a question answered) shuffle the deck while focusing on his/her question. For a general reading, the questioner should simply shuffle the cards while letting his/her mind go as blank as possible. When the cards "feel right" to the questioner, he/she should stop shuffling and either conduct the layout himself/herself or give the cards to a reader who will conduct the layout for the questioner.

The layout is normally chosen by the reader. We have included five typical layouts which are fairly easy to use. With practice, you will find that one will usually give better results than the others. You should feel free to use the layout that works best for you.

The task of the reader is to place the top cards of the shuffled deck in the correct places, as shown in the various layouts. The reader must then choose the right meaning, from the set of possible meanings, for each card. This meaning must be combined with the meaning of that card's position, to obtain the full meaning of the card.

A good reader will not only look at the individual card meanings and positions, but will also consider the various relationships between the cards in the spread (the way or order in which the cards are laid on the table). Often, the link of a card with its neighboring cards will determine which individual meaning to select. For example, the Demons of Fire could be either death or a loss. The correct choice could depend as much on the context of the card within the spread as on the question itself.

The Thirteen-Card Enochian Layout

The 13-card Enochian layout is shown in Figure 39. The 13 positions represent:

1. The present atmosphere of the questioner.

2. Masculine influences (father, son, husband, brother, friend, etc.).

3. Feminine influences (mother, daughter, wife, sister, friend, etc.).

4. Harmonious aspects. The best that can be hoped for under the present circumstances.

5. Discordant aspects. The worst that can be expected under the present circumstances.

6. Creative aspects. Creative potential of the questioner at present.

7. Emotional aspects. Emotional atmosphere of the questioner at present.

8. Intellectual aspects. Conscious/mental atmosphere of the questioner at present.

9. Hidden/repressed aspects. Influences present but not consciously known to the questioner at present.

10. The likely outcome of the question under the present circumstances.

11. General past influences and tendencies.

12. General present influences and tendencies.

13. General future influences and tendencies.

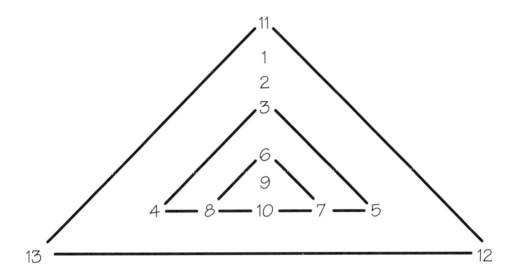

Figure 39. Thirteen-card Enochian spread

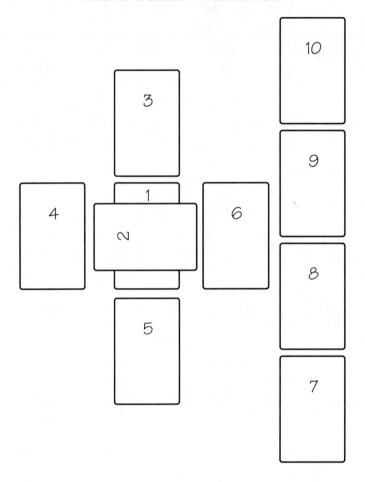

Figure 40. Traditional ten-card Celtic Cross spread

The Ten-Card Celtic Cross Layout

The traditional Celtic Cross Layout of 10 cards is shown in Figure 40. The position meanings are:

1. Present influences. Those influences currently acting on the questioner and his question.

2. Immediate obstacles. The main bar or obstacle to the questioner at present.

3. Specific goal. The purpose or motivating influence of the question.

4. Past foundation. The far past influences.

5. Past events. The near past influences.

6. Future influences. Near future tendencies.

7. The questioner at present.

8. Environmental influences.

9. Emotional influences hidden or known.

10. Result. The final outcome of the question.

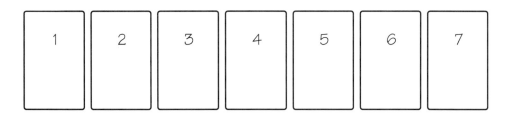

Figure 41. Seven-card Enochian spread—horizontal layout

The Seven-Card Enochian Layout

This spread can be made by laying the top seven cards in a horizontal row, beginning on the left and moving to the right, as shown in Figure 41. The position meanings are:

1. Far past influences affecting the outcome.
2. Near past influences affecting the outcome.
3. Present influences affecting the outcome.
4. Present obstacles to the questioner.
5. Present outlook. How things now stand.
6. Future influences affecting the outcome.
7. Ultimate results. The final outcome.

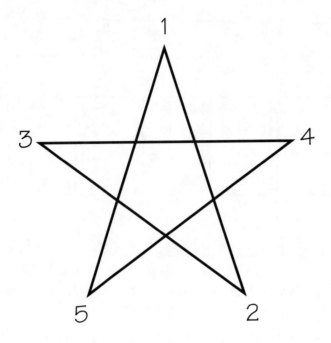

Figure 42. Five-card Enochian pentagram spread

The Five-Card Enochian Pentagram Layout

The five-card spread is ideally suited for Enochian cards, although there are times when it may be too lacking in detail. Its directness is especially good when you want quick answers. The layout consists simply in placing the top five cards in a pentagram pattern as shown in Figure 42. The position meanings are:

1. Tablet of Union—Intuition. Inner influences.
2. Watchtower of Fire—Motivation. Causal influences.
3. Watchtower of Air—Knowledge. Mental influences.
4. Watchtower of Water—Attachments. Emotional influences.
5. Watchtower of Earth—The final result. Manifested outcome.

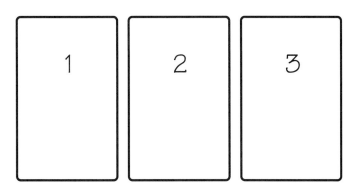

Figure 43. Three-card Enochian spread

The Three-Card Enochian Layout

This short spread is not always reliable but is often a good method to use when you are in a hurry for a direct answer. Simply place the three top cards before you from left to right as shown in Figure 43. The leftmost card represents the past influences. The center card represents the present influences. The rightmost card represents future influences. This layout has no card specifically for outcome, but quite often the general tone and probable outcome of a question can be obtained from an intuitive glance at the top three cards using this quick three-card spread.

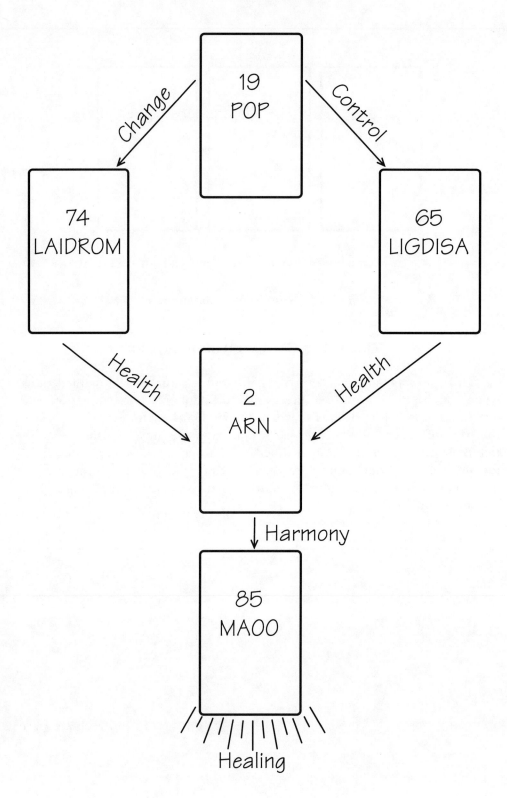

Figure 44. Tarot card arrangement to obtain health

LESSON 35

Two Tarot Meditations

Health

The Enochian Tarot cards can be used to make a meditation exercise to obtain good health. The cards are arranged as shown in Figure 44. Five cards are used as shown below.

Card No.	Name	Meaning
19	POP	A deliberate controlled change
74	LAIDROM	Good health
65	LIGDISA	Good health
2	ARN	A harmonious outcome
85	MAOO	A healing, a return to health

Sit comfortably facing the cards. Meditate on the flow of healing energy. See this energy flow from POP, the desire for change, through the two Seniors, LAIDROM and LIGDISA, who both bestow good health. Forces of health flow from these two Seniors into ARN, harmony, and a successful outcome. This healing force of harmony then flows through MAOO which reinforces the healing and radiates it outward and into your body. As you concentrate on the cards and their arrangement, feel the magical energy of healing flowing from the cards into your body. You may want to touch the bottom of the lowest card, MAOO, with the finger tips of both your hands in order to enhance the flow of healing energy into your body. Feel the power of healing flowing from the cards into your fingers, up your arms, and into your body.

As a ritual, conduct this meditation within a magic circle, and conduct the Invoking Pentagram Ritual first, and the Banishing Pentagram Ritual afterwards.

Magical Power

The Enochian Tarot cards can be used to make a meditation exercise to obtain magical power. The cards are arranged as shown in Figure 45. Four cards are used as shown below.

Card No.	Name	Meaning
31	EDLPRNAA	Magical ability and power
32	AAETPIO	Power, ability, and strength
60	LSRAHPM	Magical power, desire for magical power
3	ZOM	Mastery, self-control

Sit comfortably facing the cards. Meditate on the flow of magical energy through the cards. See this energy flow from the King of Fire, EDLPRNAA, who can bestow magical power, through the two Seniors, AAETPIO, and LSRAHPM, who also bestow magical power and ability. Forces of strong magical power flow from these two Seniors into ZOM, the Magus who has full self-mastery and fully developed magical power. This powerful force of magical power then flows outward into your body. You may want to touch the bottom of ZOM with the finger tips of your hands in order to enhance the flow of magical power into your body. Feel the power of magic flowing from the cards into your fingers, up your arms, and into your body.

As a ritual, conduct this meditation within a magic circle, and conduct the Invoking Pentagram Ritual first and the Banishing Pentagram Ritual afterwards.

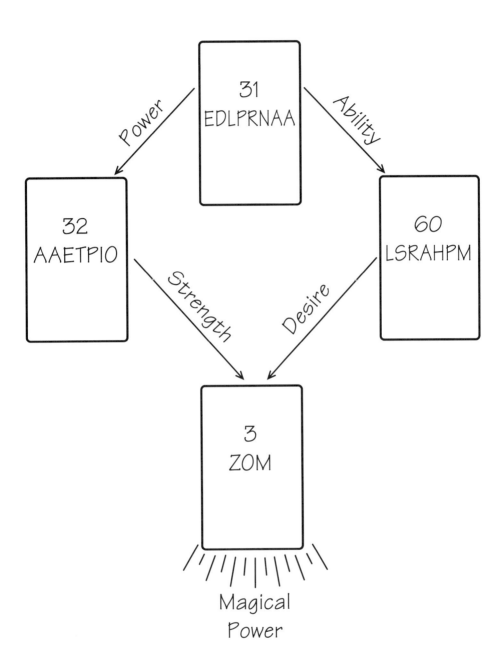

Figure 45. Tarot card arrangement to obtain magical power.

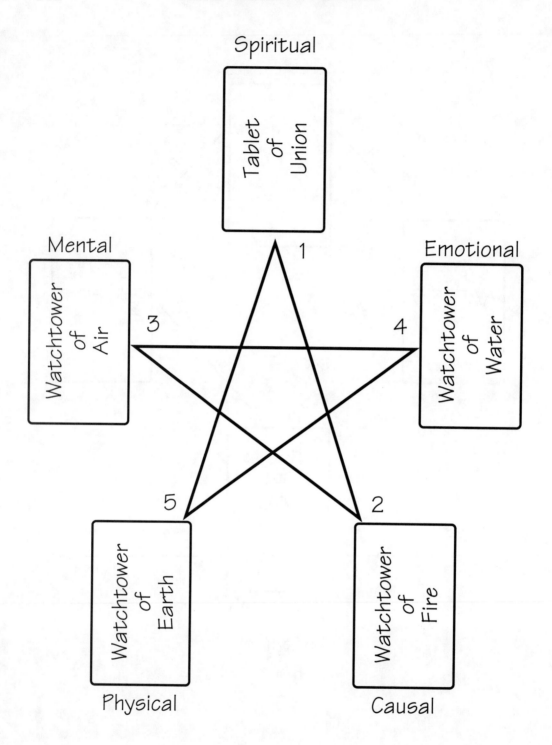

Figure 46. Layout to determine your own fate.

LESSON 36

Determine Your Own Fate Using the Enochian Tarot

Would you like to know where your life is heading? Would you like to learn what your fate has in store for you now and in your near future? Would you like to do this using a simple, straightforward, and easy method? If you answer, "yes," to these questions, perhaps you should try the following exercise using Enochian Tarot.

Everyone knows that life is not always as simple as it seems on the surface. For example, you are more than your physical body. You also have emotions and thoughts. You have causal forces ceaselessly working out your personal karma in the deepest layers of your subconscious. There are also spiritual forces at work, overshadowing the rest and usually acting unconsciously and autonomously through the deepest layers of your subconscious. How can the tarot address all of these parts of your constitution?

The Enochian Tarot is designed in such a way that it can be used effectively to address the five main parts of the human constitution: the physical body as well as the emotions, the mind, and those mysterious causal and spiritual forces which act in the background. Here's how, in four easy steps.

STEP 1. Separate the Enochian card deck (each card has a number, from 1 to 86) into five stacks as follows:

Stack No.	Card Name	Card Numbers
1	Aethyrs	1-30
2	Kings	31,45,59,73
	Seniors	32-37,46-51, 60-65,74-79
3	Sephirothic Cross Angels	38,39,52,53, 66,67,80,81
	Kerubic Angels	40,54,68,82
4	Archangels	41,55,69,83,
	Ruling Angels	42,56,70,84
5	Lower Angels	43,57,71,85
	Demons	44,58,72,86

STEP 2. Use the layout shown in Figure 46. All five parts of your constitution are addressed by dividing the deck into five stacks (this layout is an expansion of Figure 42). The number five is the number of the pentagram which is used in magic as the primary symbol for humans. Using a pentagram figure, such as that shown in the diagram, is often beneficial because it can help put your mind into a more receptive mood. Place stack one (the 30 Aethyrs, card numbers 1 through 30 as shown below) at position one, at the top or "head" of the pentagram. Place the remaining stacks on their corresponding numbers as follows:

1. Aethyrs   Spiritual
2. Kings and Seniors   Causal
3. Sephirothic Cross and Kerubic Angels   Mental
4. Archangels and Ruling Angels   Emotional
5. Lower Angels and Demons   Physical

STEP 3. Concentrate on spiritual things such as love, compassion, perfection, and so on, while shuffling stack one. When the stack "feels right" to you, turn over the top card and place it on card position one of the diagram—the "head" of the pentagram.

Concentrate on your karma, those impulses or desires which lead you to do things, while shuffling stack two. When the stack "feels right" to you, turn over the top card and place it on card position two of the diagram—the right "leg" of the pentagram.

Concentrate on your mind, and the thoughts that constantly flow through your mind, while shuffling stack three. When the stack "feels right" to you, turn over the top card and place it on card position three of the diagram—the left "arm" of the pentagram.

Concentrate on your emotions, likes and dislikes, fears and attractions, while shuffling stack four. When the stack "feels right" to you, turn over the top card, and place it on card position four of the diagram—the right "arm" of the pentagram. Concentrate on your body and your general health while shuffling stack five. When the stack "feels right" to you, turn over the top card and place it on card position five of the diagram—the left "leg" of the pentagram.

STEP 4. Consult the card meanings. These can be found in the booklet that comes with the card deck or in our *Enochian Tarot* (Llewellyn). Find at least one meaning for each of the five cards. The meanings will have a direct bearing on each of the five parts of your constitution. It is a good idea to write these down in a diary for reference. If you want to, you can use upside down cards as "reversed." This will give you an extra set of meanings because reversed cards take on reversed meanings (we prefer to use only the "normal" card meanings, but this is a personal preference). You should go through the four steps described above once a day for a month or so. Not only will the cards tell you how you are doing each day, but after a while, you will notice trends and tendencies. You will find that you have good days and bad days. You may find that the good and bad cards will show themselves in your life, especially when they repeat themselves over and over again.

Summary

The tarot is an ancient magical tool for divination and meditation. It is a powerful magical tool which is capable of harm, if used in too light a manner.

You do not have to be a master of Enochian Magic to use the Enochian Tarot deck. Enochian Magic need only be understood on a very broad, non-verbal level.

Visualization and imagination are important parts of Enochian Tarot. They can help you grasp the cosmic meaning and significance of each of the cards in the Enochian Tarot deck. With their help, you can become a part of each card you study.

The tarot is held to be the oldest book in human history. It was written in ancient Egypt, at the end of the Egyptian empire, in an attempt to save the sacred teachings. The sacred teachings were reduced to symbols and drawn on papyrus leaves. The author of the book was thought to be Hermes Trismegistus (the ibis-headed god, Thoth), and its original title was The Book of Thoth.

The Enochian Tarot was designed by us in 1988. The design combines the ancient tarot tradition with the powerful magical system of Dee—it is the ancient Book of Thoth blended with the more modern system of Enochian Magic.

Enochian Tarot is used for self-understanding. We use it as a map into the realms of psychic and spiritual reality, and as a record of our relationship with the universe. For instance, the major arcana is a symbolic map of inner space, describing the highways of consciousness, from the lofty spiritual heights of divinity, down to the material world of human beings and matter. In this respect, the traditional tarot and Enochian Tarot are identical. Although the "pathways" are slightly different, they take consciousness over the same terrain and allow the user to reach similar states and stages of consciousness.

The Enochian Tarot deck has 86 cards. The major arcana has 30 cards; one for each of the 30 Aethyrs. The 30 Aethyrs and the Qabalistic Tree of Life are both maps of the same subtle regions. Although they vary in details, they show the makeup of the subtle planes and subplanes that exist between spirit and matter. The minor arcana of the Enochian Tarot deck has 56 cards; 28 court cards and 28 suit cards. It contains the hierarchy for each Watchtower. It has seven court cards and seven suit or deity cards for each of the four Watchtowers.

Each card in the Enochian Tarot deck has an Enochian name, an English title, a card number, a gematria number, and a sexual current.

The tarot is popularly used for divination. Each card has an individual set of possible meanings—depending on its position during the layout. A good reader will not only look at the individual card meanings and positions, but will also consider the various relationships between the cards in the spread.

The Enochian Tarot is designed in such a way that it can be used effectively to address the five main parts of the human constitution: the physical body as well as the emotions, the mind, and those mysterious causal and spiritual forces which act in the background.

Further Suggested Reading

The Golden Dawn, Vol 8. Edited by Israel Regardie, Llewellyn.

Enochian Tarot. Gerald and Betty Schueler, Llewellyn.

Tarot Spells. Janina Renee, Llewellyn.

The Secrets of the Tarot. Barbara Walker, Llewellyn.

Secrets of Gypsy Fortunetelling. Raymond Buckland, Llewellyn.

The Electric Tarot. Gerald and Betty Schueler, Llewellyn.

The Magick of the Tarot. Denning & Phillips, Llewellyn.

An Introduction to the Golden Tarot. Robert Wang, Weiser.

The Rabbi's Tarot. Daphna Moore, Llewellyn.

The Witches Tarot. Ellen Cannon Reed, Llewellyn.

Buckland's Complete Gypsy Fortune Teller. Raymond Buckland, Llewellyn.

New Age Tarot. James Wanless, Merrill-West.

The Tarot Path to Self Development. Micheline Stuart, Shambala.

The Tarot of the Bohemians. Papus, Wilshire.

The Tarot. Mouni Sadhu, Wilshire.

Tarot Revelations. Joseph Campbell and Richard Roberts, Vernal Equinox.

The Pictorial Key to the Tarot. A.E. Waite, Citadel.

Things to Do for Section 9

1. Obtain a deck of Enochian Tarot cards and try all of the five layouts given in Lesson 34.

2. Use at least one layout, each day for two months, while asking questions that can be answered in the very near future. Write down the results of your readings over the two-month period and then go back and determine how well you were able to predict your future.

3. Try the two tarot meditations as given in Lesson 35. Record your results.

    Meditation 1:

    Meditation 2:

4. Try the tarot divination, described in Lesson 36, once each day for at least one month. Record your results. (Use a separate sheet of paper.)

Questions for Section 9

1. True or False: The tarot deck is a powerful tool which is capable of harm if used in too light a manner.

2. True or False: Effective utilization of the Enochian Tarot depends to a large degree on the user's ability to harness the power of Enochian Magic.

3. True or False: The tarot originated in ancient Egypt as an attempt to preserve the secret teachings of the priesthood.

4. True or False: The Enochian Tarot was created in 1988.

5. True or False: The highest purpose of the tarot is divination.

6. How many cards are in (1) the Enochian Tarot deck, (2) the major arcana, and (3) The minor arcana?

    1. _____

    2. _____

    3. _____

7. How does the Enochian Tarot deck mirror the Magical Universe?

8. Which cards make up the court cards of the Enochian Tarot minor arcana?

9. True or False: The Archangels are superior to the Sephirothic Cross Angels.

10. True or False: Each card in the Enochian Tarot deck has an Enochian name, an English title, a card number, a gematria number, and a sexual current.

11. True or False: For speed and ease of use, good results can usually be obtained by using only the major arcana cards in divination.

12. True or False: The 13-card layout will have better results than the five-card layout.

13. Multiple choice: Which layout should you use to obtain a quick response?

    a. The 13-Card Layout
    b. The Three-Card Layout
    c. The Celtic Cross Spread
    d. The Seven-Card Layout

14. True or False: Enochian Tarot cards can be used for meditation exercises.

SECTION 10

Enochian Physics

Section Outline

Learning Objectives

This section contains six lessons on Enochian Physics. Physics is a difficult subject for most students. The physics of Enochian Magic is presented here for those students who are especially interested in how the magic works. It is not essential to understand this chapter in order to practice Enochian Magic. However, an understanding of the basic laws and principles behind the magic will help to strengthen your resolve and allow you to increase your magical power. It will bring your mental body into line with your other subtle bodies. We have also included lessons on the Great Work and on the Magical Dragon so that as you end the workbook, you may gain an overall perspective of how and where Enochian Magic can fit into your life. Upon completing the reading you should be able to:

- List the ten Enochian Axioms

- List the seven Enochian Theorems

- Write a short paragraph on the theory of Enochian Physics

- Write a short paragraph on the Great Work

- Write a short paragraph on the Enochian Dragon

LESSON 37

The Cosmic Planes and Elements Model

Everything begins in the Divine Cosmic Plane of which little can be put into words because it is indescribable. Divinity is naturally creative. It expresses itself downwards and outwards into time, space, and form. This is called a continuum.

The result of divinity expressing itself downwards and outwards is a series of planes called the Seven Cosmic Planes of Manifestation. Enochian physics divides each of the six main cosmic planes into five subplanes, as shown in Figure 47, leading deeper and deeper into time, space, and form to the physical plane, the lowest plane—our material Earth.

The material makeup of our physical senses is the lowest of the seven cosmic planes. It is composed of the three subplanes or "elements" that we know as solids, liquids, and gases. Above these three states of matter is the Watchtower of Earth which is located in a region called the etheric plane. This plane is divided into five subplanes: Earth of Earth, Water of Earth, Air of Earth, Fire of Earth, and Spirit of Earth. The Watchtower of Earth is located in the etheric plane. This Watchtower does not include the physical Earth itself.

The Watchtower of Water is located in the astral, cosmic plane. The mental, cosmic plane can be thought of as divided in half; into an upper and a lower mental plane. The lower mental plane retains form and contains the Watchtower of Air. The upper mental plane (sometimes this is called the causal plane) is relatively formless and contains the Watchtower of Fire.

Separating the four Watchtowers from the Tablet of Union is the Great Outer Abyss, the home of the ArchDemon KHORONZON. The spiritual cosmic plane located above the Abyss contains the Tablet of Union.

You must keep in mind that a structural approach to reality, such as the model shown in Figure 47, is simplistic by necessity. For example, the planes and subplanes are not actually located one on top of the other with clear cut dividing lines, as it may appear from the model; rather, they overlap and interpenetrate. The thoughts of the mental plane and the emotions on the astral plane are as close to our physical body as they ever could be. The cosmic planes are not separated by spacial distance so much as by density or frequency.

Enochian Physics teaches that a host of invisible worlds exist all around us. Existence is hierarchial and spreads in a graduated, serial order from spirit into matter. The chief aspects of matter are time, space, and form. It is these three characteristics which become denser or stronger as the creative process takes place.

The Watchtowers and Aethyrs of Enochian Magic are convenient "road maps" of these invisible realms. It often helps to remember that our waking state is on the physical plane, we dream on the astral plane, and we experience deep, dreamless sleep when we enter the mental plane. Therefore, the physical, etheric, astral, and the lower mental, of the cosmic planes, are already known to us—at least to some degree.

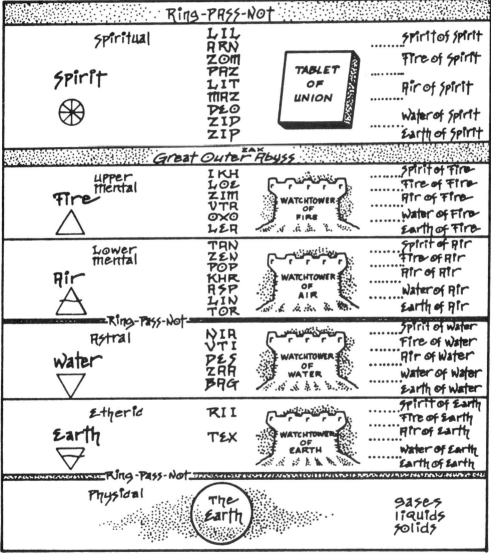

Figure 47. The cosmic planes and elements model

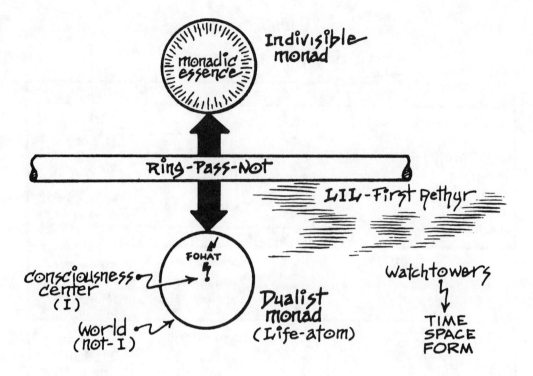

Figure 48. The monad model of Enochian physics

LESSON 38

The Monad Model

In union with the Cosmic Planes and Elements Model, Enochian physics proposes the Enochian Monad Model. These two models are dependent, and are only separated into two distinct models for simplicity.

A monad is defined as an indivisible unit; that is, it can't be broken into smaller parts. The term was used by Pythagoras as well as by Plato. Leibniz used the term to imply self-expressing centers of consciousness, or mirrors of the macrocosm. Giordano Bruno taught that the monad was the ultimate spiritual particle and all entities had a monad at their center—the core of their being. Enochian Physics uses the term in the same sense. The monad is the spiritual, indivisible essence at the center of every being. It is not the soul, but the divine spark that lies behind the soul.

The model is shown in Figure 48. Every person is inherently a monad—a divine spark. Every monad is monastic, or of single nature, above the first Aethyr, LIL. Every monad is dualistic, or of double nature, below LIL. This duality takes many forms as the monad reveals itself downward into matter. It consists of a subjective or personal Self in the center of an objective, unbiased World.

The Self is a center of consciousness having position in space, but no mass or substance. The Self is the personal, conscious side of reality. Exactly what the Self reflects, or its sense of identity, is dependent on time and position in space. Physics shows time and position to be limits or parameters of motion. Position, over time, is speed (velocity). Velocity, over time, is acceleration. When a monad enters the cosmic plane of earth, it expresses itself with mass (substance), so its expression can be said to have momentum, or stimulation, because

$$momentum = mass \times velocity = form \times (space/time)$$

However, the model separates the Self from its expressions. The Self has zero mass. The expressions of Self, however, have both substance and stimulation. It is the Self which gives things their individuality.

The other half of the monad is called the Not-I. The Self says, "I am this" and precedes to define itself accordingly. That is, the Self says, "I am John or Jane Doe." All that does not fall into its self-definition becomes the World.

The World of one monad is not the World of another, but overlapping does occur. For instance, everyone is an individual, but each individual is part of a family, a community, a state, and a country, and so our Worlds overlap.

It is because our Worlds overlap that we can form new Worlds. In fact, we can say that the probability of forming a new World is equal to the probability of overlapping Worlds in that particular region of space and time. In other words, if you are stranded alone on a deserted island, the probability of your forming a new World (child), is very remote.

A careful study of this model will reveal many interesting new ideas. The following ten principles or axioms of Enochian Physics can be formed directly from the Enochian Monad Model:

1 First Enochian Axiom: Every entity in existence is, in essence, a monad. This monadic essence expresses itself as a subjective Self and an objective World.

2 Second Enochian Axiom: The geometric equivalent of every entity is the sphere. The center of the sphere is the Self. The surface of the sphere is the World.

3 Third Enochian Axiom: The Self is conscious individuality.

4 Fourth Enochian Axiom: The World is the world in which the Self finds itself at any given point in time and space.

5 Fifth Enochian Axiom: Every geometric point in space is a Self-World monad in some stage of self-expression.

6. Sixth Enochian Axiom: Any Self can communicate with any other Self only in so far as their Worlds intersect.

7 Seventh Enochian Axiom: A world is defined as a set of intersections of countless Worlds at any given point in time and space.

8 Eighth Enochian Axiom: Subsets of Selfs are mutually exclusive.

9 Ninth Enochian Axiom: Subsets of Worlds may be either exclusive or inclusive.

10 Tenth Enochian Axiom: The monadic essence of each monad allows multitudinous expression, but no Self can ever separate itself from or exist independently of its World.

Although this model may at first appear confusing, a little study will reveal its simplicity. It expresses an old poetical and mystical definition of man as a circle whose center is nowhere and whose circumference is everywhere. If we think of the center as monadic consciousness (the Self or the I) and the circumference as infinite Space (the World or the Not-I), then it is obvious that the Enochian Monad Model is but a slight enhancement of the ancient mystical definition of man.

The Enochian Monad Model is a modern expression of an ancient idea. It does not, in itself, propose anything new. The Ancient Egyptians, for example, symbolized the Self as a winged globe; the globe was a consciousness center whose ability to move was symbolized by a pair of wings. They personified the World with the goddess, Nuit, who was often shown naked and arched over the world. She represented the sky explicitly, or exoterically, and infinite Space inexpressibly, or esoterically. The winged globe was considered a symbol for the god, Horus. Thus the Egyptians considered the center to be masculine and the circumference to be feminine. This symbolism is repeated throughout western occultism and is included in the Monad Model of Enochian Physics as well.

LESSON 39

The Theorems of Enochian Physics

The following list of seven theorems or laws summarizes the major teachings of Enochian Physics. These seven theorems are the result of using or exercising the models of Enochian Physics.

First Enochian Theorem: *Every person is a monad.*

Each of us is a star in the center of our own universe. We can change universes (individual reality) at will. For instance, the cycle of life and death is similar to the experience of reading a book. When we are reading a book, it becomes part of our universe—the action and characters appear to be part of our life. But when we finish reading the book, it quickly fades from memory. After awhile, we pick up a new book and the cycle repeats itself. So it is with the cycle of life and death. We choose an identity (a Self) for awhile, and when we are finished with that experience, we lay it down (in death) and take on a new identity (life).

Second Enochian Theorem: *Every point in space is a consciousness center.*

The Self of every monad is a consciousness center without substance or materiality. Everything in existence is composed of a collection of monads expressing themselves as molecules, cells, organs, and so forth. For instance, although we have a body, our body is composed of smaller parts, like the organs, which in turn are composed of smaller parts, cells. Each of part has own consciousness which is part of, yet separate from us. This principle is proved in the modern medical technique of cloning, where the cell of one thing (say a plant or animal) is used to produce a duplicate of the original thing.

Third Enochian Theorem: *Energy flows from one cosmic plane or subplane to an adjacent cosmic plane or subplane through laya centers, dimensionless points of space which serve as channels for the flow of energies and forces.*

Each Self must find a way to express itself materially. To do this, it has to pass through each plane from the spiritual to the material or physical. Every physical object in our universe is created by a Self expressing itself through a laya center which is a pathway joining one plane to another.

In physics, a laya center is a dimensionless point through which forces or energies from one plane or subplane can manifest in another plane or subplane. These are the white holes and black holes of astronomy. Creative energy pours into the physical plane from a white hole and drains away from the physical through a black hole.

Astronomers have observed such behavior on the cosmic scale with the birth and death of galaxies and have proposed such events for planets and stars. Enochian Physics teaches that this flowing of energy is true for all matter, though not on such a grand scale.

Fourth Enochian Theorem: *Spirit is unmanifested energy. Matter is manifested energy.*

Enochian Physics is in complete accord with modern physics on this theorem when we let spirit equal energy. Albert Einstein equated matter and energy in 1905. His famous equation, $E = mc^2$, has been proved to be true many times in laboratory experiments since that time. Matter and energy are 2 forms or states of a single substance which Enochian Physics calls the cosmic element, Spirit. In the same way, the cosmic elements Fire, Air, Water, and Earth are the quantized states of Spirit in manifestation.

Fifth Enochian Theorem: *Every manifestation within space and time is dualistic.*

With the exception of gravity, modern physics has demonstrated that all particles and forces in the physical universe are dualistic (they have two aspects). To eliminate the singular exception, some physicists have proposed the gravitron as the quantum particle of a gravitational field and antigravity as an opposing force to the gravitational force. Their existence has yet to be demonstrated in the laboratory. However, this theorem implies that antigravity is a possibility.

Magical operations, resulting in levitations of one sort or another, confirm this theorem in principle, although the mechanics can only be explained by accepting some sort of an antigravitational force. According to this theorem, all manifestation below the first Aethyr, LIL, is dualistic. Monadic essence splits the monad into a Self and a World below LIL. All of its manifestations in time and space partake of this fundamental split.

Sixth Enochian Theorem: *Space, time, and consciousness come into existence simultaneously.*

In this theorem, the term consciousness is used in the sense of the dualistic opposite of unconsciousness. The conscious Self, and the unconscious World, came into existence together. Their creation also marks the beginning of space and time. This event first occurs above the Abyss. As manifestation into time, space, and form proceeds, it approaches the physical plane (this approach must be in serial order by the third theorem). All of the "players" come together at that point and the resultant explosion begins physical expression on this plane. Consciousness, space, time, and form all began on the physical plane at a single point with the event known by modern physics as the Big Bang.

Seventh Enochian Theorem: *Every energy field and every force in our universe is directed by the True Will.*

Relativity physics has defined the spacetime continuum as a four-dimensional universe. Enochian Physics adds consciousness to this continuum as a fifth dimension (the direction of inner space). The True Will is the desire of a monad as it expresses itself in a continuum. This is usually unknown to the human being, who is but an expression on the lower cosmic planes of a monad.

Magical techniques must often be employed to attune the human consciousness with the True Will. Only after recognizing one's True Will, can one set about to attain it and satisfy the intentions of the Self. According to Enochian Magic, the True Will and the Self (poetically known as the Holy Guardian Angel) are usually seen directly in the eighth Aethyr, ZID.

LESSON 40

How the Magic Works

The Enochian Monad Model explains how Enochian Magic works, what it can do, and what it can't do. By strengthening the will, and controlling the mind (the Self or the I), the magician can bring about changes to his/her environment and/or to others around him/her (the World or the Not-I). Everything you can possibly observe anytime, anywhere, must first enter into your World. There is no such thing as "only" a hallucination or "merely" an illusion.

If you see something, then that something is real—relative to you. Dreams are real—relative to the dreamer. Hunger and poverty are real to some people, while others hardly have a concept of what they can be. Sickness and disease are real to some, while merely concepts to others. What you observe is largely controlled by your karma, both individual and collective. A magician is really a person who can consciously control his observations, and to the extent that he is successful, he is said to have "eliminated his karma."

The ultimate goal of Enochian Magic is the conscious control of your observations. In the third Aethyr, ZOM, this conscious control of Self over its World is natural and complete. By practicing Enochian Magic, you can establish this control on all of the Cosmic Planes of Manifestation, at least to a degree.

Dream control is a first step. Virtually all advanced magicians can consciously direct their dream content according to their will. Almost like a movie director, if the plot of a dream approaches something unpleasant and unwanted, the will changes it appropriately and the dream continues (it is impossible for an advanced magician to have an unwanted nightmare). This ability is relatively easier to practice in dreams than it is in the waking state. The reason for this is that with each cosmic plane into matter the collective karma (the influence of the overlapping Worlds or Not-I's) increases in strength. The Self inherently has more control over its World in the astral plane than on the physical plane. On the mental plane, the control is even stronger.

To compensate for the loss in natural ability, special techniques must be used to enhance the Self's control. This is the reason for breathing exercises and meditational rituals. The Self can be made to control its World on the physical plane to a remarkable extent (there are definite limits, however).

The key is that the Self controls, consciously or unconsciously, whatever enters into its World. In effect, it "lets" things in and then observes them and reacts to them. For example, it can let in an idea which then later expresses itself physically. The idea, "I am hungry," can eventually lead to physical eating. Magical control of the Self can prevent unwanted things from entering its World.

The mental body is extremely busy interacting with other mental bodies. Normally, we are not consciously aware of these continuous communications with other Selfs. Everyone constantly uses mental telepathy, whether they are conscious of it or not. We are literally being bombarded by thoughts and emotions all the time.

Every thought that goes through our mind came from someone else and goes out into the minds of others, who may or may not become consciously aware of them. By entertaining a thought, you give it strength. Thoughts feed on the psychic vitality of the mental body and grow according to how many people concentrate on them.

The key to controlling your World is tied to controlling the continuous flow of ideas, thoughts, and emotions that swirl through our subtle bodies. Yogic techniques are excellent tools for this task. The power of positive thinking is well known and also useful to the magician. To a large extent, just realizing that one's World can be controlled by one's thinking is a large step toward the goal.

In addition to preventing others from influencing you, the magician can also influence others (because of this, a mature responsibility is needed and ethical development encouraged). By concentration on a specific thought, the trained magician can successfully project that thought into the mental atmosphere of another Self where it can then be accepted into that other's World as a "reality." The World of another person can be influenced by the Self of the magician to the extent that their Worlds interpenetrate. This is the familiar phenomenon of spell casting that is associated with stereotyped witches and magic users. The effectiveness of such operations is directly proportional to the will of the magician and the ability of the recipient to control his/her own observations.

The Enochian Monad Model explains the mechanics of many magical operations. It suggests that the higher planes will be similar to our life on earth. When you die, for example, you will take your hopes, fears, successes, and failures with you. If you desired something during life, chances are you will continue to do so in the heavens of TEX and RII, or to wherever you gravitate. Similarly, your fears and guilts will accompany you. There is no oblivion or annihilation any more than there is "empty" space. Your karma must be worked out—now or later, here or somewhere else.

Not only do we take our problems with us, we also carry along our achievements. If we learn control over our lives, then control over our after-death experiences as well as our rebirth experiences, are equally assured. This means that spiritual development and progress can continue beyond the span of a single life on this planet. This is the great promise of Enochian Magic.

LESSON 41

The Great Work

The Great Work is the name given to the ultimate goal of the magician; to attain unto the Godhead, or in Enochian Physics' terms, to unite the Self with its World.

The Cosmic Element Model and Enochian Monad Model both show man as rooted in divinity. At the core of every person is a spark of divinity. This divine core expresses itself as a monad. The Great Work of the magician is to realize the divine spark within himself.

The magician must shift his consciousness inward, toward the monad, which is his essential being. As he progresses, he will confront his own Holy Guardian Angel and converse with him. This knowledge and conversation with the Holy Guardian Angel is a major milestone in the Great Work. It takes place in the eighth Aethyr, ZID.

Meeting the Holy Guardian Angel is similar to matter confronting anti-matter. The higher Aethyrs contain a unification of the magician and his Angel. The actual union is effected in LIL, the highest Aethyr. Such a union leads to the end or elimination of all the lower expression of the monad with a corresponding release of spiritual energy.

LESSON 42

How the Dragon Works

As physics has its physicists, so Magic has its magicians. One of the highest Adepts of Enochian Magic is called the Magical Dragon. The dragon is a special title given to one who has fulfilled certain magical requirements.

The very first ordeal of the candidate for Dragon is to learn how to travel through the spacetime-consciousness continuum in the direction of consciousness. He/she must use Spirit Vision to travel through the lower Aethyrs up to, and including, NIA. He/she must, in effect, master space, time, and consciousness, at least in so far as traveling in these five dimensions is concerned. To pass this ordeal, the candidate must be able to shift his/her consciousness to the astral body. The astral body must travel successfully through the six directions of space (forward, backward, right, left, upward, and downward), the two directions of time (past and future) and the two directions of consciousness (upward, through the planes, toward the spiritual, and downward, through the planes, toward the physical).

Shifting consciousness, to the astral body, is itself traveling in one direction of consciousness. Returning consciousness to the physical body, is traveling in the other direction of consciousness. We all travel through space and time whenever we move about. We also all travel through the inward direction of consciousness, during sleep, but such traveling is usually done subconsciously, as an automatic reflex of consciousness working through its lower vehicles. In this ordeal, the candidate must be able to shift consciousness at will, and retain memory of all experiences throughout the exercise. This is the first step toward the title of Dragon. It involves learning and mastering the mechanics of Spirit Vision. The Self, and its relationship to its World, must be examined in depth. As the candidate explores the World, he/she really learns about him/herself.

In the second ordeal, the candidate must learn to differentiate between the Self and the World. He/she must also learn to cultivate a sense of humor. When sufficiently prepared, he/she must enter the 14th Aethyr, VTA, make observations there, and return with full memory of his/her experiences. Each of the Aethyrs emphasizes a different aspect of our universe and its operations. Some stress the Self (subjectivity) while others stress the World (objectivity). In VTA, the tendency is to focus consciousness on the Self, and ignore the World as an illusion—the maya of Eastern occultism. If the candidate gives in to this suggestion he/she will be tempted to join with the other inhabitants of this region, and thereby risk the possibility of never returning to the physical body. Physically he/she will simply enter a coma from which he/she may never recover.

However, the damage to consciousness, by remaining in VTA, is worse, in the long run, than physical death (which will come to us all anyway in the natural course of things).

The candidate for Dragon faces death, and even worse than death, in the second ordeal. He/she must learn to balance the Self with its World. Neither is more or less important than the other.

The candidate learns the Law of Periodicity in the 20th Aethyr, KHR, where he/she observes the universe as a giant revolving wheel. He/she learns the Law of Duality in the 17th Aethyr, TAN, where he/she observes the polarized forces and energies of the universe in the form of a giant, two-pan balance. He/she learns the Law of Identity in a confrontation with KHORONZON in the 10th Aethyr, ZAX. This Aethyr is the Great Outer Abyss and the candidate must safely cross this Abyss, and retain full memory of the experiences. ZAX is the region where formless spiritual ideas take on psychic forms. It is the highest region conceivable by the human mind. It is a Ring-Pass-Not for the mental body. The candidate must shift consciousness, from the upper mental or causal body to the spiritual body, in order to successfully complete this ordeal.

After crossing the Abyss, the candidate must enter the eighth Aethyr, ZID, and observe and communicate with his/her World in this spiritual region. In ZID, the World takes the form of a highly developed persona. It is actually a direct projection of the Self, but it is usually observed as another being, separate from the candidate. This being is the Holy Guardian Angel, a spiritual personification, and is an Angel in the true sense of the True Will of the Self.

The Self, in ZID, projects its True Will onto the World in the form of a personification. The candidate must encounter this personification, when entering ZID, and commune with it. In this way he/she will learn his/her True Will which is the real beginning of his/her magical work.

However, the candidate does not gain the full title of Dragon until one more ordeal is undergone. He/she must enter the next Aethyr, DEO, and learn the meaning of Love. All of the many aspects of Love are contained in DEO, and the candidate will only become a Dragon if he/she can learn from all of them. The highest aspect of Love is compassion—what the successful candidate must cultivate in DEO.

After successfully completing these ordeals, the candidate becomes a Magical Dragon. He/she acquires a new magical name and Word in order to accomplish his/her Great Work. He/she becomes a teacher and travels the Cosmic Planes of Manifestation proclaiming his/her Word and helping others wherever he/she can—a practitioner of Enochian Magic. The ordeals of the Enochian Dragon are described in detail in *Enochian Yoga* (Llewellyn).

Summary

Everything begins in the Divine Cosmic Plane of which little can be put into words because it is indescribable. Divinity is naturally creative. It expresses itself downwards and outwards into time, space, and form.

The result of divinity expressing itself downwards and outwards is the seven Cosmic Planes of Manifestation. Each of the planes is divided into subplanes, leading deeper and deeper into time, space, and form to the physical plane.

The planes and subplanes overlap and interpenetrate. The cosmic planes are not separated by spacial distance so much as by density or frequency.

A monad is defined as an indivisible unit, that is, it can't be broken into smaller parts. A monad is the divine spark that lies behind the soul.

The Self is a center of consciousness having position in space, but no mass or substance. The Self is the personal, conscious side of reality. Exactly what the Self reflects, or its sense of identity, is dependent on time and position in space.

While the Self has zero mass, the expressions of Self have both substance and stimulation. It is the Self which gives things their individuality.

The other half of the monad is called the Not-I. The Self defines itself, and all that does not fall into its self-definition becomes the World.

The World of one monad is not the World of another, but overlapping does occur. It is because our Worlds overlap that we can form new Worlds.

There are ten principles or axioms of Enochian Physics formed from the Enochian Monad Model which is a modern expression of an ancient idea. They are:

1. Every entity in existence is, in essence, a monad.

2. The geometric equivalent of every entity is the sphere.

3. The Self is conscious individuality.

4. The World is the world in which the Self finds itself at any given point in time and space.

5. Every geometric point in space is a Self-World monad in some stage of self-expression.

6. Any Self can communicate with any other Self only in so far as their Worlds' intersect.

7. A world is defined as a set of intersections of countless Worlds at any given point in time and space.

8. Subsets of Selfs are mutually exclusive.

9. Subsets of Worlds may be either exclusive or inclusive.

10. The monadic essence of each monad allows multitudinous expression, but no Self can ever separate itself from or exist independently of its World.

Seven theorems summarize the major teachings of Enochian Physics. They are:

1. Every person is a monad.

2. Every point in space is a consciousness center.

3. Energy flows from one cosmic plane or subplane to an adjacent cosmic plane or subplane through laya centers.

4. Spirit is unmanifested energy; matter is manifested energy.

5. Every manifestation within space and time is dualistic.

6. Space, time and consciousness come into existence simultaneously.

7. Every energy field and every force in our universe is directed by the True Will.

The Great Work is the name given to the ultimate goal of the magician; to attain unto the Godhead, or in Enochian Physics' terms, to unite the Self with its World—to realize the divine spark within himself.

The highest Adepts of Enochian Magic are called Magical Dragons; a special title given to one who has fulfilled certain magical requirements. The candidate for Dragon faces great danger in the quest to realize the divine spark within.

Further Suggested Reading

The Secret Doctrine. H. P. Blavatsky, Theosophical University Press.

The Cosmic Doctrine. Dion Fortune, Helios (Society of the Inner Light) and also by Aquarian Press.

Fountain-source of Occultism. G. de Purucker, Theosophical University Press.

Magick in Theory and Practice. Aleister Crowley, Castle.

Liber Aleph: The Book of Wisdom or Folly. Aleister Crowley, Stellar Visions.

Things to Do for Section 10

1. Study the two models of Enochian Physics, the Cosmic Planes and Elements Model, and the Monad Model. Try to see how the axioms and theorems were derived from the models. Try to develop some corollaries of these axioms and theorems on your own.

2. Study the axioms and theorems of Enochian Physics. How do these relate to your own life? How can you use them to make your life better?

3. Now that you are familiar with the fundamentals of Enochian Magic, determine for yourself if you would like to earn the title of Dragon and take up the Great Work.

Questions for Section 10

1. True or False: The Cosmic Planes and Elements Model graphically shows the cosmic planes containing the Watchtowers and Aethyrs.

2. How many Cosmic Planes of Manifestation does Enochian Magic recognize?

3. Each cosmic plane is divided into how many subplanes?

4. True or False: The Watchtower of Water is located in the astral cosmic plane.

5. What separates the four Watchtowers from the Tablet of Union?

6. What is Fohat?

7. What is Kundalini?

8. What is the First Enochian Axiom?

9. What duality is contained within the monad, below the First Aethyr, LIL?

10. What is the Great Work?

11. What is the Holy Guardian Angel?

12. What is the first ordeal of the Enochian Dragon?

13. True or False: The Holy Guardian Angel is located above the Great Outer Abyss.

SECTION 11

Invocation

Section Outline

Learning Objectives

This section is presented last, because it includes almost everything that has gone before. It can be considered the highest operation of the ritual magician. Upon completing the reading you should be able to:

• Describe the difference between invocation and evocation

• Invoke an Enochian Angel

LESSON 43

How to Invoke
an Enochian Angel

Invocation and Evocation

Invocation and evocation are probably the best-known magical operations of ritual magic. When most people think of ritual magic, they visualize a magician calling upon a demon or angelic entity and making that entity obey his will. While the stereotype invocation and evocation are well known in literature, they are the most difficult to do properly.

When you conduct an invocation, you call a discarnate entity into your body. When you conduct an evocation, you call a discarnate entity to you, but keep it restrained or confined and safely external to you. The invocation can be a significant help to the Great Work of a magician. By invoking a being with certain powers or abilities, you bring those powers or abilities into yourself, and thus acquire them—at least temporarily.

Assuming a God-Form

Assuming a god-form is very similar to conducting a ritual invocation. In both cases, the result is the same—you temporarily take on the characteristics of a particular discarnate entity. For beginners, it cannot be stressed too much to limit your invocations to friendly and loving entities. As a general rule, invoke friendly entities—ones whose qualities you would like to share. Avoid invoking demonic beings, or those who have qualities that could harm you or those around you.

Enochian Angels

Enochian Angels include the Kerubic Angels, the Sephirothic Cross Angels, the Archangels, the Ruling Angels, and the Lesser Angels. Each of these can be invoked in a similar manner. The ritual to invoke an Angel includes the Calls and the use of the pentagram as shown in Figure 49. The pentagram has five points, each of which corresponds to an element and to an Enochian Tablet. To invoke an Angel, trace a pentagram toward that point which corresponds to the Angel's location. To banish an Angel, trace a pentagram away from that point which corresponds to the Angel's location. This is shown in Figure 50.

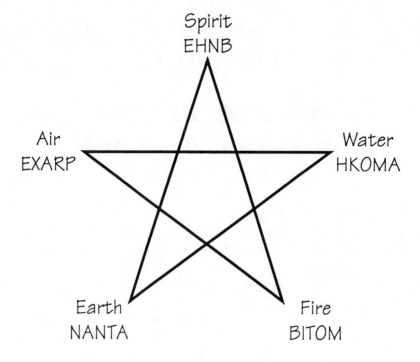

Figure 49. Pentagram for invocation and banishment of angels

How to Invoke Enochian Angels

The following steps can be used as a general guide to invoke any of the Lesser Angels or Ruling Lesser Angels of the four Watchtowers:

1. Select the Angel to be invoked.
2. Determine its location in the Watchtowers, using Figures 1-7.
3. Use the information in Lesson 17 to determine the appropriate Call(s) to use.
4. Determine the correct Names of Power to speak. This consists of the names of the hierarchy the Angel is in, as given in Lesson eight (correct pronunciations are in Lesson 5). Always begin with the Great Holy Name, the King, and the six Seniors of the appropriate Watchtower.
5. Determine the correct pentagram to trace, using Figures 49 and 50.
6. Construct a Magic Circle. Stand within the circle and face the Watchtower where the Angel is located as follows: Earth in the North, Water in the West, Air in the East, and Fire in the South.
7. Conduct the Enochian Invoking Pentagram Ritual, as given in Lesson 22.
8. Recite the Call(s) out loud.
9. Use your Wand (see Lessons 13 and 21) to trace an invoking pentagram in the air before you (see Figures 49 and 50). Begin at the correct starting

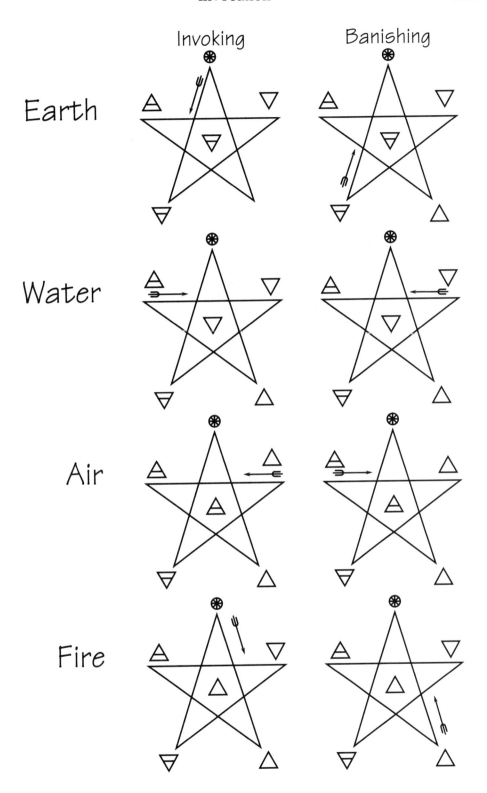

Figure 50. Invoking and banishing pentagrams for angels of the four elements

point and use one continuous line. Visualize the line being drawn in the appropriate color: Earth, black; Water, blue; Air, yellow; and Fire, red. After drawing the pentagram, draw the appropriate element symbol in the center, visualizing the same color. The element symbols are:

Earth
Water
Air
Fire

10. Vibrate the Holy Name while drawing the pentagram (see Lesson 19 for how to vibrate the names). Vibrate the King's name while drawing the inner element symbol. Vibrate the names of the six Seniors while clearly visualizing the pentagram before you. Finish by vibrating the two Sephirothic Cross Angels, the Archangel, and the Kerubic Angel. The names of all of these Angels are given in Lesson 8.

11. Vibrate the name of the Angel to be invoked. Feel his/her presence. If you desire an evocation, then visualize the Angel taking form within the pentagram. If you desire an invocation, then feel his/her presence within yourself. If the invocation is successful, you will feel his/her presence and you will partake in some degree of his/her characteristics, qualities, and powers. If you are unable to invoke the Angel, trace his/her sigil in the pentagram overtop of the element symbol. Use the Enochian Rose, as shown in Figure 51, to determine the sigil. The sigil of any Watchtower Angel is found by tracing the name of the Angel, using the letters on the petals of the rose.

12. Banish the Angel back to his/her Watchtower region by tracing the banishing pentagram, as shown in Figure 50. As you trace the banishing pentagram, imagine that your Wand is erasing it. When complete, the pentagram, and the Angel, should be gone.

13. Conduct the Enochian Banishing Pentagram Ritual, as given in Lesson 22.

A Sample Invocation of the Earth Angel AXIR

The following is a typical example of an invocation. Although it is specifically designed for the Earth of Earth Angel, AXIR (pronounced Ah-tzee-ar), the principles can be used to invoke any Watchtower Angel.

STEP 1. Construct a magic circle and consecrate with by conducting the Enochian Invoking Pentagram Ritual from Lesson 22. Burn a heavy, musk-type incense. The use of incense during magical operations is optional, but many students insist that it helps. The following incense can be used during Watchtower operations:

Earth: storax, musk, sandalwood, any dull, heavy odor.

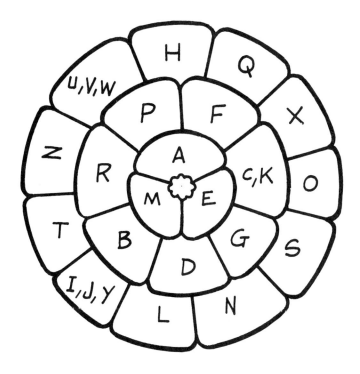

Figure 51. Enochian Rose for sigils of the watchtower deities

Earth: storax, musk, sandalwood, any dull, heavy odor.
Water: myrrh, onycha, ginger, any cool, watery odor.
Air: galbanum, peppermint, lemon, orange, any light, airy odor.
Fire: olibanum, cinnamon, any spicy or fiery odor.
STEP 2. Hold your Wand in your right hand, face South and say,

> I see the holy and formless Fire which darts through the hidden
> depths of the universe. I hear the Voice of Fire. OIP-TEAA-
> PDOKE (Oh-ee-peh-Teh-ah-ah-Peh-doh-keh) I invoke you,
> Angels of the Watchtower of the South.

Hold your Cup in your right hand, face West and say,

> I see the holy and formless Water which flows through the
> hidden depths of the universe. I hear the Voice of Water. MPH-
> ARSL-GAIOL (Em-peh-heh-Ar-ess-el-Gah-ee-oh-leh) I invoke
> you, Angels of the Watchtower of the West.

Hold your Dagger in your right hand, face East and say:

I see the holy and formless Air which blows through the hidden depths of the universe. I hear the Voice of Air. ORO-IBAH-AOZPI (Oh- roh-Ee-bah-Ah-oh-zeh-pee) I invoke you, Angels of the Watchtower of the East.

Hold your Pantacle in your right hand, face North and say:

I see the holy and formless Earth which lies at the hidden depths of the universe. I hear the Voice of Earth. MOR-DIAL-HKTGA (Moh-ar-Dee-ah-leh-Heh-keh-teh-gah) I invoke you, Angels of the Watchtower of the North.

STEP 3. Recite the Fifth Call out loud.

STEP 4. While still facing North, use your Wand to draw the invoking pentagram of Earth in the air before you. See the black pentagram clearly before you. While tracing this, vibrate the Holy Name MOR-DIAL-HKTGA.

STEP 5. Trace the element for Earth (a downward pointing triangle with a horizontal line through it) in the center of the pentagram, also with a black color. While tracing, vibrate the name of the King of Earth, IKZHIKAL (Ee-keh-zeh-hee-kal).

STEP 6. Vibrate the names of the 6 Seniors of the Watchtower of Earth while clearly visualizing the pentagram before you.

LAIDROM (Lah-ee-deh-roh-em)
AKZINOR (Ah-keh-zee-noh-ar)
LZINOPO (El-zee-noh-poh)
ALHKTGA (Ah-leh-heh-keh-teh-gah)
AHMLLKV (Ah-heh-meh-el-el-keh-veh)
LIIANSA (Lee-ee-ah-ness-ah)

STEP 7. Vibrate names of the two Sephirothic Cross Angels, the Archangel, the Kerubic Angel, and the Ruling Lesser Angel of Earth of Earth:

ABALPT (Ah-bah-leh-peh-teh)
ARBIZ (Ar-bee-zeh)
NRONK (Neh-roh-en-keh)
RONK (Roh-en-keh)
TAXIR (Tah-etzee-ar)

STEP 8. Vibrate the name of the Angel to be invoked, AXIR (Ah-etzee-ar). Feel his presence. If the invocation is successful, you will feel his presence and you will partake in some degree of his characteristics, qualities, and powers.

Sometimes it helps to say a few words such as, "O mighty and powerful Angel AXIR, I call you. I bind you, in the name of your King, IKZHIKAL, I call

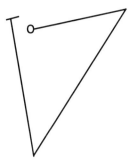

you to me. Come to me and purify my earthy self with your presence." If you are still unable to invoke the Angel AXIR, trace his sigil in the pentagram overtop of the element symbol and then repeat the invocation. The sigil of AXIR, from the Enochian Rose, is shown above.

STEP 9. Banish AXIR by tracing the banishing pentagram so that the pentagram and Angel both disappear. Conduct the Enochian Banishing Pentagram Ritual as given in Lesson 22.

Summary

Invocation and evocation are probably the best-known magical operations of ritual magic but they are difficult to perform properly. When you conduct an invocation, you call a discarnate entity into your body. When you conduct an evocation, you call a discarnate entity to you, but keep it restrained or confined and safely external to you. The invocation can be a significant help to the Great Work of a magician. By invoking a being with certain powers or abilities, you bring those powers or abilities into yourself, and thus acquire them—at least temporarily.

Assuming a god-form is very similar to conducting a ritual invocation. In both cases, the result is the same—you temporarily take on the characteristics of a particular discarnate entity. Beginners should limit their invocations to friendly and loving entities. As a general rule, invoke friendly entities—ones whose qualities you would like to share. Avoid invoking demonic beings, or those who have qualities that could harm you or those around you.

Enochian Angels include the Kerubic Angels, the Sephirothic Cross Angels, the Archangels, the Ruling Angels, and the Lesser Angels. Each of these can be invoked in a similar manner. To invoke an Angel, trace a pentagram toward that point which corresponds to the Angel's location. To banish an Angel, trace a pentagram away from that point which corresponds to the Angel's location.

Further Suggested Reading

Techniques of High Magic: A Manual of Self-Initiation. Francis King and Stephen Skinner, Doubleday.

The Book of the Goetia of Solomon the King. Trans. by Aleister Crowley, Magickal Childe.

The Key of Solomon the King. Trans. S. Liddell MacGregor Mathers, Weiser.

The Magus. Francis Barrett, Citadel.

The Book of the Sacred Magic of Abramelin the Mage. S. Liddell MacGregor Mathers, Dover.

Liber O. Aleister Crowley.

Things to Do for Section 11

1. Conduct the ritual to invoke the Angel AXIR, as given in Lesson 42. Record your results.

2. Experiment with the invoking ritual. Make any changes that you think would improve the ritual. For example, you could add things to say to AXIR when he appears, or things to say to coax him into appearing. Use the correspondences given in the other lessons to embellish the ritual. Always record your results.

3. Use the invoking ritual, with suitable changes, to invoke other Angels. Record your results.

Questions for Section 11

1. True or False: There is no difference between an invocation and an evocation.

2. True or False: It is easy to invoke Enochian Angels.

3. Multiple choice: Beginners should limit invocations to:
    a. unknown entities.
    b. entities who are friendly.
    c. entities who are powerful.
    d. Kings and Seniors.

4. Multiple choice: Which group is not an Enochian Angel:
    a. Kerubic Angels.
    b. Seniors.
    c. Devils.
    d. Archangels.

5. What are the names of the two Sephirothic Cross Angels of the Earth sub-quadrant of the Watchtower of Earth.

6. True or False: During an invocation, you bring an entity into yourself, and allow it to become a part of yourself.

7. True or False: To invoke an Enochian Angel, you must recite the proper Call or Calls.

8. What is used to determine the sigil of a Watchtower Angel?

9. What are the Names of Power that are spoken during an invocation?

10. True or False: If an invocation is successful, an entity will appear before you and converse with you.

11. Multiple choice: The color to trace an invoking pentagram for an Earth Angel is:
    a. black.
    b. vermilion.
    c. blue.
    d. amber.

12. True or False: When invoking an Angel, trace the corresponding element symbol in the center of the pentagram.

13. True or False: When invoking an Angel, trace the Angel's sigil in the center of the pentagram.

Glossary

Abramelin Magic A type of magic described in *The Book of Abramelin the Mage*, translated by S.L. MacGregor Mathers.

adepts Individuals who are masters of magic.

Aethyrs Name given to 30 special regions of the Magical Universe according to Enochian Magic.

Air A cosmic element found in the mental plane.

Angelic language The language of Enochian having 21 letters.

angels Rulers of various regions of the Magical Universe.

astral body The body of emotions.

astral plane The cosmic plane of emotions symbolized by the element Water.

astrological Pertaining to the heavenly planets and their influences.

Black Cross A cross of Squares that separates the four Watchtowers. The Squares of the cross containing letters are used to comprise the Tablet of Union.

Body of Light General term for the aura or subtle body.

Calvary Cross Name given to 16 special regions within the four Watchtowers.

causal plane The cosmic plane immediately below the Abyss which karmically causes rebirth.

correspondences Magical relationships between two things.

Cosmic Planes of Manifestations Seven major states of being from divinity to physicality.

crystal ball A magical device used for skrying. A type of shewstone.

Cup The magical weapon of the Watchtower of Water. It signifies understanding.

Dagger The magical weapon of the Watchtower of Air. It signifies the penetrating power of the intellect.

Dee, Dr. John Dee was a famous magician and intellectual who discovered and carefully recorded the basics of Enochian Magic.

demons Residents of the Lesser Watchtower Squares who appear to be demonic because their nature is to oppose the rulers of those regions.

divination Using magic to predict future events. Foreseeing the future.

duality Doctrine of polar opposites, central to Buddhism.

Earth Cosmic element. In Enochian Magic, it symbolizes the etheric plane.

Egyptian deities Gods and goddesses of the ancient Egyptians.

elements The primary substance of the cosmic planes.

Enochian language The Angelic language, the language of Enochian Magic that has 21 letters.

ethereal body The aura or Body of Light.

etheric plane A cosmic plane symbolized by the element Earth.

etheric body The subtle body which is the lowest within the Body of Light.

exoterically Visibly or outwardly. That which can be expressed in words.

Fire Cosmic element. In Enochian Magic it symbolizes the causal plane.

gematria A magical method of converting letters and words into numbers.

glyphs Magical signs or letters.

god-forms The form or likeness of a deity.

Golden Dawn Name of an occult school which is still active today. Also called the GD.

Great Outer Abyss Name given to the barrier between form and formlessness. It separates the four Watchtowers from the Tablet of Union.

Great Cross Central region within each Watchtower.

hexagram A star-shaped figure with six equidistant points.

Holy Tablets Devised by Dee and Kelly as maps of the Magical Universe.

Holy Guardian Angel Name given to the spark of divinity within every human being.

karma Doctrine of cause and effect.

Kelly, Edward Kelly was the psychic partner of John Dee. He was clairvoyant and channeled Enochian Magic through skrying a crystal ball.

Kerubic Square Important regions within the four Watchtowers that lie directly above the arms of the Calvary Crosses.

layout The laying down of the Tarot cards into a spread or special pattern.

Lesser Squares The lowest regions of a Watchtower.

Lesser Angels Rulers of the Lesser Squares.

magic The art and science of making your experiences conform with your will.

magical weapons Equipment used as devices for mental focus in magical operations.

magical act Any act that is done consciously in accordance with the will.

magical operations Specific magical acts that use ritual.

Magical Will The focused will of the magician.

Magical Universe The subtle and invisible worlds that exist between divinity and our physical world.

magus A high adept.

Mathers, S. L. MacGregor Mathers was one of the founders and chiefs of the Golden Dawn.

mental body A subtle body within the Body of Light that corresponds to the mind.

mental plane Cosmic plane of thought symbolized by the element Air.

Not-I Everything that is not yourself.

Nuit (Nut) Egyptian goddess of the night sky.

occultism Study of the hidden or invisible side of life.

Ordo Templi Orientis A magical organization once headed by Aleister Crowley and active, in several forms, today. Also known as the OTO.

Pantacle Old spelling of pentacle. Magical instrument used for operations dealing with the Watchtower of Earth.

pentagram A star-shaped figure with five equidistant points.

physical plane Our everyday world of gross matter.

physical body Our gross body of flesh and bones.

planetary Having to do with the planets.

primary value The key value of something that has several possibilities.

psychic circle A magic circle made by your mind by visualization.

psychic Mental.

pyramid A four-sided structure where each side is a triangle. Pyramids were made famous by the ancient Egyptians who used them as both tombs and places of initiation.

Qabalah (Qabbala, Kabala, Kabbala, Cabala, or Cabbala) Name of popular Western school of magic and occultism based on the Hebrew Scriptures.

questioner Person who shuffles Tarot cards while asking a question.

reader Person who spreads the Tarot cards and reads them for the questioner.

Regardie, Israel Regardie was a Golden Dawn magician who first published the school's secret teachings and rituals.

Ring In Enochian Magic, a special ring worn for protection.

secondary (alternate) value A value that is possible but not probable. In Enochian gematria, the letters T and Z have alternate or secondary values.

Sephirothic Cross Another name for the Calvary Cross. Name given to 16 special regions within the four Watchtowers.

shewstone A stone used for skrying such as a crystal ball.

sigils Signs of deities made from their names. Used in invocations and evocations.

signposts Generally known things that are experienced or encountered by everyone in the Magical Universe.

skrying Magical technique of gazing into a reflective substance to obtain visions.

sphinx Magical animal used to block progress until knowledge is obtained.

Spirit Cosmic element. This is the highest element, symbolizing the substance of the spiritual plane.

spiritual plane Great region of the Magical Universe whose substance is Spirit.

spread The pattern created by the layout of Tarot cards.

Square Region of the Magical Universe.

subquadrant A division of a Watchtower. Each Watchtower has four subquadrants.

subtle regions Areas of the invisible worlds that surround our physical Earth.

Sword A magical weapon used in operations that concern the Watchtower of Air symbolizing the power of thought. Similar to the Dagger.

Tablet of Union The highest region of the Magical Universe.

Tablets Same as Holy Tablets

Tarot A deck of cards used for meditation or divination.

telepathy Power to communicate mentally over long distances.

The Law of Duality The law of magic that divides manifestation into polar opposites.

The Law of Identity The law of magic that equates all monads and by which the spiritual essence of everything is the same.

The Law of Periodicity The law of magic by which all things manifest in cycles.

theosophic addition A way of reducing large numbers to a number between one and nine. Also called the Qabala of Nine Chambers or Aiq Bqr.

True Will The will of the inner god, the Holy Guardian Angel.

visualization Magical technique used to create vivid mental images such as god-forms.

Wand Magical weapon used in operations that concern the Watchtower of Fire.

Watchtower Used in Enochian Magic as a special region of the Magical Universe.

Water Cosmic element symbolizing the substance of the astral plane.

Will Desire or resolve. In Enochian Magic, can be the True Will or the Magical Will.

World As used in Enochian Physics, the world is everything that is not yourself (same as Not-I).

yoga Eastern school of meditation which seeks to unite the human with the divine.

yogi Someone who practices yoga.

yogic meditation Type of meditation used by yogis that includes visualization and breathing techniques.

Appendix A

Answers to Questions

Section 1

1. There are several definitions. For example, Crowley called it the science and art of bringing about change in accordance with the will.
2. True according to Crowley's definition of magic.
3. Science is repeatable, while magic is not necessarily repeatable.
4. True.
5. (1) The Law of Duality
   (2) The Law of Periodicity
   (3) The Law of Identity
6. True.
7. True.
8. Aleister Crowley.
9. In descending order, these are the seven planes: Divine, Spiritual, Fire, Air, Water, Earth, Physical.
10. The four Watchtower Tablets and the Tablet of Union.
11. Spirit, Fire, Air, Water, and Earth.
12. False. The Watchtower of Air is located on the metal plane, but is not identical with it.
13. True.

Section 2

1. True.
2. The letter S can be pronounced either seh or ess.
3. c. Shewstone.

4. False. Kelly was a psychic, but not John Dee.
5. True.
6. d. No one knows for sure (Dee and Kelly channeled it from Angels, but did not actually create it themselves).
7. The letter H. The letter B.
8. The letter T (9 and 3) and the letter Z (also 9 and 3).
9. True.
10. The primary value is 16. The secondary value is 10.
11. True.
12. True.
13. 110. BABALON.

Section 3

1. True.
2. False. The region of strong life-creating forces is the Watchtower of Water. The Watchtower of Earth is sustentative rather than creative.
3. Earth—Moon
   Water—Venus
   Air—Mercury
   Fire—Sun
4. Spirit.
5. Air—BATAIVAH
   Water—RAAGIOSL
   Earth—IKZHIKAL
   Fire—EDLPRNAA
6. True.
7. True.
8. Sothis.
9. Osiris.
10. c. Only one element.
11. d. The Enochian letter of the Square.
12. ZAX. This Aethyr contains the Great Outer Abyss, and the archdemon KHORONZON.
13. The ka contains emotions, symbolized by upraised arms. The ba is the mind or soul, symbolized by a human-headed hawk. The ka corresponds to the astral body while the ba corresponds to the mental body.
14. True.
15. True (large wings)
16. Michael.
17. Horus because all four sides of this pyramid have the element Earth.
18. Mestha because the sides of this pyramid are: two Earth, one Water, and one Fire.
19. Kerubic Angels of Earth: BOZA, PHRA, RONK, IAOM.
    Kerubic Angels of Water: TAAD, TDIM, MAGL, NLRX
    Kerubic Angels of Air: RZLA, YTPA, TNBA, XGZD

Kerubic Angels of Fire: DOPA, ANAA, PSAK, ZIZA

20. Sphinx in A of AXIR: cow (feminine)

Sphinx in X of AXIR: human-headed cow (feminine)

Sphinx in I of AXIR: hawk-headed cow (feminine)

Sphinx in R of AXIR: lion-headed cow (feminine)

21. Qebhsennuf. The sphinx is human-headed with a bull's torso and a lion's legs and tail. It does not have wings and its sex is neutral.

Section 4

1. True. Magical weapons are devices which help, but are not essential. For example, you can use your finger as a Wand, but for most people, a real Wand is better.
2. 1 = d, 2 = c, 3 = f, 4 = a, 5 = e, 6 = b
3. a = c, 2 = e, 3 = d, 4 = a, 5 = a, 6 = b

Section 5

1. An amulet is worn on the body while a talisman is not. Also, an amulet is made from a natural material (such as a rabbit's foot), while talismans are generally metal. The power of an amulet comes from its material and its shape. A talisman is like a battery and must be charged.
2. True.
3. True.
4. True.
5. A person who progresses sufficiently in Enochian Magic or Enochian Yoga is called a Dragon. A Magical Dragon is therefore a high Adept.

Section 6

1. Use only the fifth Call for Earth of Earth.
2. Use the third Call and then the seventh Call for Water of Air.
3. "The Heavens that are in the 29th Aethyr, RII, are mighty in those regions of the universe, and they carry out the Judgement of the Highest. ..." and so on as given in The Call for the Aethyrs in Lesson 17.
4. Opening up a veil or barrier and forcing yourself through.
5. Leaving through a veil or barrier and closing it up after you.
6. The Sign of Rending the Veil.
7. True, it can be, but only if you visualize it clearly.
8. (2) Water
9. (3) Air
10. (4) Fire
11. (1) EXARP
12. (4) IKZHIKAL
13. True.

Section 7

1. b. Seeing
2. True.
3. True.
4. They serve as road maps or guides to assure that you don't get lost, or wander off into your own inner world.
5. With crystal gazing, your Body of Light remains in your physical body. With Spirit Vision, your Body of Light actually leaves your physical body.
6. The mental body. The causal body.
7. True.
8. False. It is harder and more dangerous.
9. False. You should recite the proper Call prior to entering an Aethyr to establish the correct psycho-magnetic links. However, after experience is gained in an Aethyr, the recitation for that Aethyr can be mental rather than verbal.
10. False. You should specifically address each Governor. They personify the primary forces that will be encountered.
11. TEX has four Governors: TAOAGLA, ADUORPT, DOZIAAL, and GEMNIMB.
12. The lowest, TEX.
13. The lowest, the Watchtower of Earth.

Section 8

1. True.
2. 36 (four sets of nine each).
3. Spirit. Osiris.
4. Isis.
5. Black.
6. Knight's Pawn—Qebhsennuf
   Bishop's Pawn—Hapi
   Queen's Pawn—Tuamautef
   Castle's Pawn—Mestha
7. True.
8. King—one square at a time in any direction.
   Queen—three squares at a time in any direction.
9. True.
10. False because pawns must only move one square forward, while in regular chess, they may open by moving two squares.
11. c. Three players.
12. False because the play goes clockwise, and therefore to the left of each player.
13. Because Shu is closely associated with the element Air. He is also more familiar to most people.
14. No one knows, but it was certainly one of the original founders of the Golden Dawn.

Section 9

1. True.
2. True.
3. True, according to tradition.
4. True.
5. False, the highest purpose is a focus for meditation.
6. The Enochian Tarot deck has 86 cards. There are 30 cards in the Major Arcana, and 56 cards in the Minor Arcana.
7. By the magical theorem, "as above so below." The cards are a microcosm of the macrocosmic universe.
8. The 28 court cards are the Kings and Seniors of the Watchtowers (one King and six Seniors for each of the four Watchtowers).
9. False, the Sephirothic (Calvary) Cross Angels are superior to the Archangels.
10. True.
11. True, but you should try both ways to see which works best for you.
12. False, the results will have more detail, but the "bottom line" should be the same.
13. b. The Three-Card Layout
14. True.

Section 10

1. True.
2. Seven planes as follows: Divine, Spiritual (Spirit), Causal (Fire), Mental (Air), Astral (Water), Etheric (Earth), and physical.
3. Five.
4. True.
5. The Great Outer Abyss.
6. Fohat is the psycho-electric connecting link between the subjective self and the objective world.
7. Kundalini is the primary creative force or energy in the universe. It is a feminine Fohatic energy.
8. The first Enochian Axiom is: Man, and every entity in existence is in his essence a monad. This monadic essence expresses itself as a subjective Self and an objective World.
9. Below LIL, the monad splits into a subjective Self and an objective World.
10. The Great Work is the on-going task of spiritualization and en-lightenment. It is an eternal process whereby the human approaches divinity.
11. The Holy Guardian Angel is the name given to the inner god, the spark of divinity that lies latent within every man and woman.
12. The very first ordeal of the candidate for Dragon is to learn how to travel through the spacetime-consciousness continuum in the direction of

consciousness. He must use Spirit Vision (astral traveling) to travel through the lower Aethyrs up to and including the Aethyr, NIA. He must, in effect, master space, time and consciousness at least in so far as traveling in these five dimensions is concerned.

13. True.

Section 11

1. False. An invocation brings an entity into your body while an evocation brings it to you while keeping it external to you.
2. False. Although this operation is the main stereotype for ritual magic practice, it is probably the most difficult to do successfully.
3. b. Entities who are friendly
4. c. Devils
5. ABALPT and ARBIZ
6. True.
7. True.
8. Sigils are determined from the Enochian Rose.
9. The Names of Power are the Holy Name, and the names of the King and six Seniors together with the Sephirothic Cross Angels, Kerubiuc Angels, and so on for the Watchtower in question.
10. False. This will happen if an evocation is successful, not an invocation.
11. a. black
12. True.
13. This is also true. Use the element first, and then use the sigil if necessary as an alternative.

Appendix B

Questions and Answers on Enochian Magic

The following questions have been asked by curious students of Enochian Magic. Many of these question and answers have been published in "The Enochian Forum" in the *Llewellyn New Times*.

Question 1. *What would happen if, instead of wrapping a charged talisman in white cloth, you wore it as a necklace?*

Answer. A talisman is generally charged with a specific force for a one-time specific purpose. The idea is to charge it when you have time and conditions are ready for charging (astrological and so on). Then you wrap it in white linen to keep the charge from dissipating until it is needed (such as during one of the rituals given in our *An Advanced Guide to Enochian Magick*). When removed from the cloth and used in a ritual, most talismans are often discharged so much that they can't be used effectively a second time. In other words, they must be recharged. Obviously such talismans are not to be used lightly.

Objects charged and then worn on the body for protection, healing, or other purpose, are called amulets. In fact, this is the main difference between an amulet and a talisman. In general, amulets have a general type charge while talismans are charged for very specific uses with a specific type of charge or force. An object charged for general protection, such as the Egyptian Amulet of Isis, would be an amulet that you could wear as a necklace, for example. Usually an amulet is made from material that naturally supports or holds the charge given. The Amulet of Isis, for example, should be made from the wood of a sycamore tree, the tree sacred to the goddess Isis and naturally inclined to hold a general protective force for long periods. Also, the shape of the amulet should be such that its form stimulates your subconscious whenever you look at it or think about it. This helps to maintain the charge while increasing its effectiveness.

Question 2. *Does it do any harm to let other people see a talisman that I have charged?*

Answer. In our book, *Coming into the Light*, there is a curious statement made in the rubric of the Papyrus of Nu concerning the Amulet of Isis. It says, "You must not let any man or woman see you place it, or it will not work for you." This suggests that the idea of not letting any other person see your amulet/talisman is a very old idea. This idea is true for most branches of magic, including Enochian Magic. There is a very subtle telepathic transfer between you and anyone seeing your talisman. In our book, *Enochian Physics*, we call this phenomenon an overlapping of Not-I's. The fact is this: if one sees your talisman who is not a believer, his very unbelief will degrade the effectiveness of your talisman to some degree, even if no words are spoken. However, if someone sees your talisman who is a believer, a fellow magician or New Ager for example, then little or no harm will be done.

Question 3. *Can I use a ritual from another source, such as from* Buckland's Practical Color Magick, *to charge an Enochian talisman?*

Answer. The idea of using other magical rituals for charging Enochian talismans is interesting. Theoretically it should work. Although many branches of magic exist, they all basically teach the same things. We have tried to show in our *Enochian Physics* that the same universal laws and principles exist throughout all branches of magic and occultism. Our suggestion to you is to experiment with some talismans and see what happens. Make two talismans and charge one with an Enochian ritual, and one with another ritual (*Practical Color Magic* has some very good ones to use). Then see if one works while the other doesn't, or if both work, and so on. Unbiased scientific experimentation of this sort is encouraged in most magical schools.

Question 4. *In your book,* Enochian Tarot, *you describe how each card represents a formula which is determined from the letters in the name. But you left out the Seniors. Could you give me an example of a formula using the name of a Senior?*

Answer. The Enochian language is such that almost all names express magical formulas. The formula of a name is found by looking at the letters which comprise it. Names with three or four letters are relatively easy to convert to a formula. Names with seven or more letters can get messy. We deliberately left out the Kings and Seniors, from the formulas, because we felt that they were too complicated for the average reader. For those readers who are interested, it is a good idea to try these things yourself, once you get the idea of how to do it. For example, lets look at the Third Senior of Earth, LZINOPO (card number 76). His formula can be determined from the seven letters of his name (see Table 10 in *Enochian Tarot*) as follows: L=Chariot in Cancer, Z=The High Priestess in

Caput Draconis, I=Art/Temperance in Sagittarius, N=Death in Scorpio, O=Justice in Libra, and P=Strength in Leo. Remember, the formula is derived from the meanings of the letters as well as from their arrangement in the name. The formula here has to do with the meaning of initiation (The High Priestess in Caput Draconis). In plain words, the formula of LZINOPO is that all true esoteric initiation acts with the ability to resemble death, and this will bring strength to one who is immersed in karma. (Notice how the P between two O's is interpreted as strength from an immersion in karma) This is the Formula of Obtaining Psychic Abilities. Esoteric initiation, which resembles death, often leads to psychic abilities and spiritual insight. Remember though, such abilities are always accompanied by a high karmic price. Using this example, try to determine useful formulas for the other Court Cards.

Question 5. *Is Enochian Magic the most powerful type of Magic?*

Answer. There are many who think that it is. Of course, it is really a matter of personal choice. We do think that Enochian Magic attracts more powerful magicians than any other school. For example, two of the most powerful magical schools, the Golden Dawn and the O.T.O., both include Enochian Magic. Aleister Crowley, perhaps the most powerful magician in modern days, practiced it regularly. Israel Regardie gave it very high regard. Most schools of Magic have similar or even identical teachings, and employ similar techniques. But the variations are enough for some people to feel at home with one branch, while at sea with another. It seems to us that those who feel at home with the Enochian school, are those who are either already advanced, or have an inherent potential to advance in Magic.

Question 6. *Can you suggest a method for divination? I have tried several with little success.*

Answer. Divination, like most psychic processes, requires at least some intuitive ability in order to get successful results. Whether you use the I Ching, Tarot, Crystal Gazing, geomancy, or whatever makes little difference: these are all devices that we use, more or less effectively, to focus consciousness and the intuitive processes that lie beneath the surface of consciousness. In truth, it is our own minds that look into the future or past, and the methodology used to point consciousness in the proper direction, so to speak, is an aid, but has no real power in itself. A high Adept, for example, will not need cards, or a crystal ball. S/he would be able to see directly into the future without external aids. Most of us, however, are not so fortunate, so we use aids of one kind or another. Our own favorite is the Tarot. We have developed an Enochian Tarot card deck and instruction manual, just for this purpose. We would suggest that you give it a try (available from Llewellyn).

Question 7. *I have been studying witchcraft for years. Is Enochian Magic compatible with witchcraft? Can I practice both together?*

Answer. The basic teachings of Enochian Magic are very similar to those of Wicca. Even the practice has similarities, especially as presented in Scott Cunningham's excellent book, *Wicca, A Guide for the Solitary Practitioner* (Llewellyn). If you compare the teachings of Wicca, as presented by today's leading authorities such as Cunningham, Ray Buckland, Janet and Stewart Farrar, and Arnold and Patricia Crowther, with the laws and theorems of Enochian Magic, as presented in our *Enochian Physics*, you will find many similarities. Nevertheless, there are several differences between the two. Enochian Magic does not employ coven-type groups like Wicca, but organizations do exist, and most rituals can certainly be performed in groups. Wicca does not teach evocations, and reserves invocations only for the God and Goddess. These are likely the two biggest differences that you will find. In general, witches center themselves on the Earth, while magicians leave the Earth and explore the subtle invisible worlds that surround the Earth. Both accept the doctrines of reincarnation and karma in some form or another. Both accept the Law of Periodicity, the Law of Duality, the Law of Identity, (these three laws are fully explained in our *Enochian Physics*) and so on. Ellen Reed's *The Witches' Qabala* (Llewellyn) shows how Wicca and magic can come together in harmony. In short, we think that the theories are very similar, but the practice tends to be quite different. To answer your question; yes, we think that you could probably practice both without difficulty. After all, both are paths toward the same ultimate destination.

Question 8. *I read a lot nowadays about psychism. Some books say that certain dangers are associated with it. At the same time, many books are available which teach that anyone can develope psychic powers. What is the truth?*

Answer. The truth is that psychic development is associated with dangers; dangers which many New Age books fail to mention to the reader, while other books go to great lengths to discourage such development altogether. The truth is probably somewhere in the middle of these two extreme views. There are indeed many books available that purport to give lessons on psychic development to any and all. Certainly anyone can develop their psychic abilities, if they want to, and if they practice at it. Our own view is that you should ask yourself what you want such "powers" for in the first place. In short, what is your motive? If it is to exercise power or control over others (a type of Black Magic), then you are on the road to a lot of trouble in the form of what we often call "karmic backlash." Every deed that we do generates karma, and bad karma, that comes to us from our own misguided actions, is what we call karmic backlash. If your motives are to help others, or simply to gain an understanding of yourself and the world, then you will probably have little difficulty. The same is true for practicing magic, and especially Enochian Magic which is a very powerful and effective branch of magic. The best, and safest, path to take is to develop your spiritual senses and moral/ethical character. On such a path, you will find that psychic abilities will come to you naturally, without effort, and that you will then have the maturity to handle them wisely. Most Adepts use the analogy of matches—obtaining psychic powers is lot like obtaining a box of matches. You can use the matches to keep warm and to cook your food, but also, if you are not careful, you can burn yourself and others very badly.

Question 9. *What is the origin of the Enochian language and of Enochian Magic? Where did the teachings come from?*

Answer. We know that John Dee, court astrologer to Elizabeth I, together with his psychic partner, Edward Kelly (sometimes spelled Kelley) gave us several tablets of letters, an entire alphabet, and some fragments of a translated language; a language which he called Enochian after the Biblical patriarch, Enoch. Little was done with the language, that we know of, until the Golden Dawn introduced it to its membership at the turn of the last century. The Golden Dawn's version of Enochian had many important embellishments. Aleister Crowley also added some embellishments of his own. Basically, the Golden Dawn carefully described the Watchtowers, while Crowley described the Aethyrs. But where did Dee and Kelly get their information? According to Dee's written records, the language was channeled through Angels to Kelly. This is why it is often called the Angelic Language. Some Golden Dawn members believed the language to have originated on the sunken continent of Atlantis, and Kelly merely rediscovered it in modern times. Whatever the case for the language, the teachings of Enochian Magic are almost certain to have come down to us from Egypt. The teachings of the ancient Egyptians have often been called the "fountain-source of Western occultism," because all true Western occult groups teach ideas that originated with the Egyptians. For example, the ancient Egyptians taught the doctrines of reincarnation and karma. They taught that man is a microcosm of the macrocosmic universe, and many other occult doctrines. We have detailed this in our *Coming into the Light* (Llewellyn). This, of course, begs the question, where did the Egyptians get their teachings? Unfortunately, the origin of ancient Egyptian teachings is lost in time. Some say it came from Atlantis. Others that is came from the East. Some say that it originated with the Egyptians themselves, who are far older than we now think. Our own view is that the flame of truth has always been held alight in the world by some group or other, and always will be.

Question 10. *I have a strong desire to realize the truth of my existence, but I also have doubts and hesitations about Enochian Magic. Your books are full of warnings and cautions. Could you give me some prescriptions for how to go about this safely?*

Answer. Your wish to realize the truth of your existence is a noble one, and we wish you success. Certainly Enochian Magic can help. When you say that your mind fills with doubt and hesitation you are simply being honest with yourself, and we probably wouldn't believe you if you said otherwise. If you are sincere at all, then your mind will certainly be filled with doubt and fear. That is normal. The journey through the Watchtowers and Aethyrs of Enochian Magic is not an easy one, nor does it hold out rash promises for the human ego. As for some prescriptions, they are few and simple: Be as selfless and loving as possible, and start with the fundamentals and gradually work up to the harder material. Don't jump into the higher Aethyrs before you have mastered the lower ones. Don't jump into the Abyss until you fully know what you are doing. If you want to invoke, invoke friendly deities and leave the nasty ones alone. Don't lust for magical power, let it come naturally without force. Our own journey has been a long one, and we are still treading the Path. Don't be in a hurry for anything except the truth. Lastly, try to live a balanced life; don't make Magic an obsession, but when you learn things, try to relate them to your everyday life (this is a lot harder than you think).

Question 11. *I would like some information on demons. Can they attack me when I am practicing Enochian Magic? If so, can they cause physical harm? How can I protect myself? What can happen if I am interrupted in the middle of an invocation and don't get to finish it?*

Answer. Enochian deities (especially demons) can attack you astrally, but not physically. However, sometimes a psychic attack can have physical effects. The only way to invoke them is to establish a psychomagnetic link, and they can use this link too, especially if you don't use a good banishing ritual after each invocation. The purpose of a banishing ritual is to sever the link created during the invocation. You should always banish a deity, even if you don't think the invocation was successful. Deities and demons cannot normally enter the physical plane. During evocation, a suitable substance such as smoke is often provided to allow temporary manifestation. During invocation, your body is used to provide a temporary incarnation. They do not have physical bodies, and would need to have a suitable substance provided for them. They normally converse through the mind. Certainly there is protection. Knowledge of what you are doing is one. Lack of fear is itself a powerful protection. We have found that love is probably the very best protection of all. Greed, egotism, revenge, hate, and so on tend to attract the most unsavory demons and so should be avoided. If you don't finish an invocation, the results will depend on the circumstances. Who is being invoked? Did you establish a link? If you failed to use a banishing ritual of some kind, for example, the connecting psychomagnetic link would remain. In that case, the deity or demon would be free to possess your body whenever you drop your guard. Enochian Magic is relatively safe to practice providing you are prepared beforehand and you employ a few necessary safeguards.

Question 12. *How can you prove your theory of monads as expressed in your* Enochian Physics?

Answer. First of all, it is probably impossible to adequately prove the Enochian theory to everyone's satisfaction. Einstein's view of relativity, for example, is still a theory. *Enochian Physics* describes the Enochian Monad Model. This scheme, like any scientific model, is only an approximation of reality, and is only as good as the assumptions that go into it. Like most models, the Enochian

Monad Model can be used to make predictions. By testing these predictions in some fashion, we can determine if the model holds up or is flawed in some way. For example, the model predicts that the disintegration (decay) constant of radioactive materials is not truly a constant, but is increasing for most materials albeit very slowly. However, until this is demonstrated in a scientific laboratory (so far the increase has been too small to measure), it will have to be taken on faith. We will leave such proofs to others. Our advice is to study the Enochian model and, using your intuition, decide for yourself.

Question 13. *How can your Enochian Tarot cards show what is going to happen in the future?*

Answer. The rationale behind Tarot cards is known as the Law of Correspondences. So long as the cards reflect the universe (that is, so long as they are structured in the form of a microcosm) they can show probabilities of past, present, and future events and/or conditions. The Enochian Tarot deck is so structured, as described in our *Enochian Tarot*. The idea is that the cards are a microcosm of the macrocosmic universe, and thus reflect in miniature, the processes of the outer universe. The mechanics of rendering the reflection include the questioner shuffling the deck. This randomizes the cards in such a way that at a specific point in time (i.e., sooner or later), they can truly express our lives in the world. The real question is, How do we know exactly when such an expression occurs? The traditional answer is that the questioner knows subconsciously, and thus is told to stop shuffling when the cards "feel right." In this sense, the Tarot deck is a key that can open a door into our subconscious thought processes, where all of our future possibilities can ultimately be found. But the deck itself must be microcosmic in its structure. We have carefully structured the Enochian Tarot deck to express the magical universe as defined by Enochian Magic (see our *Enochian Physics*), and for this reason, the cards can actually show windows into the future.

Question 14. *How important is pronunciation of Enochian names? Must the names be pronounced exactly correct for success?*

Answer. The truth is, no one really knows the "correct" pronunciation of Enochian today. The rules established by the Golden Dawn (see pages 14-15 of our *Enochian Magic: A Practical Manual*) were slightly bent by Crowley and others. Today, they have undergone even more changes in other groups. For example, Z was pronounced zod (like zoad or zode) by the G.D., but it is often heard as zeh today. It is often uncertain when R is to be pronounced ar or rah, or even reh. Similarly, S can be ess or seh. Israel Regardie clearly stated that as far as he knew, there was no right or wrong way to pronounce Enochian, though he followed the general G.D. rules. Our own advice is to use whatever you feel is sonorous or melodic within the general rules. The syllables should flow with a rythym that is almost musical. Success in a magical operation depends on more than just properly pronouncing the words or names. You must also concentrate strongly on their meanings while speaking them. The names of the deities, for example, must be vibrated rather than spoken (see pages 63-64 of our *Advanced Guide* for details).

Question 15. *What is the Enochian view on evolution? Does evolution exist or is time an illusion so that all things exist simultaneously?*

Answer: Obviously, it takes time for evolution to occur. Evolution is a growth process that takes place in (or through) time. Without time, there can be no evolution (or reincarnation for that matter). The concept of motion (evolution is a specific type of motion) through a spacetime continuum, and especially through a spacetime-consciousness continuum, is detailed in our *Enochian Physics*. According to Enochian Physics, everything in our universe is evolving, not only physically but mentally and spiritual as well. Nevertheless, time is indeed an illusion, and it only exists in a relative sense; relative to the consciousness that experiences it. Time is variable, and its speed differs in each Watchtower. Above the first Aethyr, LIL, there is no sense of time at all, and evolution there, as we know it, is neither necessary nor possible. The answer to your question therefore, is that yes, evolution does exist, but only in the same sense that time can be said to exist. Both are ultimately what Eastern yogis call Maya.

Question 16. *I am a beginner. How should I begin invocations? Who can I invoke safely?*

Answer: The magical process of invocation is used to allow an external entity to enter into your physical body and temporarily merge its self with your self. The true magical goal is to be able to shift your sense of identity from the human to the divine. Therefore, you should only invoke beings of a high and spiritual nature. Whoever you invoke will inevitably affect you in subtle ways that you may not even notice. If you invoke loving entities, then you will tend to become a more loving person. However, if you invoke hateful or selfish entities, then you will tend to become like them. The magician must always be on guard to invoke only those entities who will help him/her in the Great Work of spiritual awareness. If an Angel, for example, is conceited but has magical power that you want, you may indeed get power from invoking him, but you will become more conceited as an unwanted by-product. For beginners, we recommend a general invocation ceremony such as An Enochian Invoking Ritual found on page 88 of *An Advanced Guide to Enochian Magick*. Rather than invoking a specific entity, this ritual allows you to invoke the general forces of the Watchtowers. If done properly, you should find it stimulating and invigorating, and perfectly safe to practice. As a general rule, always invoke peaceful wise beings whose contact will stimulate your spiritual growth. Avoid those entities whose contact will cloud your aura. If you must contact lower entities, then use evocation rather than invocation.

Question 17. *I would like to invoke AHMLLKV, a Senior of Earth. I have tried* *several times without success. Could you give me some advice or hints that would help me?*

Answer. We sympathize with your attempt to invoke AHMLLKV. Seniors are not easy to invoke (Kings are just about impossible). We have found it much easier to enter the Body of Light and travel to the Seniors and Kings in their own "natural habitats." They do not like to take on physical manifestation, even temporarily. It might help you if you learn some "signposts" of each deity before invoking him/her. For example AHMLLKV has a scarlet color and wears a transparent red robe. These colors are expressive of his solar nature; his presence is similar to a beautiful blood-red sun at sunrise. Like all the Seniors, he is male. However, he has a lot of feminine characteristics such as grace and beauty. He holds a ram's horn in his right hand and a tiger lily in his left hand. This horn is called the Horn of AHMLLKV. When he blows it, all who are in his presence are purified; cleansed of doubts, fears, and karmic burdens. The tones of this horn bestow purity and spiritual power to those who can hear it. AHMLLKV also likes geraniums, especially their smell. During an invocation, try to permeate your circle with the odor of either geraniums or tiger lilies. We hope this helps. The data for AHMLLKV and other deities can be obtained from known signposts as well as from experience. We suggest you consult Crowley's *Liber 777*, or similar book of correspondences. A lot of this data can be found in our *Enochian Yoga*.

Question 18. *Why are all of the deities of Enochian Magick males? Is this form of Magick chauvinistic? Why are there no Queens to complement the four Kings?*

Answer. We think this is an extremely good question. In former days, such an idea would never even occur. In the past, virtually all magicians were men, and women had little say in things. However, the question touches on an interesting philosophical idea and certainly needs to be answered. We suspect that male chauvinism did indeed influence the choice of all male deities. However, if you look closely at Enochian deities you will notice that many "male" deities have feminine characterisitics. For example, BATAIVAH, the King of Air, is kindly and merciful and for most practical purposes can be considered feminine. Similarly with RAAGIOSL, the King of Water. On the other hand, the Kings of Earth and Fire are decidedly masculine. This same situation can be found with the Seniors; of the six Seniors of each Quadrant, three are masculine and three feminine. In the Aethyrs, the duality of sex is explicit—Babalon and the Beast being but one instance. Thus when we look behind the outer lables of Enochian Magick we find that the creative and sustaining forces of our universe are both masuline and feminine, and therefore in agreement with other branches of Magick.

Question 19. *Where can I find a group of practicing Enochian Magicians?*

Answer. This is the most frequently asked question that we receive from students. Quite frankly, we don't know. However, the need for sharing experiences is obviously a real one. We would like to point out that the Enochian magician is typically a loner, preferring solitary contemplation and practice of his or her craft. Working in groups has many advantages, but the group Karma (yes, Karma exists collectively as well as individually) of a magical organization sometimes results in problems and stress factors that can override these advantages. When joining such groups, you must assume the group Karma, at least to a degree. So take care and be selective.

Question 20. *I am confused about the term "truncated pyramid." Do the lines of the Tablets line up with the "pyramid" lines?*

Answer. The term "truncated pyramid" is literally just what it says. Take a pyramid and lop off the top. What remains is a truncated pyramid. There is a lot of occult symbolism in the pyramid. In one sense, it is a tomb, a place or death. In another sense, it is a temple, a place of initiation or new life. In the sense of Watchtower pyramids, they represent regions of inner space—the invisible worlds that surround and interpenetrate our physical world. When you look straight down on a truncated pyramid, you will see five planes—the four sloping sides and the cutaway top. The correspondence with the four Watchtowers and five cosmic elements should be obvious. The pyramids are thus "wheels within wheels" each a microcosm partaking of, and in turn expressing, the cosmic totality. The general rule in this sort of thing is "as above so below." The actual regions themselves are not shaped like little cutoff pyramids. The pyramid shape is used only in a symbolic sense. The earth is not square, yet a yellow square is often used to symbolize it. In the same way, the Tablets themselves are symbols (in fact they are symbolic maps).

Question 21. *Why is it that the names of Enochian deities are spelled differently by different people?*

Answer. The names of Enochian deities are found from the letters that are in the Squares of the Watchtower Tablets. Dee and Kelly (sometimes spelled Kelley) made several changes to some of the letters in the squares. The Golden Dawn handled this problem by showing all the possible letters in the Squares. We have adopted this view, and also show all of the possible letters (see Figures 1 through 4 of this book). We explained in *An Advanced Guide* that multiple letters in a square are due to the complex nature of that region of the magical universe. This causes a problem when we try to use those letters to form the name of the Angel, Archangel, or Demon of that region. Which letter should we use? As a guide, the general rule is to use the first letter of any group of multiple letters. However, gematria also comes into play. In some cases, the first letter will not give the name of a significant gematria value, while another letter will. This process is further complicated by the fact that there are at least four major gematria systems available (see Table III of *An Advanced Guide*). The fact is, you can use other letters to make variant spellings if you want to. You can even use two or more letters from a multiple-lettered Square to give a more sonorous sound during the pronunciation and thus have a Senior's name with eight or nine letters rather than seven.

Question 22. *In* Enochian Physics *you say that it is possible to do levitation. Can you levitate?*

Answer. We have never tried to levitate, nor have we seen a levitation. Our physics book discusses the scientific rationale for levitation and concludes that it is theoretically possible. We do not discuss how to go about putting this theory into practice. We leave that for others. According to the theory, gravity, like all natural forces, must have an opposite, or antigravity. When science discovers gravitons, then the theory will become more firm. The idea is this: by holding a certain frequency of thought, we can attract enough gravitons into our body that it will rise up into the air, repulsed by the earth rather than attracted to it. According to Enochian physics, all of the occult powers attained by yogis and magicians throughout history can be explained by the conscious control of subatomic particles within or around the physical body. Modern physics, unfortunately, leaves consciousness out of its equations. By factoring consciousness into the equations of modern physics, the principles of Magic are revealed.

Question 23. *Can I use a ritual from another source, such as* Buckland's Color Magick, *to charge an Enochian talisman?*

Answer. The idea of using other magical rituals for charging Enochian talismans is interesting. Theoretically, it should work. Although many branches of magic exist, they all basically teach the same things. We have tried to show in *Enochian Physics* that the same universal laws and principles exist throughout all branches of magic and occultism. Unbiased scientific experimentation is encouraged in most magical schools.

Question 24. *Your book,* Enochian Magic, *says that the Holy Guardian Angel is your own spiritual self or genius, but Aleister Crowley has said that we should realize the Holy Guardian Angel as an objective entity. How do you resolve this?*

Answer. Your question about the H.G.A. is a good one. We know that this may sound like a paradox, but the H.G.A. is both your own spiritual self and an objective entity. Crowley taught that we should regard all Angels/Deities as objective external independent beings. The Magic works better that way. However, many are actually psychic projections from our own subconscious, and thus, in a psychological sense, are part of ourselves. With regard to the H.G.A., it is a part of our spiritual Self, a reflex of the divine spark that exists within us all. This fact, however true, will not help us much in a magical sense. For example, if we told you that you make your own dreams, and that they are caused by your own thinking, that fact probably would not help you much tonight when you go to sleep. It is more effective, for most magical operations, if we consider the H.G.A. to be an independent deity. If you ask, "Which is it, an external deity or a part of myself?" the answer is really impossible to determine. Such a question is of the nature of a Zen Buddhist Koan. It could be one, or the other, or neither, or both, all depending on perspective. Crowley said that it is more convenient to consider Angels to be independent entities, not that they actually are. In most magical groups, a magician would first learn to see Angels and such as external independent entities. At a very high grade he would be told that the H.G.A. is actually himself (because we are each more than human). The truth of the relationship is only clearly seen in the eighth Aethyr, ZID, and this usually takes many years of hard work to attain.

Question 25. *I have been studying the use of sex in Magic. Could you tell me why karmic effects will take place if I use sex in any of my rituals?*

Answer. We have found that sex in Magic does indeed have strong karma attached to it. It could be because our society still is not open to using sex for reasons other than procreation (therefore it often leads to an unconscious sense of guilt, etc.), but we think that there is more to it. Crowley called sex "indescribably dangerous" in the hands of a magician, but never elaborated what the dangers are. The bottom line of any branch of sex magic is this: you cannot have pleasure without pain, because pleasure and pain are two poles of a duality. If sex, in any form, gives you physical pleasure, then sooner or later you will encounter physical pain. To try and get pleasure such as the bliss and ecstasy promised by sex magic (and yes, the bliss or amrita produced is very real), without pain is futile. The reason for this is the Law of Dualities which we have explained in *Enochian Physics*. If you look at Tibetan Yoga, for example, which has close parallels with Enochian Magic (as shown in our *Enochian Yoga*), you will discover that after achieving several degree of bliss, they seek corresponding degrees of emptiness or empties. The great Tibetan yogi Milarepa taught that once bliss is achieved, you have to continue on and achieve emptiness. This is to say that all physical pleasure must be transmuted into spiritual joy. We warn all students—sex magic is dangerous. Having said that, its practice is up to you.

Appendix C

Magic and
its Dangers

The following article on magic and its inherent dangers was written by the authors for the newsletter, *Quintessence*. Because it contains material which is ideally suited to beginners, it is included here.

Magic

Magic, or Magick, to differentiate it from simple parlor games, has many connotations. Many people see Magic as evil or sinister. Some people, theosophists for example, see it as a bad thing, not because it doesn't work, but because its working tends to inflate the human ego. Most all authorities define magic as both an art and a science. As a science it comes under the general heading of Occult Science. Magic has rules, principles, laws, and so on which operate just as surely as physical laws (see our *Enochian Physics*). Magic is scientific in the sense that these laws explain how things work in the magical universe as well as the interface between the magical universe and our physical universe.

Let's define the magical universe in a broad sense as the world in which the magician works. In a very large sense, it includes the invisible worlds that surround our physical planet. The magical universe is essentially the etheric, astral, mental, and causal planes. Sometimes the spiritual planes are included, but sometimes these are exempt.

According to magic, man possesses an aura. The aura is a subtle envelope or body that surrounds and interpenetrates the physical body. Magic, especially Enochian and Golden Dawn Magic, calls this the Body of Light. The Body of Light is essentially identical to what occultists call the auric egg. It is comprised of the very same matter that comprises the magical universe. In other words, the Body of Light includes an etheric counterpart, an astral counterpart, a mental/psychic counterpart, a causal counterpart, and a spiritual counterpart. In a very real sense, the Body of Light can be thought of as consisting of a separate body for each cosmic plane in the magical universe. Running through each of these "bodies" and cementing them together, so to speak, is consciousness. In addition, there is a psycho-magnetic link which connects the bodies together through which consciousness moves and focuses. In the West, this is called the Silver Cord. In the East, it is called the Sutratman. The points where this cord is said to connect the higher bodies to the etheric body is called the chakras, lotuses, or psychic centers. Kundalini Yoga has brought the tradition of the chakras and their connecting channels (called nadis) to the attention of the West. However, theosophists have long known of this teaching. It is found in Vol 12 of HPB's *Collected Writings*, and was considered a part of her "esoteric instructions" to the inner circle of theosophists. Apparently HPB considered knowledge of the bodies, chakras, and connecting pathways, to be too dangerous to give out publicly. However, Charles Leadbeater published his famous book on the chakras in 1927 (it is still selling well today), which freely gave out this information, as it was known to theosophists at that time.

Probably the main point to the entire theory of subtle bodies, planes, and chakras, is the teaching that this knowledge can be used to actually experience the magical universe. Consciousness can be made to leave the physical body, and travel in one or more subtle bodies in the magical universe, while retaining full memory. This is where the "art" comes in (remember that magic is both a science and an art). Traveling in the Body of Light is the hallmark of magic. HPB, while fully aware of this, was skeptical of giving out detailed information. She feared many would try the operation, with unsuccessful results. The science aspect of magic contains the theory. The art aspect contains the practical applications. Theory, by itself, is relatively safe. Practice, on the other hand, can be dangerous.

Putting aside these apparent dangers for a moment, let's look at the theory. Magic teaches that man has subtle bodies, and that these correspond to subtle worlds. It teaches that consciousness can be shifted to these bodies, and that experiences can be obtained in the invisible globes/worlds that surround our physical Earth. As far as the magical universe is concerned, HPB gave us the Gupta Vidya Model of the universe in *The Secret Doctrine*. Qabalists have described the Tree of Life consisting of ten globes or Sephiroth, and 22 connecting pathways. And we have presented the Enochian version in our *Enochian Magic, An Advanced Guide to Enochian Magick*, and *Enochian Physics*. Together, these three models are probably the best known "maps" of the magical universe. The ancient Egyptians also had a version, but it is fragmented and relatively unknown (see our *Coming Into the Light* for details).

Now, back to the dangers. Probably the two main possibilities that discourage magical "astral traveling" is death and madness. Both are possible results for the unprepared. Either signifies failure. And if neither of these are attained, if rather one is successful, the very real possibility of an overinflated ego looms large on the horizon. For these reasons, many occultists will not condone the attempt. Nevertheless, the challenge awaits one who is prepared and who is willing to "dare."

Why death or madness? Because the very act of astral traveling is exactly what happens at death (also sleep, which is death's "brother"). At death, or sleep, consciousness leaves the physical body and enters one of the subtle bodies of the aura. The only real difference between death and sleep is that when we sleep the silver cord remains intact, while when we die this psycho-magnetic link is severed permanently. In astral traveling (sometimes called an out-of-body experience or OBE) this link remains fixed, making astral traveling much like daydreaming. Becoming lost in the magical universe, or so bogged down that return to the physical is impossible, will result in death. Also, the aura/Body of Light is often called a mirror (the "magic mirror" of classical magic and folklore) because it mirrors what is in the magical universe. In other words, when we travel about in the magical universe we will, sooner or later, encounter our worse fears and confront our most deeply embedded horrors. We may have dream-like experiences, but on the other hand, we may also have nightmares of the very worst kind (this is where karma comes into the picture). Such en-counters can result in insanity—the instability and ultimate degeneration or frag-mentation of the human personality due to the unwillingness of consciousness to confront specific contents of the unconscious. According to magic, the only safe way to astral travel is to be prepared beforehand. Such preparation includes the cultivation of both morals and compassion.

Traveling in the magical universe has many rewards. For one thing, the temporary nature of the human ego is seen directly. As consciousness rises to higher planes/Globes, one's sense of identity shifts away from the human personality toward something else. Whether by death, by insanity, or by spiritualization, the human personality will give way, sooner or later, for each one of us. The personality gives way to the individuality. Clinging to the personality is fruitless in the long run, yet is essential in the short run of one lifetime. One of the techniques used in magic to effect this shift in identity is to adopt a magical name. The magician chooses a magical name for the individuality, and then slowly shifts consciousness over to it. This technique, if misused, can lead to multiple-personality disorders. The golden rule in magic is "do not confound the planes." In other words, always remain conscious of who you are and where you are. Otherwise the business of shifting your sense of identity can lead you to grief (insanity in one form or another). The ancient Egyptians, for example, were adept at this form of magic. Their hieroglyphics are filled with such lines as "I am Tem" or "I am Horus" where the human personality is made to shift to that of a god or goddess. Consciousness is made to focus on an aspect of the inner divinity, and then unites with it. The result, if successful, is a mystical experience in which consciousness rises to the highest regions of the magical universe.

It appears then, that we can "try" and "damn the torpedoes," or we can be timid, believe that the dangers are too great and discourage any attempt to practice magic. Each individual should decide for himself/herself which road to take. To help make that decision, lets look briefly at karma. Because magic is practical application, and this involves action, all magic is highly karmic. This is the chief reason why moral development is essential to success in magic. You can practice magic successfully without moral development for the short run, but in the long run, your karma will surely catch up with you.

As a barometer, look at your dreams. If you have nightmares, chances are high that you will have unpleasant experiences in the magical universe, and probably shouldn't try. If you have reached a stage where your dreams are always pleasant or at least interesting to you, then chances are you will have pleasant experiences in the magical universe. If you have progressed to the point where you can consciously control your dreams, then chances are you will control your experiences in the magical universe as well. If you belong to that small group of people who don't dream (i.e., who don't remember their dreams—everyone dreams whether they remember or not) then you should not try magic at all and probably wouldn't want to, because this group generally won't believe in magic. In this way, dreams can be used as a rule of thumb for predicting success (after all, dreams are only unconscious OBEs). Dreams, especially dream contents, are also highly karmic.

Another barometer is motive. We must honestly ask ourselves, why do we wish to practice magic? Why hasten our evolutionary development? To gain fame and fortune? Or, to gain information? To better understand the inner nature of ourselves and our universe? How we answer this question will go a long way to determining how successful we will be.

Appendix D

Enochian Gematria
Arranged by Order of Gematria Values

Word	Gematria Primary	Secondary	Meaning
F	3		to visit
D	4	31	one third
A	6		I, my
G	8		not
L	8		first
P	9		eight
PD	13		thirty-three
SA	13		within
AG	14		no
AP	15		the same as before
GAH	15		spirits
TA	15	9	is, as, like
ZA	15	9	within
ATH	16	10	works
ES	17		one-fourth
AFFA	18		empty
EL	18		first
GE	18		not
TAFA	24	18	poison
SALD	25		wonder
BAHAL	26		to shout out loud
BALT	28	22	justice
PAEB	30		an oak

Word	Gematria Primary	Secondary	Meaning
PASHS	30		children
ASPT	31	25	before, in front, prior
PAGE	33		to rest
DO	34		name
ADPHAHT	36	30	unspeakable
OS	37		twelve
LO	38		first
OL	38		to make
HOL	39		to measure
BABAGE	40		south
TOH	40	34	triumph
EFAFAFE	41		vessels
ELZAP	42	36	course, way, path
TABGES	45	39	a cave
GLO	46		things
HOATH	47	41	true worshiper, devotee
SOE	47		savior
TOL	47	41	all
ELO	48		first
OBZA	50	44	one half
QAA	52		creation
TALHO	54	48	a cup
DODSEH	56		vexation
GOSAA	57		a stranger
BOGPA	58		to govern
BALTOH	59	53	righteous
I	60		not, is
ODO	64		to open
BI	65		voice
ADNA	66		obedience
IA	66		truth
IL	68		Aethyr, Aire
GOHO	69		to say, to speak
IP	69		not
ZEN	69	63	sacrifice
IAD	70		God
OADO	70		to weave
BIA	71		voices
AAI	72		within you
FAFEN	72		to train
IAL	74		to consume
ED-NAS	77		receivers
THIL	78	72	seat

	Gematria		
Word	**Primary**	**Secondary**	**Meaning**
TOTO	78	66	cycles
HOLQ	79		are measured
PAID	79		always
NAPEA	81		two-edged sword
NAZPS	81	75	a sword
TABAAN	82	76	governor
LAIAD	84		Secrets of Truth
OLLOG	84		men
PIAP	84		scale, balance
TOOAT	84	72	to provide
VLS	85		the ends
DAZIS	86	90	heads
NETAAB	86	80	government
BALIT	88	82	the just
BUZD	88	82	glory
APILA	89		to live forever
BALIE	89		salt
FIFALZ	89	83	to eliminate, to weed out
LUSD	89		feet
PON	89		to destroy
ZON	89	83	form
BAGHIE	90		fury
SONF	90		to reign
VPAAH	92		wings
GNETAAB	94	88	government
EM	100		nine
FABOAN	100		poison
IAOD	100		the Beginning
MAD	100		your god
OIAD	100		god, the just
PLAPLI	100		partakers, users
LONSA	101		everyone
MAL	104		arrow
TOANT	104	92	love, union
FAONTS	105	99	to dwell in
MAZ	105	99	appearances
PAM	105		beginning
AR	106		the sun, to protect
EOPHAN	106		sorrow
BAMS	108		forget
OTHIL	108	102	seat
DOSIG	109		night
BABALON	110		evil, wicked

Word	Gematria Primary	Secondary	Meaning
BAZM	110	104	noon
IN	110		void
LAMA	110		the Path
MATB	110	104	a thousand
NI	110		twenty-eight
TOANTA	110	98	lust
BABALOND	114		harlot
EOLIS	115		to make
HARG	115		to plant, to sow
ONDOH	115		kingdoms
ZAR	115	109	ways, paths, courses
MABZA	116	110	a robe
POILP	116		to be divided
NANBA	117		thorns
ZIZOP	117	105	vessels
GONO	118		faith
RAAS	119	the	East
ZIN	119	113	waters
ALAR	120		to settle down
GRAA	120		moon
OM	120		to know, understanding
HOM	121		to live
NANTA	121	115	earth
OHIO	121		woe, alas
DARBS	122		obedience
LONDOH	123		kingdoms
GNAY	124		to do, does
LRASD	125		to dispose of
ENAY	126		Lord
FARGT	126	120	homes
OMA	126		understanding
IADNAH	127		knowledge
PRGE	127		fire
QUASB	128		to ruin, destroy
MOZ	129	123	joy
OMP	129		understanding
SOBOLN	130		the West
VNPH	130		anger
ETHAMZA	131	119	to be covered
OVOF	133		to be magnified
ANANAEL	136		Secret Wisdom
IAIDA	136		the Highest
IPSI	136		to tie, to fasten

Word	Gematria Primary	Secondary	Meaning
NOAN	136		to become
FISIS	137		to do, to perform
ORS	137		darkness
SIBSI	139		covenant
IA-IAL	140		consume with truth, truth that consumes
TIANTA	140	128	a bed
ABRAASSA	143		provided, to provide
MOLAP	143		men
MA-OF-FAS	145		not to be measured
NOIB	145		yes, affirmation
BRGDO	147		sleep
ORSBA	148		drunken, intoxicated
TIBIBP	148	142	sorrow
POAMAL	149		palace
GROSB	150		a bitter sting
IM	150		apply
MI	150		power
GIGIPAH	152		living breath
OLLAR	152		man
OOAONA	152		eyes
OLANI	154		twice, two times
VAUL	154		to work
MOSPLEH	155		horns
ADONIAN	156		a face
DAMPLOZ	156	150	variety
LONSHI	156		power
OLPRT	156	150	light
ZORGE	157	151	love, friendship
NOQOL	158		servants
IO-IAD	160		Eternal God
IOU	160		the indwelling soul
VONPH	160		wrath
VAOAN	162		truth
QANIS	163		olives
SALMAN	167		a house
PIR	169		bright
RIT	169	163	mercy
ZIR	169	163	I am
PAMIS	172		end
LNNIA	174		Beast, animal
OLORA	174		man
BASGIM	176		day

Word	Primary	Gematria Secondary	Meaning
APOPHRASZ	177	171	motion
INSI	177		to tread, to walk on
NIIS	177		to come
BLIAR	179		with comfort
LIMLAL	180		treasure
NEMO	180		Master of the Temple
BLIARD	183		with comfort
BAEOUIB	186		righteousness
V-MA-DEA	186		strong towers
MOOOAH	187		repent, rejoice
ZILDAR	187	181	to fly
VNIG	188		to require, need
NORZ	189	183	six
QUASAHI	190		pleasure, delight
VONPHO	190		wrath
IAL-PRG	191		burning flames
AMMA	192		cursed
ANGELARD	192		thoughts
LORSLQ	193		flowers
BITOM	194	188	fire
EMETGIS	194	188	seal
PARADIZ	194	188	virgins
ETHARZI	195	183	in peace
DLUGAR	196		to give
ISRO	197		promise
LAS-OLLOR	197		a rich man
VRELP	197		a strong seer
DOALIM	198		sin
PIDIAI	199		marble
SAMVELG	199		the righteous
LIALPRT	200	194	the First Flame
VIV	200		second
PIAMOL	203		righteousness
ZIRDO	203	197	I am
PAPNOR	204		remembrance
NIBM	205		season
PARM	205		to run, flow
NIISO	207		to come away
BLIORA	209		comfort
BALZIZRAS	210	198	judgement
IA-IDON	210		all-powerful
VNIGLAG	210		to descend
IALPOR	213		flaming

Word	Gematria Primary	Secondary	Meaning
SIAION	213		a temple
HUBARDO	216		living lamps, lanterns
TORZU	218	206	to rise up
ZIRN	219	213	wonder
MALPRG	221		fiery, flames
TRANAN	221	215	the marrow
IADNAMAD	226		God of your God
LRING	226		to stir up
URAN	226		to see
VRAN	226		elders
ILONON	228		branches
PRDZAR	228	222	to decrease, to take away from
SAANIR	229		parts, sections, regions
ROR	230		the sun
HOMIN	231		age
PANPIR	234		increase
QURLST	234	228	a handmaiden
VIRG	238		nests
MATORB	240	234	echo, repeat
AVINY	246		millstone
MOMAO	246		crown
PI-BLIAR	248		places of comfort
SIATRIS	249	243	scorpions
MIR	250		torment, upon, on
VABZIR	250	244	an eagle
VOHIM	251		a hundred
MONONS	257		heart
ZAMRAN	261	255	to appear
MADRID	264		iniquities
ZONRENSG	264	258	to deliver
YRPOIL	267		division
ABRAMIG	275		to be prepared
VOVIN	280		dragon
VOVIN	280		dragon
MALPIRG	281		Fires of Life
PRIPSOL	283		the heavens
RIOR	290		a widow
ZUMVI	299	293	seas
KAB	311		rod
KAL	314		to solidify
NOR-MOLAP	323		Sons of Men
YARRY	326		fate, providence
RIPIR	329		nowhere, no place

	Gematria		
Word	**Primary**	**Secondary**	**Meaning**
LEVITHMONG	336	330	beasts of the field
DODRMNI	338		vexed
ZOKH	340	334	the past
KAOS	343		physical
KAOSG	351		Earth
TELOKH	358	352	death
IKH	361		tension
NOR-QUASAHI	370		Sons of Pleasure
OBLOK	373		a garland
KAOSGO	381		Earth
SIASKH	381		brothers
ESIASKH	391		brothers
LUKAL	392		north
KONST	396	390	thunder
KHIDAO	401		diamonds
KHR	401		wheel
AX	406		name
DAX	410		loins
NOKO	410		servant
KAFAFAM	414		to abide
KRAL	414		joy
LONKHO	419		to fall
ZAKAR	421	415	move, mobility
KNILA	424		blood
PARAKH	425		equal
HKOMA	427		water
OX	430		twenty-six
OVKHO	431		to confound
ZAKARE	431	425	move, mobility
NONKP	439		a place
PARAKLEDA	449		marriage, wedding
KOMO	450		a window
KOMSELHA	452		a circle
MIKA	456		powerful, mighty
YOLKI	458		to bring forth
KIAOFI	459		terror, terrible
OXO	460		dance
UNKHI	481		to confound
OXI	490		mighty
IOLKAM	494		to bring forth
DOBIX	499		to fall
MIKALZO	503	497	power, strength, might

Word	Gematria Primary	Secondary	Meaning
MOSPLEH-TELOCH	513	507	Horns of Death
KOMMAH	517		to bind up together
LUKIFTIAS	523	517	brightness
EXARP	525		air
KHIRLAN	525		joy
KORMFA	529		numbers
KORMP	529		to number
KOAZIOR	535	529	to increase
PATRALX	538	532	rock, stone
GIZYAX	543	537	mighty earthquakes
ZIXLAY	543	537	to stir up
DRIX	564		to bring down
RAKLIR	574		weeping, crying
MOMKAOSGO	591		Moss of the Earth
IAIADIX	596		honor
KOKASB	648		time
KOKASG	651		times
MADRIAAX	672		heavens
KIKLE	678		mysteries
OXEX	840		to vomit out, emanate, ejaculate
KAMLIAX	870		to speak
KA-KAKOM	1032		to thrive, to flourish

Appendix E

A Short Master Index

The index below should help you locate information from our previous books. For example, information on the Abyss can be found beginning on page 243 of *An Advanced Guide*. This is coded to II:243. The Roman number before the colon refers to the book, while the number following the colon refers to the beginning page number.

The following index is coded for each source book as follows:

I = *Enochian Magic: A Practical Manual*

II = *An Advanced Guide to Enochian Magick*

III = *Enochian Physics*

IV = *Enochian Tarot*

V = *Enochian Yoga*

Index

STAY IN TOUCH

On the following pages you will find listed, with their current prices, some of the books now available on related subjects. Your book dealer stocks most of these and will stock new titles in the Llewellyn series as they become available. We urge your patronage.

To obtain our full catalog, to keep informed about new titles as they are released and to benefit from informative articles and helpful news, you are invited to write for our bi-monthly news magazine/catalog, *Llewellyn's New Worlds of Mind and Spirit*. A sample copy is free, and it will continue coming to you at no cost as long as you are an active mail customer. Or you may subscribe for just $7.00 in U.S.A. and Canada ($20.00 overseas, first class mail). Many bookstores also have *New Worlds* available to their customers. Ask for it.

Stay in touch! In *New Worlds'* pages you will find news and features about new books, tapes and services, announcements of meetings and seminars, articles helpful to our readers, news of authors, products and services, special money-making opportunities, and much more.

Llewellyn's New Worlds of Mind and Spirit
P.O. Box 64383-719, St. Paul, MN 55164-0383, U.S.A.
* * *

TO ORDER BOOKS AND TAPES

If your book dealer does not have the books described on the following pages readily available, you may order them direct from the publisher by sending full price in U.S. funds, plus $3.00 for postage and handling for orders *under* $10.00; $4.00 for orders *over* $10.00. There are no postage and handling charges for orders over $50.00. Postage and handling rates are subject to change. UPS Delivery: We ship UPS whenever possible. Delivery guaranteed. Provide your street address as UPS does not deliver to P.O. Boxes. UPS to Canada requires a $50.00 minimum order. Allow 4-6 weeks for delivery. Orders outside the U.S.A. and Canada: Airmail—add retail price of book; add $5.00 for each non-book item (tapes, etc.); add $1.00 per item for surface mail.

FOR GROUP STUDY AND PURCHASE

Because there is a great deal of interest in group discussion and study of the subject matter of this book, we feel that we should encourage the adoption and use of this particular book by such groups by offering a special quantity price to group leaders or agents.

Our Special Quantity Price for a minimum order of five copies of *Enochian Workbook* is $44.85 cash-with-order. This price includes postage and handling within the United States. Minnesota residents must add 6.5% sales tax. For additional quantities, please order in multiples of five. For Canadian and foreign orders, add postage and handling charges as above. Credit card (VISA, MasterCard, American Express) orders are accepted. Charge card orders only ($15.00 minimum order) may be phoned in free within the U.S.A. or Canada by dialing 1-800-THE-MOON. For customer service, call 1-612-291-1970. Mail orders to:

LLEWELLYN PUBLICATIONS
P.O. Box 64383-719, St. Paul, MN 55164-0383, U.S.A.

MAGICIAN'S COMPANION
A Practical and Encyclopedic Guide to Magical and Religious Symbolism
by Bill Whitcomb

The Magician's Companion is a "desk reference" overflowing with a wide range of occult and esoteric materials absolutely indispensable to anyone engaged in the magickal arts!

The magical knowledge of our ancestors comprises an intricate and elegant technology of the mind and imagination. This book attempts to make the ancient systems accessible, understandable and useful to modern magicians by categorizing and cross-referencing the major magical symbol-systems (i.e., world views on inner and outer levels). Students of religion, mysticism, mythology, symbolic art, literature, and even cryptography will find this work of value.

This comprehensive book discusses and compares over 35 magical models (e.g., the Trinities, the Taoist Psychic Centers, Enochian magic, the qabala, the Worlds of the Hopi Indians). Also included are discussions of the theory and practice of magic and ritual; sections on alchemy, magical alphabets, talismans, sigils, magical herbs and plants; suggested programs of study; an extensive glossary and bibliography; and much more.
0-87542-868-1, 522 pgs., 7 x 10, illus., softcover   **$19.95**

SECRETS OF A GOLDEN DAWN TEMPLE
The Alchemy and Crafting of Magickal Implements
by Chic Cicero and Sandra Tabatha Cicero
Foreword by Chris Monnastre
Afterword by Donald Michael Kraig

A Must-Have for Every Student of the Western Magickal Tradition! From its inception 100 years ago, the Hermetic Order of the Golden Dawn continues to be *the* authority on high magick. Yet the books written on the Golden Dawn system have fallen far short in explaining how to construct the tools and implements necessary for ritual. Until now.

Secrets of a Golden Dawn Temple picks up where all the other books leave off. This is the first book to describe *all* Golden Dawn implements and tools in complete detail. Here is a unique compilation of the various tools used, all described in full: wands, ritual clothing, elemental tools, Enochian tablets, altars, temple furniture, banners, lamens, admission badges and much more. This book provides complete step-by-step instructions for the construction of nearly 80 different implements, all displayed in photographs or drawings, along with the exact symbolism behind each and every item. Plus, it gives a ritual or meditation for every magickal instrument presented. It truly is an indispensable guide for any student of Western Magickal Tradition.
0-87542-150-4, 592 pgs., 6 x 9, 16 color plates, softcover   **$19.95**

ENOCHIAN MAGIC
A Practical Manual
by Gerald J. Schueler

The powerful system of magic introduced in the 16th century by Dr. John Dee, Astrologer Royal to Queen Elizabeth I, and as practiced by Aleister Crowley and the Hermetic Order of the Golden Dawn, is here presented for the first time in a complete, step-by-step form. There has never before been a book that has made Enochian Magic this easy!

In this book you are led carefully along the path from "A brief history of the Enochian Magical System," through "How to Speak Enochian," "How to Invoke," "The Calls," "Egyptian Deities" and "Chief Hazards" to "How to visit the Aethyrs in Spirit Vision (Astral Projection)." Not a step is missed; not a necessary instruction forgotten.

0-87542-710-3, 288 pgs., 5 1/4 x 8, illus., softcover　　　　　　　**$9.95**

ENOCHIAN PHYSICS
The Structure of the Magical Universe
by Gerald J. Schueler

Gerald Schueler has taken the latest discoveries of modern physics and compared them to the laws of Enochian Physics. He shows how the magical universe is a natural extension of Einstein's space/time continuum. The only ingredient that Einstein left out was consciousness. When this factor is included, the magical universe is revealed. According to modern physics, matter is a form of energy. In *Enochian Physics* you will see that this same energy, the energy of modern physics, is the very substance, or "matter," of the magical universe.

The book incorporates magick and the latest concepts in the ever-changing field of theoretical physics. Quantum mechanics, black and white holes, alchemy and levitation, quarks and the Big Bang, the four elements and the four elementary forces are all brought together within a Grand Unified System of the magical universe. Included are such tantalizing scientific puzzles as the fluidity of time, the possibility of parallel universes, matter and antimatter, and the fate of the stars and galaxies. Those seeking a clear explanation of magical phenomena such as invisibility, astral travel and psychic healing will find it in the pages of *Enochian Physics*. Anyone practicing magick or interested in how magick works should read this book.

0-87542-712-X, 400 pgs., 5 1/4 x 8, illus., softcover　　　　　　　**$12.95**

Prices subject to change without notice.

ENOCHIAN YOGA
Uniting Humanity and Divinity
by Gerald & Betty Schueler

Here is the only book currently available that combines magick and yoga, and Western and Eastern thought, into a single, easy-to-use system that is suitable for everyone, from beginners to advanced magicians and yogis. Eight graduated paths of development are described, and the book includes a complete description of the subtle Centers and Channels of Enochian Yoga, which are equivalent to the chakras and nadis of kundalini Yoga. The application of the Enochian worlds to the meditation techniques and philosophy of yoga makes this magical development more accessible to those having a cultural or educational background in the Eastern religions. A thorough method for spiritual attainment.

0-87542-718-9, 408 pgs., 5 1/4 x 8, illus., softcover   **$12.95**

THE ENOCHIAN TAROT
by Gerald and Betty Schueler

The popular deck of cards known as the Tarot has been used for many centuries for divination, fortunetelling and self-initiation through meditation. The Enochian Tarot, an 86-card deck, is the first to utilize the mystery and magical power inherent in Enochian Magic.

The Enochian Tarot explains in detail the meaningful correspondences behind the structure of this deck. It discusses, for example, the difference between the 22 Paths on the Qabalistic Tree of Life, on which traditional Tarot decks are based, and the 30 Aethyrs of Enochian Magick (the Enochian deck has 8 extra cards because there are 8 more Aethyrs than Paths). The book also includes tables and figures for easy comprehension of an otherwise difficult subject, as well as tips for reading the cards for fun or profit.

The unique system of Enochian Magick was revealed to John Dee, court astrologer to Queen Elizabeth I of England, and his partner Edward Kelly by the Enochian Angels who inhabit the Watchtowers and Aethyrs of the subtle regions of the universe. The authors are foremost authorities on this subject and have published a number of books that have made a fascinating magical system accessible to a wide audience.

0-87542-709-X, 352 pgs., 5-1/4 x 8, illus., softcover   **$12.95**

THE ENOCHIAN TAROT DECK
Created by Gerald and Betty Schueler
Painted by Sallie Ann Glassman
The Enochian Tarot is a deck of cards which is primarily used to foretell the future. Forecasting the future, however, is only a superficial use of the massive powers of the Enochian Tarot. Here is a powerful tool which allows you to look deep inside your subconscious and "see" the direction your life is taking. The Enochian Tarot is an easy-to-use system of self-discovery which allows you to see your relationship to God and the universe.

The Tarot is your map of life. With it you can choose the road you want to wander. Instead of being an uninformed victim of your subconscious will, you can gather your inner strength and consciously change the path your life is to take. The Tarot is your key to self-determination, and with that key you can open any door.

The Enochian Tarot Deck consists of 86 cards which are divided into 2 main sections: a Major Arcana and a Minor Arcana. The Major Arcana is a set of 30 picture cards which are also called The Greater Arcana, Trumps, Atouts, or Triumphs. These cards are symbolic representations of various cosmic forces such as Doubt, Intuition, Glory, etc. The Minor Arcana contains 56 cards which represent the Four Enochian Watchtowers. The Minor Arcana is divided into 4 "suits" called Earth, Water, Air, and Fire.
0-87542-708-1, boxed set: 86 cards with booklet   **$12.95**

GOLDEN DAWN ENOCHIAN MAGIC
by Pat Zalewski
Enochian magic is considered by most magicians to be the most powerful system ever created. Aleister Crowley learned this system of magic from the Hermetic Order of the Golden Dawn, which had developed and expanded the concepts and discoveries of Elizabethan magus John Dee. This book picks up where the published versions of the Enochian material of the Golden Dawn leave off.

Based on the research and unpublished papers of MacGregor Mathers, one of the founders of the Golden Dawn, *Golden Dawn Enochian Magic* opens new avenues of use for this system. New insights are given on such topics as the Sigillum Dei Aemeth, the Angels of the Enochian Aires applied to the 12 tribes of Israel and the Kabbalah, the 91 Governors, the Elemental Tablets as applied to the celestial sphere, and more. This book provides a long-sought break from amateurish and inaccurate books on the subject; it is designed to complement such scholarly classics as *Enochian Invocation* and *Heptarchia Mystica*.
0-87542-898-3, 224 pgs., 5 1/4 x 8, illus., softcover   **$12.95**

THE MAGICAL PHILOSOPHY, VOLUME 1
The Foundations of High Magick
by Denning & Phillips

The long-awaited re-publication of *The Magical Philosophy Series* is now complete—this time improved and revised with additional material. *The Foundations of High Magick* is a structured and progressive curriculum of Qabalistic and Ogdoadic Magick based upon the wide practical experience and extensive researches of the Order Aurum Solis. The *Foundations of High Magick* contains the revised Book I, "Robe and Ring," which explores the philosophy of the magical art and the ethics of Western Occultism. It also contains Book II, "The Apparel of High Magick," which discusses the symbolism and introduces the concept of "the correspondences." It makes a preliminary study of some of the objective materials of the magical art, both on the physical and other levels, and introduces some of the laws which link those levels.

The Aurum Solis was founded in 1897 as a practical school of ceremonial magick. Its philosophy is rooted deeply in the Western esoteric tradition. Founded on the Ogdoadic Tradition rather than on the Rosicrucian mold, the Aurum Solis is distinctive and unique, yet remains harmonious with the work of other Qabalistic orders.

0-87542-174-1, 408 pgs., 6 x 9, illus., softcover   **$15.00**

THE MAGICAL PHILOSOPHY, VOLUME 2
The Sword and the Serpent
by Denning & Phillips

This is the comprehensive guide to the Magical Qabalah, with extensive correspondences as well as the techniques for activating the centers, use of images and the psychology of attainment.

In this volume, histories from contemporary life, together with references to the works of mystics, poets, artists, philosophers and authorities in psychology are cited to illustrate the action and interaction of the functions of the psyche as identified in Qabalistic teaching.

The real meaning of adepthood is clearly set forth: in relation to this, frequent enigmas of occult literature such as the Abyss, the Knowledge and Conversation of the Holy Guardian Angel, and the supernal attainments are presented in their true meaning and significance. The natural dignity and potential of life in this world is your birthright. In this volume, its splendor and power are made unmistakably manifest.

0-87542-197-0, 540 pgs., 6 x 9, illus., softcover   **$15.00**

THE MAGICAL PHILOSOPHY, VOLUME 3
Mysteria Magica
by Denning & Phillips

For years, Denning and Phillips headed the international occult Order Aurum Solis. In this book, they present the magickal system of the order so that you can use it. Here you will find rituals for banishing and invoking plus instructions for proper posture and breathing. You will learn astral projection, rising on the planes, and the magickal works that should be undertaken through astral projection. You will learn the basic principle of ceremonies and how to make sigils and talismans. You will learn practical Enochian magick plus how to create, consecrate and use your magickal tools such as the magickal sword, wand and cup. You will also learn the advanced arts of sphere-working and evocation to visible appearance.

Filled with illustrations, this book is an expanded version of the previous edition. It is now complete in itself and can be the basis of an entire magickal system. You can use the information alone or as the source book for a group. If you want to learn how to do real magick, this is the place you should start.

0-87542-196-2, 480 pgs., 6 x 9, illus., softcover   **$15.00**

THE GOLDEN DAWN
The Original Account of the Teachings, Rites & Ceremonies of the Hermetic Order
As revealed by Israel Regardie

Complete in one volume with further revision, expansion, and additional notes by Regardie, Cris Monnastre, and others. Expanded with an index of more than 100 pages!

Originally published in four bulky volumes of some 1,200 pages, this 6th Revised and Enlarged Edition has been entirely reset in modern, less space-consuming type, in half the pages (while retaining the original pagination in marginal notation for reference) for greater ease and use.

Corrections of typographical errors perpetuated in the original and subsequent editions have been made, with further revision and additional text and notes by noted scholars and by actual practitioners of the Golden Dawn system of Magick, with an Introduction by the only student ever accepted for personal training by Regardie.

Also included are Initiation Ceremonies, important rituals for consecration and invocation, methods of meditation and magical working based on the Enochian Tablets, studies in the Tarot, and the system of Qabalistic Correspondences that unite the World's religions and magical traditions into a comprehensive and practical whole.

This volume is designed as a study and practice curriculum suited to both group and private practice. Meditation upon, and following with the Active Imagination, the Initiation Ceremonies are fully experiential without need of participation in group or lodge. A very complete reference encyclopedia of Western Magick.

0-87542-663-8, 840 pgs., 6 x 9, illus., softcover   **$19.95**

THE EQUINOX & SOLSTICE CEREMONIES OF THE GOLDEN DAWN
by Chris & Pat Zalewski
Throughout time, the Spring and Fall Equinoxes and Summer and Winter Solstices have been the basic reference points for the seasons and the major times for celebration in both the Christian and Pagan calendars. Yet until now, there has been little in the way of detailed information on the magical effects of the Equinox and Solstice.

The Equinox & Solstice Ceremonies of the Golden Dawn is a valuable contribution to magical literature. It defines and explains the Equinox and Solstice, along with the Golden Dawn concept of them. It presents a scientific evaluation of the magnetic fields they produce, along with the astrological data connecting them and how they relate to spiritual development. It investigates myths and festivals from the time of the Egyptians and how the theology of that time related specifically to the Sun and the change of the seasons. Jewish, Christian, Celtic and Norse festivals are also explored along with the different timing of these ceremonies in different climatic conditions. The authors then present the full Golden Dawn rituals and give their expert commentary, which reveals many unpublished teachings associated with the ceremonies.
0-87542-899-1, 192 pgs., 6 x 9, illus., softcover   **$12.95**

MODERN MAGICK
Eleven Lessons in the High Magickal Arts
by Donald Michael Kraig
Modern Magick is the most comprehensive step-by-step introduction to the art of ceremonial magic ever offered. The eleven lessons in this book will guide you from the easiest of rituals and the construction of your magickal tools through the highest forms of magick: designing your own rituals and doing pathworking. Along the way you will learn the secrets of the Kabbalah in a clear and easy-to-understand manner. You will discover the true secrets of invocation (channeling) and evocation, and the missing information that will finally make the ancient grimoires, such as the "Keys of Solomon," not only comprehensible, but usable. This book also contains one of the most in-depth chapters on sex magick ever written. *Modern Magick* is designed so anyone can use it, and it is the perfect guidebook for students and classes. It will also help to round out the knowledge of long-time practitioners of the magickal arts.
0-87542-324-8, 592 pgs., 6 x 9, illus., index, softcover   **$14.95**

A GARDEN OF POMEGRANATES
by Israel Regardie

What is the Tree of Life? It's the ground plan of the Qabalistic system—a set of symbols used since ancient times to study the Universe. The Tree of Life is a geometrical arrangement of ten sephiroth, or spheres, each of which is associated with a different archetypal idea, and 22 paths which connect the spheres.This system of primal correspondences has been found the most efficient plan ever devised to classify and organize the characteristics of the self. Israel Regardie has written one of the best and most lucid introductions to the Qabalah. *A Garden of Pomegranates* combines Regardie's own studies with his notes on the works of Aleister Crowley, A. E. Waite, Eliphas Levi and D. H. Lawrence. No longer is the wisdom of the Qabalah to be held secret! The needs of today place the burden of growth upon each and every person . . . each has to undertake the Path as his or her own responsibility, but every help is given in the most ancient and yet most modern teaching here known to humankind.

0-87542-690-5, 160 pgs., 5 1/4 x 8, softcover $8.95

Z-5: SECRET TEACHINGS OF THE GOLDEN DAWN
Book I: The Neophyte Ritual
by Pat Zalewski

This book is the first in a series on the grade rituals of the Hermetic Order of the Golden Dawn. It is designed to show the type of procedure one encounters when he or she joins a Golden Dawn temple. It focuses on the secret, Inner Order techniques for performing the Neophyte initiation ritual, which is the essence of the Golden Dawn's Z-2 magical instructions.

Z-5 is a tool and a helpful guide based on the observations of a number of Adepts from the Golden Dawn, the Stella Matutina, and the Smaragdum Thalasses. Originally intended as a document restricted to members of the Inner Order of the Thoth-Hermes Temple, the Z-5 material includes many of the "word of mouth" teachings passed on from Inner Order Adepti. These teachings go beyond the step-by-step mechanics of ritual on the mundane level and unveil the deeper meanings, allowing access into the Golden Dawn's "magical current" which is the source of the true power of ritual.

0-87542-897-5, 240 pgs., 6 x 9, illus., softcover $12.95

Z-5: SECRET TEACHINGS OF THE GOLDEN DAWN
Book II: The Zelator Ritual 1=10
by Pat & Chris Zalewski

Two of the Golden Dawn's highest initiates reveal the hidden mysteries of the best-known occult system in the world. Pat and Chris Zalewski show what actually happens when one is initiated into the Golden Dawn's second grade ceremony—the Zelator Ritual.

In the first book in this series, *Z-5 … The Neophyte Ritual 0=0*, Pat Zalewski showed the whole process of initial initiation. Now, in *Z-5 … The Zelator Ritual 1=10*, Pat and his wife Chris take things a step further as the candidate embraces the forces of the Earth Element and the effects it has on him. In this ceremony, the postulant has his aura magnetically earthed and his physical body revitalized.

Unlike any other book written on the Golden Dawn, *Z-5 … 1=10* presents in enormous detail all the higher explanations given on the Zelator Ceremony in one package. For those who want to study ritual magic in a group, this book provides firm guidelines of the dos and don'ts of Hermetic Ritual. For those who wish to utilize magic in the privacy of their own homes, this book explains the shortcuts that can be applied on a solo basis.
0-87542-896-7, 224 pgs., 6 x 9, illus., softcover $12.95

COMING INTO THE LIGHT
Rituals of Egyptian Magick
by Gerald & Betty Schueler

Coming Into The Light is the name that the ancient Egyptians gave to a series of magickal texts known to us today as *The Book of the Dead. Coming into the Light* provides modern translations of these famous texts, and shows that they are not simply religious prayers or spells to be spoken over the body of a dead king, but rituals to be performed by living magicians who seek to know the truth about themselves and their world. Basic Egyptian philosophical and religious concepts are explained and explored, and ritual texts for a wide variety of magickal use are presented. For example, the Ritual of the Opening of the Mouth, perhaps the most well-known of Egyptian rituals, allows a magician to enter into the higher regions of the Magickal Universe without losing consciousness. Enough of this ancient wisdom has been passed down to us so that today we may gain a unique insight into the workings of those powerful magicians who performed their operations thousands of years ago.
0-87542-713-8, 378 pgs., 6 x 9, 24 color plates, softcover $14.95